Getting Started with Unity 5.x 2D Game Development

Build a tower defense game and earn delectable C# treats by baking cupcakes and fighting fearsome sweet-toothed pandas

Francesco Sapio

BIRMINGHAM - MUMBAI

Getting Started with Unity 5.x 2D Game Development

First published: February 2017

Production reference: 1080217

Published by Packt Publishing Ltd.
Livery Place
35 Livery Street
Birmingham
B3 2PB, UK.

ISBN 978-1-78439-717-3

www.packtpub.com

Credits

Author

Francesco Sapio

Reviewer

Lauren S. Ferro

Commissioning Editor

Ashwin Nair

Acquisition Editor

Larissa Pinto

Content Development Editor

Mayur Pawanikar

Technical Editor

Dinesh Pawar

Copy Editors

Vikrant Phadkay
Safis Editing

Project Coordinator

Nidhi Joshi

Proofreader

Safis Editing

Indexer

Mariammal Chettiyar

Production Coordinator

Aparna Bhagat

About the Author

Francesco Sapio obtained his computer science and controls engineering degree from Sapienza University of Rome, Italy, with a couple of semesters in advance, graduating *summa cum laude*; he is currently studying there for a master's of science and engineering degree in artificial intelligence and robotics.

He is a Unity 3D and Unreal expert, skilled game designer, and experienced user of major graphics programs. He developed *Game@School* (Sapienza University of Rome), an educational game for high-school students to learn concepts of physics, and the *Sticker Book* series (Dataware Games), a cross-platform series of games for kids. In addition, he worked as consultant for the (successfully funded by Kickstarter) game *Prosperity – Italy 1434* (Entertainment Game Apps, Inc) and for the open online collaborative ideation system titled *Innovoice* (Sapienza University of Rome). Moreover, he has been involved in different research projects such as *Belief-Driven Pathfinding* (Sapienza University of Rome), which is a new technique of path finding in video games that was presented as a paper at the *DiGRA-FDG Conference 2016*; and *perfekt.ID* (Royal Melbourne Institute of Technology), which included developing a recommendation system for games.

Francesco is an active writer on the topic of game development. Recently, he authored the book *Unity UI Cookbook*, Packt Publishing. It teaches readers how to develop exciting and practical user interfaces for games within Unity, and he wrote a short e-guide, *What do you need to know about Unity*, Packt Publishing. In addition, he co-authored the book *Unity 5.x 2D Game Development Blueprints*, Packt Publishing, which has also been transformed in the video course *Unity 5.x Game Development Projects*, Pack Publishing. He has also been a reviewer for the following books: *Game Physics Cookbook*, Packt Publishing, *Unity 5.x by Example*, Packt Publishing, and *Unity Game Development Scripting*, Packt Publishing.

Francesco is also a musician and a composer, especially of soundtracks for short films and video games. For several years, he worked as an actor and dancer, where he was a guest of honor at the Teatro Brancaccio in Rome. In addition, he has volunteered as a children's entertainer at the Associazione Culturale Torraccia in Rome. Finally, Francesco loves math, philosophy, logic, and puzzle solving, but most of all, creating video games—thanks to his passion for game designing and programming.

You can contact him at www.francescosapio.com.

Acknowledgment

I'm deeply thankful to my parents for their infinite patience, enthusiasm, and support throughout my life. Moreover, I'm thankful to the rest of my family, in particular to my grandparents, since they have always encouraged me to do better in my life with the Latin expressions *Ad maiora* and *Per aspera ad astra*.

I also want to thank Lauren S. Ferro, the reviewer, for her fantastic feedback and help, which have enhanced the quality of this book. Another important person, without whom this book couldn't have seen the light, is Mayur Pawanikar, the content development editor, who supported me throughout the whole process.

Finally, a huge thank to all the special people around me whom I love. In particular to my girlfriend: I'm grateful for all of your help in everything, I love you.

About the Reviewer

Lauren S. Ferro is a gamification consultant and designer of game and game-like applications. She has worked, designed, consulted, and implemented strategies for a range of different purposes from professional development, recommendation systems, and educational games. She is an active researcher in the area of gamification, player profiling, and user-centered game design. Lauren runs workshops both for the general public and companies that focus on designing user-centered games and game-like applications. She has written a book about implementing gamification within Unity titled *Gamification with Unity 5.x* and is the developer of the game design resource Gamicards, which is a paper prototyping tool for both game and game-like experiences.

www.PacktPub.com

For support files and downloads related to your book, please visit www.PacktPub.com.

Did you know that Packt offers eBook versions of every book published, with PDF and ePub files available? You can upgrade to the eBook version at www.PacktPub.com and as a print book customer, you are entitled to a discount on the eBook copy. Get in touch with us at service@packtpub.com for more details.

At www.PacktPub.com, you can also read a collection of free technical articles, sign up for a range of free newsletters and receive exclusive discounts and offers on Packt books and eBooks.

https://www.packtpub.com/mapt

Get the most in-demand software skills with Mapt. Mapt gives you full access to all Packt books and video courses, as well as industry-leading tools to help you plan your personal development and advance your career.

Why subscribe?

- Fully searchable across every book published by Packt
- Copy and paste, print, and bookmark content
- On demand and accessible via a web browser

Customer Feedback

Thank you for purchasing this Packt book. We take our commitment to improving our content and products to meet your needs seriously—that's why your feedback is so valuable. Whatever your feelings about your purchase, please consider leaving a review on this book's Amazon page. Not only will this help us, more importantly it will also help others in the community to make an informed decision about the resources that they invest in to learn.

You can also review for us on a regular basis by joining our reviewers' club. If you're interested in joining, or would like to learn more about the benefits we offer, please contact us: customerreviews@packtpub.com.

Table of Contents

Preface

When Packt asked me to write this book, we had in mind something more modest than the book that you have today. While I was writing, I realized how many books can be found on the shelves that teach the basics without giving any practical insight on how to use that knowledge to actually make a game. Therefore, I slightly deviated the course of this book. As a result, it has changed into a somewhat solid manual about Unity, with a particular focus on 2D game development. The book that you are holding in your hands (either hard copy or on your tablet) is the outcome of a lot of effort trying to create something that is easy for the readers to understand, without sacrificing completeness or practical use of the different tools learned. Thus, everything is explained in detail, along with many examples of usage.

Also, I felt that another big deficiency of many books is the lack of *Homework* sections that provide the reader with exercises to improve her/his skills. In fact, I believe that these sections are important, since they provide a common ground in case you want to challenge yourself and take the discussion beyond the book with your friends, course mates, or colleagues. In the field of game development, it's important to collaborate, because a game is often the result of the coordinate efforts of many talented and passionate people.

For this book, I decided to support the learning of the different tools we will face by building a tower defense game on the joyful and sugary theme of cupcakes, sprinkles, and sweet-toothed pandas who will try to bite the delicious player's cake. This project will guide the reader through the book, and help her/him to develop a practical skillset as well.

Whoever you are, a hungry student of knowledge, a professor looking for a book to adopt in your classes, an expert in game development trying out Unity (or willing to extend your understanding of Unity), or just a passionate hobbyist, I hope you will enjoy this book.

What this book covers

Chapter 1, *A Flat World in Unity*, is an introduction to the 2D world of Unity. You will discover how to set up your project, import assets, and make them ready to use. In particular, we will go through in detail on how to use the Sprite Editor.

Chapter 2, *Baking Cupcake Towers*, teaches you how to integrate code within your game. We will cover the important and fundamental concepts of Unity and we will see how to script game objects by starting to create the behaviors of our cupcake towers for the tower defense game we are building.

Chapter 3, *Communicating with the Player – the User Interface*, deals with the important task to provide feedback to your players through the use of user interfaces (UIs). You will learn how to design them by discovering the general principles behind them, and learn how to implement any UI within the UI system of Unity.

Chapter 4, *No Longer Alone – Sweet-Toothed Pandas Strike*, introduces us to the terrible sweet-toothed Pandas, who will try to steal the player's cake. You will learn how to bring characters to life by using the powerful animation system of Unity *Mechanim*, starting from Sprite-sheets.

Chapter 5, *The Secret Ingredient Is a Dash of Physics*, takes you by hand deep down into the secrets of physics and explains them in a clear and easy way. You will grasp the basics of physics, and learn how to use the 2D Physics engine of Unity.

Chapter 6, *Through a Sea of Sprinkles – Navigation in Artificial Intelligence*, is an introduction to the universe of artificial intelligence applied to video games. You will learn the basics principles and how to implement a navigation system in Unity for 2D (or even 3D) games, so that we can make our terrible sweet-toothed Pandas move!

Chapter 7, *Trading Cupcakes and the Ultimate Battle for the Cake – Gameplay Programming*, wraps everything we saw and learned in the previous chapters to conclude the tower defense game. In particular, we will deal with gameplay programming, which is the glue between the different parts of your game.

Chapter 8, *What Is beyond the Cake?*, explores different aspects of our game and game development in general. You will discover different tips, tricks, and suggestions on how to improve the game we built in this book, along with improving your own skills to become a better game developer. Then, the chapter will give you an understanding of parts of the game development pipeline, which are not strictly tied to the development of the game itself. Thus, you will dive into different topics ranging from playtesting, optimizations, team management and work, documentation, getting ready to publish your game, marketing, social media, game protections, to even localization.

What you need for this book

To go through the topics covered in this book, you will need two important things:

- Any version of Unity, possibly 5.x since it was the range of versions that this book has been written for. As you already know, and Chapter 1, *A Flat World in Unity*, will repeat, you can get it from the Unity official website: http://www.unity3d.com.
- Your enthusiasm and passion, in order to take an awesome journey in the world of game development together!

Who this book is for

Anyone including students, game enthusiasts, and academic professors who want to adopt this book as part of their course and classes.

Conventions

In this book, you will find a number of text styles that distinguish between different kinds of information. Here are some examples of these styles and an explanation of their meaning.

Code words in text, database table names, folder names, filenames, file extensions, pathnames, dummy URLs, user input, and Twitter handles are shown as follows: "All of them are placed inside a folder named Assets, which can be found inside the Project folder."

A block of code is set as follows:

```
public AwesomeUnityDeveloper GettingStarted(Yourself you) {
  you.ReadThisBook();
  return you;
}
```

When we wish to draw your attention to a particular part of a code block, the relevant lines or items are set in bold:

```
public AwesomeUnityDeveloper GettingStarted(Yourself you) {
  you.ReadThisBook();
  return you;
}
```

New terms and **important words** are shown in bold. Words that you see on the screen, for example, in menus or dialog boxes, appear in the text like this: "First of all, if you ever need to switch between 2D and 3D mode, you can do so by navigating to **Edit | Project Settings | Editor**."

Warnings or important notes appear in a box like this.

Tips and tricks appear like this.

Reader feedback

Feedback from our readers is always welcome. Let us know what you think about this book-what you liked or disliked. Reader feedback is important for us as it helps us develop titles that you will really get the most out of. To send us general feedback, simply e-mail feedback@packtpub.com, and mention the book's title in the subject of your message. If there is a topic that you have expertise in and you are interested in either writing or contributing to a book, see our author guide at www.packtpub.com/authors.

Customer support

Now that you are the proud owner of a Packt book, we have a number of things to help you to get the most from your purchase.

Downloading the example code

You can download the example code files for this book from your account at http://www.packtpub.com. If you purchased this book elsewhere, you can visit http://www.packtpub.com/support and register to have the files e-mailed directly to you.

You can download the code files by following these steps:

1. Log in or register to our website using your e-mail address and password.
2. Hover the mouse pointer on the **SUPPORT** tab at the top.
3. Click on **Code Downloads & Errata**.

4. Enter the name of the book in the **Search** box.
5. Select the book for which you're looking to download the code files.
6. Choose from the drop-down menu where you purchased this book from.
7. Click on **Code Download**.

Once the file is downloaded, please make sure that you unzip or extract the folder using the latest version of:

- WinRAR / 7-Zip for Windows
- Zipeg / iZip / UnRarX for Mac
- 7-Zip / PeaZip for Linux

The code bundle for the book is also hosted on GitHub at `https://github.com/PacktPubl ishing/Getting-Started-with-Unity-5.x-2D-Game-Development`. We also have other code bundles from our rich catalog of books and videos available at `https://github.com/P acktPublishing/`. Check them out!

Downloading the color images of this book

We also provide you with a PDF file that has color images of the screenshots/diagrams used in this book. The color images will help you better understand the changes in the output. You can download this file from `https://www.packtpub.com/sites/default/files/downloads/GettingStartedwithUnity5 x2DGameDevelopment_ColorImages.pdf`.

Errata

Although we have taken every care to ensure the accuracy of our content, mistakes do happen. If you find a mistake in one of our books-maybe a mistake in the text or the code-we would be grateful if you could report this to us. By doing so, you can save other readers from frustration and help us improve subsequent versions of this book. If you find any errata, please report them by visiting `http://www.packtpub.com/submit-errata`, selecting your book, clicking on the **Errata Submission Form** link, and entering the details of your errata. Once your errata are verified, your submission will be accepted and the errata will be uploaded to our website or added to any list of existing errata under the Errata section of that title.

To view the previously submitted errata, go to `https://www.packtpub.com/books/conten t/support`and enter the name of the book in the search field. The required information will appear under the **Errata** section.

Piracy

Piracy of copyrighted material on the Internet is an ongoing problem across all media. At Packt, we take the protection of our copyright and licenses very seriously. If you come across any illegal copies of our works in any form on the Internet, please provide us with the location address or website name immediately so that we can pursue a remedy.

Please contact us at `copyright@packtpub.com` with a link to the suspected pirated material.

We appreciate your help in protecting our authors and our ability to bring you valuable content.

Questions

If you have a problem with any aspect of this book, you can contact us at `questions@packtpub.com`, and we will do our best to address the problem.

1
A Flat World in Unity

This is the beginning of our journey in to the world of 2D game development with Unity. This book is structured to guide you through the creation of an entire 2D game from scratch, in particular a tower defense game.

Despite the fact that we will focus on 2D game development, our final goal is to learn how to use Unity, and therefore this means that we will also have a glance at how Unity handles 3D. So, if later on you want to dedicate some time to 3D games, by the end of this book you will have the necessary background for doing so. In fact, the book is structured to contain as much detail as possible for each topic, and this includes historical overviews and references to further readings.

In every chapter, we will face different challenges that will improve our skills. Furthermore, this book doesn't stop by telling you just what needs to be done (like many others), but it also explains the different tools that we will encounter and how to use them. In this way, we will learn how to use and apply them in different contexts as well. Thus, you can use this book as a reference manual, in order to speed up your workflow. To help you out, I recommend that you use the index, to quickly locate each one of the specific topics we will face.

At the end of each chapter, there is a *Homework* section, which leaves you with some exercises that are related to the topics that we have dealt in that chapter. Of course, you are free to skip this section, but I recommend that you do the exercises if you feel that you need to improve your skills even more.

For now, this chapter is an introduction to the 2D world inside Unity, and what needs to be done in order to create our game. In particular, we will look at the following topics:

- What are 2D games?
- What does designing and developing 2D games mean?
- Where to get Unity and its different versions
- Downloading a graphical package from an external source
- How to organize a project in Unity
- Understanding Unity when it is set in 2D
- What are Sprites?
- The Sprite Renderer component
- Import settings for Sprites
- How to use the Sprite Editor with all its different modes
- Preparing the assets for our game
- Setting up scenes and proportions

One last thing. Sometimes I'll refer to the player and to characters in order to make examples or explain concepts. As such, sometimes I'll refer to them as if they were males, and at other times as if they were females (and sometimes both). The reason derives from my personal point of view so as to not to discriminate between the two genders.

And with this said, let's get started!

Learning game development

Game development and design are some of the most extensive works of art around. This is due to the large amount of expertise that is required to bring a game to life. You can get an idea of this by just looking at any credits in a game. They are extensive and contain a lot of names of people who have dedicated a lot of their time to the game in various roles.

Like most things in life, game development can be learned not only through practice, but iteration as well. And even when you master one of the many branches in game development, there is still something new to learn.

Regardless of your level of knowledge of Unity, I strongly suggest that you follow each step in this book, even if you think you know the topic. You just never know, there is always something new to learn!

Tower defense games

Tower defense games come in many different styles. For example, in the following screenshot of *Defense Grid: The Awakening* and *Unstoppable Gorg*, both are top-down isometric style games. However, they are set in different worlds, with different objectives. So, given this, what makes a tower defense game? For one, they are centered on the idea of defending something, whether it is buildings, resources, weapons, and so forth. This is the main mechanism that defines the genre and drives the gameplay. Secondly, most tower defense games require economic and resource management. For example, after each wave of enemies, you may obtain a certain amount of virtual currency that you must then allocate to either the purchase of new defenses (weapons, towers, and so on) or upgrades. Each has their benefits depending on a range of factors such as weak points in your defense as well as the anticipated amount and strength of enemies that will be in the next wave. The number and difficulty of enemies increases after each wave, therefore challenging the player to manage resources and build defenses strategically. The idea is to build up enough resources to upgrade your defenses and to outlast the incoming wave. Sometimes, the player must stop the enemies (or an opponent) from destroying their own base.

In other cases, the player must prevent the enemies from reaching the end, as each enemy that manages to get through cause damage to the player's health bar.

(Top) *Defense Grid: The Awakening* and (bottom) *Unstoppable Gorg*

There are many places on the Internet where you can find tower defense games. For example, Kongregate (http://www.kongregate.com/) and Newgrounds (http://www.newgrounds.com/) are examples of sites where a varied array of free tower defense games exist (such as *Kingdom Rush* or *Bloons Tower Defense 5*). However, many exist for iOS (App Store) and Android (Play Store), operating systems such as Linux, OSX, and PC (for example, Steam), and consoles (Playstation, Xbox), and so on.

Designing our game

Before you even think about turning your computer on, you need to design your game. It's not enough to have a rough idea in mind. You need to write down all your ideas before hand to start working. The first phase of game design is **brainstorming**. There are different techniques and methodologies of brainstorming that, unfortunately, we don't have the time, in this small section, to describe. However, the final outcome should be tons of paper with thousands of ideas written down. It's not meant to be a work of art, but the foundations upon which your game will be built.

> Some information about brainstorming can be found also in a practical book, *Gamification with Unity*, by *Packt publishing*. You can find it here: https://www.packtpub.com/game-development/gamification-unity-5x.

The next step is to refine your ideas, discard (or keep for other projects) the ones that you don't need, and organize them in a coherent form.

The final result should be something like the following.

> *Panda Invasion is a 2D tower defense game. In fact, hungry pandas are invading to steal all the sugar from the player. He or she has to push back the pandas by using cupcake towers. There are different kinds of cupcake towers that the player can decide to place in the map. In every level, there will be a path that pandas will follow. Furthermore, they are spawned at the beginning of this path. At the end, there is the ambitious sugar castle that the player has to defend. If the pandas steal too much, bringing the sugar-meter to zero, the player has failed his or her important mission. On the contrary, if he or she is able to push all of them back, the player will gain victory. However, cupcake towers are not free. In fact, the player has to buy them by using candy. Every time that a panda is pushed back, then the player will earn a certain amount of candy. Furthermore, the player can use candy to upgrade the cupcake towers and make them even stronger!*

From this excerpt, you are now able to understand what we are going to do in this book. You also have a basic idea of how to write down your ideas. I strongly suggest that you always do this step, even when you are the only developer, and especially when you have a team.

Getting ready

Now that we have our idea, the next thing to do is to get Unity. It comes in different versions: Personal (which is free), Plus, Professional, and Enterprise. The last three contain more features than the Personal one. However, all the topics covered in this book can be done with the free version. In any case, you can get or buy Unity on the official website: www.unity3d.com.

This is the comparison screen between the different versions of Unity on the Unity Technologies website (if you scroll down, you will find which feature is included in which version):

This is a very short summary of how model pricing for Unity has varied in recent years. In fact, to become a developer also means to be aware of the world around you, and having basic marketing knowledge could also help.

At the beginning, the model price of Unity didn't allow developers to publish commercial games with the free version. In addition, the game engine didn't have all the features, such as the Profiler or the Movie Textures.

Epic Games, the company that owns Unreal Engine, changed its model prices by making its game engine free in March 2015, also for commercial use (although it will take in return the 5% of the game's gross revenue). After a period of time, Unity Technologies also allowed developers to publish commercial games even with the free version, but it was still watermarked. From Unity 5.x, features that were only in the Pro version became available in the free version as well.

During the beginning of 2016, Unity used to come in two different versions: Free (or Personal) and Professional. The latter contains more features than the Personal one, and here is the comparison screen of the two:

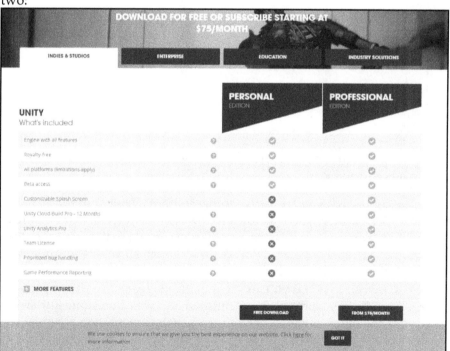

In June 2016, Unity changed its price model in the one described earlier.

Once we have installed Unity, we can begin creating new projects. If we click on the **New project** button in the top-right corner of the window, Unity will ask us to insert the details for our project. We can name it `Panda Invasion` and choose the destination path, which is where the files of the project will be stored. There is another an important thing to note. Unity gives us the possibility to choose between a 3D and a 2D project. This is not important decision, since it can be changed at any time. However, it is useful to already have in mind whether or not the game will be 2D or 3D. By selecting the 2D mode, Unity adapts the default settings to the game that we have in mind. We will see these settings in the following sections. For now, you should have a screen that looks like the following:

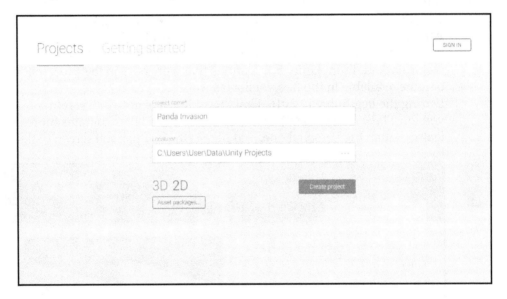

Now, we can press the **Create project** button, and we have successfully created our project and are ready to build it.

This book assumes that you are fairly familiar with the Unity interface and with C# code. If you are not, don't worry. There are different ways that you can learn before continuing on with this book. For example, I wrote a small free e-guide that briefly goes through the main interfaces and concepts of Unity. Don't expect to learn all you need from there, but it is a good start. You can find it at `https://www.packtpub.com/packt/free-ebook/what-you-n eed-know-about-unity-5`. If you are a complete newcomer to Unity, please read that small e-guide. I'll still be here once you have finished and we can resume our awesome journey. Furthermore, the official manual of Unity and its documentation are great companions in the Unity game development world. You can find them both on the official website, at `https://docs.unity3d.com/Manual/index.html`.

Since we don't have the time to create our own graphics for the game that we are going to develop, we need to download a custom package. Of course, you are free to choose the one you like most. For this book, we are going to use the `Tower Defence Pack 2` package, which can be downloaded from `http://player26.com/`.

`Tower Defence Pack 2` features a delicious assortment of cupcakes ranging from infamous fluffy white frosting and colorful sprinkles, to decadent chocolate chip, not to mention an all-time favorite, lemon meringue with silver dragees. It also features the Sugar Castle, a home away from home for candy lovers! In addition to all this sugary goodness are trees, mountains, rainbows, and various other assets to populate your sugary environment. Just be beware, there are some hidden dangers among it all with the pandas, so be careful to keep your stash well protected from thieving sweet-toothed animals!

The package includes all the basic assets that we need to create our tower defense game. It is free, even for commercial use, and even if credits are required. There is also a premium version that contains more assets and some of the decorations in different Sprites to increase customizability. In particular, in the free version we can find:

- Maps designed for tower defense games
- Evil pandas (with animation)
- Three different upgrading levels for cupcakes towers
- Multiple icons for each object in the package
- And many more assets to populate the level with!

The following image can give you an idea of the kind of graphics this package contains:

So, download this package before moving on to the next section.

Remembering the past to build the future

If you are new to Unity, or you have only used Unity 5.x, you can skip this section or read it just for curiosity.

In Unity 4.x (before version 4.6) and other previous versions, building 2D games was a bit harder. In fact, you needed to use a range of different methods and tricks to achieve the illusion on 2D. All the 2D objects were actually 3D objects viewed in a particular perspective or with a particular camera, which gave the illusion of a 2D object.

From Unity 4.6 on, and especially since Unity 5.x, this is not needed any more. There is built-in support for 2D games. So now, there are special components to deal with 2D objects, and the following sections will explore some of them.

Organizing the project

There are different ways to organize a project within Unity, therefore giving a bit more freedom. In this section, we propose one method, which we will use during the development of the project in this book.

The key idea is to organize the different assets by type (and not, as in other methods, by their position within the level).

First of all, let's understand how Unity organizes assets. All of them are placed inside a folder named `Assets`, which can be found also inside the `Project` folder. Therefore, all our assets should be contained in this folder or subfolder. In order to create a new folder, right-click on the **Project** panel and then **Create | Folder**. As a result, a new folder is created within the folder you clicked. Since we don't have any folders, it will be a subfolder of the **Assets** one. We have the option to rename it as we want. If you miss this, you can just select it and then click on it again (but not too fast, otherwise Unity will consider this as a double-click and it will open the folder), as shown in the following screenshot:

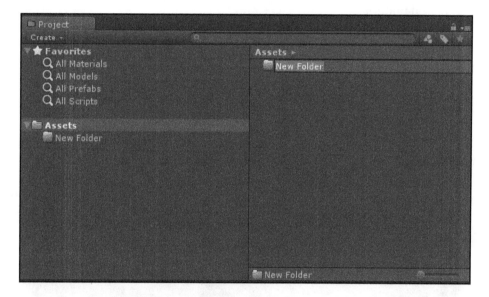

It is important to note that Unity will ignore the following categories, in order to avoid importing system files:

- Hidden folders and files
- Folder and files that starts with ~ and with .
- Folders and files named `cvs`
- Files which have a `.tmp` extension

We need to create the following folders (you should only create the ones in bold, since we will not use the other ones):

- Fonts
- **Graphics**
- Materials
- **Animations** (we will see them in more detail in `Chapter 4`, *No Longer Alone – Sweet-Toothed Pandas Strike*)
- Music and sounds
- Other assets (to store, for instance, `.txt` assets)
- Physical materials
- **Prefabs** (we will see what they are in the next chapter)
- **Scenes**
- **Scripts**

 If you are planning to create a 3D game, the folders will be different and they will include other kind of assets, such as 3D models and textures.

At the end, we should see the following in our **Project** panel (I'll add the `Animation` folder in `Chapter 4`, *No Longer Alone – Sweet-Toothed Pandas Strike*, when we will see animations, but feel free to add it immediately if you like):

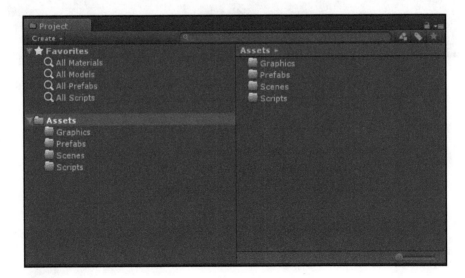

There is something else to know about the folders in your projects. If you create folders with some specific names, Unity will treat them in a special way. We are not going to use them; however, it's worth giving them a quick look:

- `Editor` (or a subfolder within it): This contains editor scripts rather than runtime scripts. These are designed to implement new functionality in Unity during the development of your games, and will not be included in the published game. As a result, you cannot use any of the scripts inside this folder within your `Scene`. Furthermore, it's possible to use more than one `Editor` folder in your project (even if this affects the execution order).

- `Editor Default Resources`: This contains resources that can be loaded on-demand by editor scripts by using the `EditorGUIUtility.Load()` function.

- `Resources` (or a subfolder within it): This contains all the assets that can be loaded on demand from a script by using the `Resources.Load()` function. In fact, you may need to load an asset that is not present in the scene yet. As with the `Editor` folder, you can have as many as you want in your project.

- `Plugins`: This contains native DLLs, written in C/C++, which can access third-party libraries, system calls, and other functions that Unity doesn't provide directly. As the name suggests, it is used to implement or import plugins.

- `StreamingAssets`: This contains assets that will not be included in your main game file, but that can be streamed from a script.

- `WebPlayerTemplates`: This contains custom host pages to use when the target platform is the `WebPlayer`. Scripts in this folder will not be compiled.

Coming back to our folder, we need to import the package that we have downloaded. This can be done in a number of different ways, but the easiest way is to drag and drop the folder of the package within our `Graphics` folder.

If you need to select an asset to use, in the bottom-left corner of the **Project** panel, there is a slider that allows you to increase the size of the icons in the **Project** panel. This function is useful when there are a lot of assets and we need to find the right one without knowing the name, or when exploring new packages we don't know yet. The slider is highlighted in the following screenshot for your convenience:

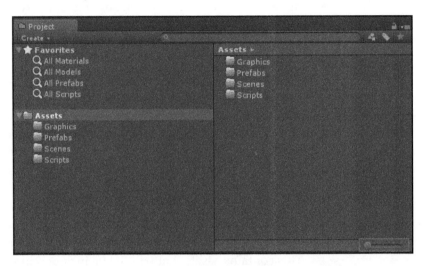

A 2D world

There are few things to notice in our project when it is set to 2D mode, which we are going to explore in this section.

First of all, if you ever need to switch between 2D and 3D mode, you can do so by navigating to **Edit** | **Project Settings** | **Editor**. If you go in to the **Default Behavior Mode** settings, you can change the **Mode**, as shown in the following screenshot:

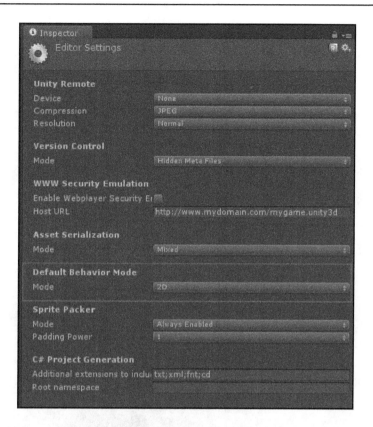

Coming back to our main interface, let's see the main differences between 2D and 3D mode. The **Scene** view is set by default to **2D**, as you can see in the following screenshot:

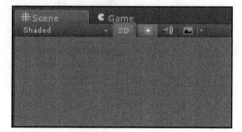

This allows us to have the **Scene** view locked on to the *xy* plane.

The *z* axis is used to determine which object should be rendered first. This decides which objects are in the foreground and which ones are in the background.

Then, every time we create a new scene, the default camera that comes with it is always set in **Orthographic** mode. Furthermore, its position is set to (0, 0, -10), whereas in 3D mode, it is set to (0, 1, -10). You can also check this by selecting the **Main Camera** in the **Hierarchy** panel and seeing its properties in the **Inspector**, as shown in the following screenshot:

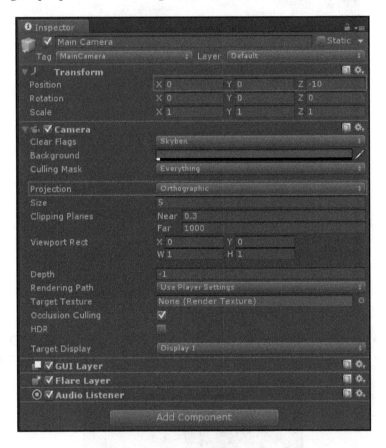

Other differences are the options to use the **Sprite Packer** or the default objects that don't have real-time directional lights. There are also changes in the **Lighting** settings (you can access them from **Window/Lighting**). In particular, the **Skybox** is disabled for new scenes and **Precomputed Realtime GI**, **Baked GI**, and **Auto-Building** are set to off. In addition, the **Ambient Source** comes with a dark grey color.

In the following screenshot, you can see the default **Lighting** settings:

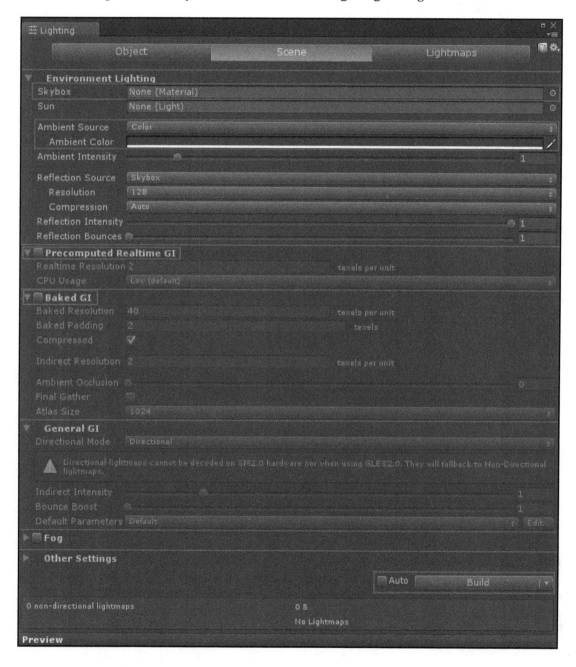

The RGB code of the color of the **Ambient Source** that is set by default in the 2D mode is (54, 58, 66).

However, the most important difference is how Unity imports new 2D assets, but we are going to see this in detail in the following sections.

Sprites

The fundamental bricks of a 2D game in Unity are the Sprites. You can think of them as pictures, but actually as we are going to see, they are something more. In fact, one image can contain more than one Sprite. Usually, this kind of image takes the name of a Sprite Sheet. Here is an example of a Sprite Sheet within our package:

There are different reasons why we want to have all the Sprites on a single image, rather than display them separately. The most important one is efficiency. Every time you want to render something on the screen, this has to be rendered by the graphics card in your computer. If all the Sprites are in separate images, the graphics card will have to process a lot of images. As a result, your game will run slowly.

Another reason for having Sprite Sheets is for animations. While 3D animations are made of data that describes how a 3D model has to be moved, 2D animations are made of frames. Like a movie or a cartoon, an animation is made of different images, or in this case, Sprites. Each of them describes a moment, and if you change them quickly enough, such as 25 per second, you can give the illusion of movement. Having all of the frames in a unique image is both efficient and well organized.

Naturally, there are other reasons for Sprite Sheets, but the two preceding reasons should be enough to convince you that Sprite Sheets are the best practice. On the other hand, there is a tradeoff to pay: the game engine needs to be able to distinguish between them on the image. We will see how Unity handles this in the following sections. But before we move on, there are other important concepts to learn about Sprites in Unity.

Like a 3D object, a Sprite also has a pivot point. Usually, this is located in the middle, but it can be changed in the Sprite Editor. The pivot point is where Unity starts to do all the calculations from. For instance, when you give a position for the Sprite to be within the Scene, Unity places the pivot point in that specific location, and then draws the Sprite around it. The pivot point is also important for rotations. Every time we rotate the Sprite, the rotation will be around the pivot point. In other words, during a rotation, the pivot point is the only point that does not change position.

This can be better explained with a screenshot, where the arrow is indicating the location of the pivot point:

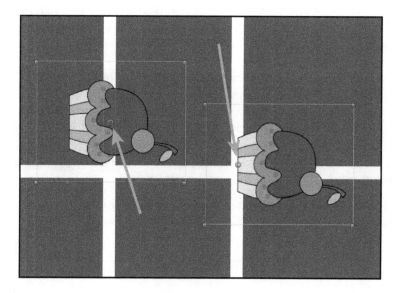

As you can see, there is the same Sprite rotated by 90 degrees clockwise. The one on the left has the pivot point in the middle, whereas the one on the right has it toward the left-hand side (the pivot point can be identified by the blue circle). Of course, you can make them coincide with a translation, but it is important to keep where it is in mind, especially when we code, in order to easily achieve what we want.

Now, there is another aspect to take into account about Sprites. In a 2D game, both the background and the character who is moving around the world are considered Sprites. However, we would like to render the background behind the character, and not vice versa. Therefore, the Sprites are rendered in a certain order that determines which one should render on top of the others.

In Unity there are two main ways to decide this order:

- **Sorting Layers**: Each **Sprite Render**, which is a component attached to a game object that renders the Sprite selected, has a variable called **Sorting Layer**. There, we can chose on which layer the Sprite will be rendered. The order of the different sorting layers can be determined in the Tags and Layers Settings (we will see how to access this menu later on in the chapter). Furthermore, Sorting Layers can offer an internal order for Sprites within the same layer by using the **Order In Layer** variable, which is always in the **Sprite Render** component.
- **Z-Buffering**: Since a 2D object only needs two coordinates to describe its position (the x and y axes), we have the z axis to describe depth. Unity uses depth to determine which Sprite should be rendered first. Since you need to imagine this as a depth, it's good practice to use only negative values. The greater the negative value, the closer the character or object is to the camera.

There aren't any great differences between these methods in terms of computational efficiency. Therefore, both can be used. Actually, they can also be used together. A general approach is to use the z axis for visually structuring characters. Imagine a character who is carrying a weapon. Depending on which hand the weapon is held in and in which direction the character is facing, the weapon should be rendered behind the character or in front of it. Sorting Layers, instead, are used for organizing the Sprites at a higher level, such as background, foreground, player, enemies, and so on.

However, for the sake of learning, in this book we will not use Sorting Layers, but only Z-Buffering, since it can be easily changed within the code.

Sprite Renderer

Before we mention this component, it might be worth discussing it a bit more.

This component will be automatically attached every time we add a Sprite to the scene. It should look like the following screenshot:

Let's break down the different parameters:

- **Sprite**: This holds the Sprite that it has to render.
- **Color**: This is a color that is multiplied to the Sprite image. If you know bit about shaders and renderers, this is actual the vertex color of the rendered mesh.
- **Flip**: This defines on which axis the Sprite needs to be flipped. This is a new function from Unity 5.3.
- **Material**: This is the material Unity should use to render the Sprite. The default one is more than enough for our needs. If you are an expert in shaders, there are two kinds of built-in shader. Both are simple alpha-blended shaders, but the Diffuse one interacts with light, generating a (0, 0, −1) front-facing normal vector.
- **Sorting Layer**: This is in which Sorting Layer the Sprite should be rendered (as discussed previously).
- **Order in Layer**: This is the order within that particular Sorting Layer (as we discussed previously).

Importing new friends

If you have downloaded and imported the package from the *Getting ready* section, we should now have all the files inside our `Project` folder. If you go to the `Graphics/towers` folder and select `cupcake_tower_sheet-01`, we should see the following in the **Inspector**:

These are the **Import Settings**, where different options can be set. After we have changed something, we need to press the **Apply** button at the bottom to confirm the changes. Likewise, if we are not happy, we can press the **Revert** button to discard our changes.

It is important to note that the **Texture Type** is **Sprite (2D and UI)**. In 2D mode, Unity always imports image files as Sprites and not as Textures.

The other important parameter that we need to take into consideration is the **Sprite Mode**. By default, it is set to **Single**, but it can be changed to **Multiple** or **Polygonal** (only from Unity 5.3). As the names suggests, the first is used when the image contains a single Sprite, and the second mode is used when we have a Sprite Sheet with more than one Sprite. The last one is used to identify a polygonal Sprite with a custom number of edges.

Furthermore, the **Pixel Per Unit** parameter determines how big the Sprite will be in the Scene. It represents how many pixels are needed to have a unitary length in the **Scene View**. By default, it is set to **100**, but you should modify this value when you need to adapt your assets and change them to the right dimensions. However, if you already have a scale in mind, creating the graphics accordingly could be a useful time saver for the later stages of development.

With regard to the other settings (**Packing Tag**, **Generate Mip Maps**, **Filter Mode**, **Max Size**, and **Format**), we will see them in detail in the last chapter of this book, when we will talk about optimization.

Since the file that we have selected contains more than one Sprite, let's set the **Sprite Mode** to **Multiple** before we move on to the next section.

The Sprite Editor

In **Import Settings**, there is also a button named **Sprite Editor**. If we press this button, a new window appears. This is the **Sprite Editor**, as we can see in the following screenshot:

If we mess things up, we can always revert them back by clicking on the **Revert** button in the top-right corner of the **Sprite Editor**. Next to it, you can also find an **Apply** button, which you use to confirm your choices, so be careful which one you press!

For your own reference, they are highlighted in the next screenshot:

Near these two buttons, you can find some features that might help you when working in the **Sprite Editor**. The first is a button that is easy to miss, but that allows you to switch from the colored asset (RGB channels) to B/W (alpha channel). This is particularly useful when you need to define contours and the image has transparency, as we will see later. So that you avoid missing it, you can find it highlighted in the following screenshot:

To the right of it, there are two sliders, which allow you to either zoom in/out or increase/decrease the resolution (number of pixels). These features are shown in the following screenshot:

The **Sprite Editor** allows you to do different things. For single sprites, it gives the possibility to change the pivot point. For Sprite Sheets, such as in this case, it is the way for Unity to understand how many Sprites there are and where they are located on the image.

Now, there are different ways to do this, so let's have a look at them in more detail.

Manual mode

In manual mode, it's you that selects each Sprite in the image, and tells Unity where it is and how big it is.

To create a new selection, you need to click in a corner of your Sprite and drag the mouse until you have selected the whole Sprite. A green rectangle appears, showing you the selected area, and you can see how the Sprite changes in real time while dragging the mouse. If you release the mouse button, the green rectangle becomes blue and Unity will interpret everything that is inside it as a Sprite.

You can create as many selections (rectangles) as you want. Also, by clicking on them, you can move them around the image and change their dimensions. Here is an example of our Sprite Sheet with some manual selections:

If you have made a rectangle that is bigger than the Sprite, Unity can try to trim it. In the top-left corner of the Sprite Editor, there is the Trim button, as shown in the following screenshot:

It is active only when a selection is highlighted. If you don't like the final result, you can always modify the selection.

Furthermore, in the middle of each selection, there is a small blue circle. This is the Pivot Point of that selection. We are free to drag it to another position. However, other than very specific cases, having the pivot point in the middle is common and useful. So at the moment, don't worry much about it, and just leave it in the middle.

Another thing you may notice is four small green squares in the middle of each edge of the rectangle. We will need them to do 9-slice scaling in a few sections.

Once we have highlighted a selection, it is possible to modify it in more detail by using the menu that appears in the bottom-right corner of the Sprite Editor. Here is what it looks like:

From this menu, you can modify the name of the selection, which will be reflected in the name of the Sprite when we use it. By typing numeric values, you can precisely set the dimension, the position, and the Pivot Point of the selection.

To conclude, manual mode is particularly useful when the shape and the dimensions of the Sprite in the Sprite Sheet are different. Even if the designer of the picture is careful and avoids placing single Sprites close to each other, the objects can still have very different dimensions.

Automatic mode

In automatic mode, Unity tries to slice the Sprites, which means it creates the different selections for you. However, to get a better result, you need to give some information about the image. In any case, once Unity has offered its selections for the image, you can still modify them as you would in manual mode.

In the top-left corner of the **Sprite Editor**, next to the **Trim** button, we can see the **Slice** button, as shown here:

By clicking on it, a menu appears that looks like this:

As you can see, we can select different types. Let's go through them.

The **Automatic** type is the best guess of Unity about the selections. Besides the method that we will see in a bit, and where to place the pivot points of the selections, there is nothing else to set. Unity will do everything automatically, and if we don't need our Sprites to be the same size, this way works pretty well. Here is the final result applied to our image:

The **Automatic** type comes with three different methods:

- The **Delete Existing** method erases all the previous selections before slicing the image
- The **Smart** method tries to create selections for the Sprites that are not yet in a selection
- The **Safe** method creates new selections without erasing the previous ones

The **Grid By Cell Size** type, instead, divides the image into a grid of selections. From the menu, you can select the dimension of each cell. As a result, the number of cells will depend on how big they are.

The **Grid By Cell Count** type, again, divides the image into a grid of selections. However, this time, you can set from the menu how many cells will be in the image, and their dimensions will depend on this. Here is our image sliced using a 4 x 4 grid:

Polygonal mode

From Unity 5.3, you can have access to this new feature of the Sprite Editor. In order to use it, you need to set the Sprite Mode to Polygonal in the import setting of the asset.

In this mode, Unity automatically slices the Sprite as a polygon. Once we open the Sprite Editor, we will immediately be able to set the number of sides or edges of the polygon. If we miss this, we can always press the **Change Shape** button in the top-left corner of the Sprite Editor, as shown here:

If we select an octagon (eight-sided polygon), this is the final result we would get in our image:

Sprite Editor for UI-9-slice scaling

There is another important feature of the Sprite Editor, called 9-slice. It is used when a UI element needs different scaling in different parts of it. This feature is in the Sprite Editor because UI elements are treated as Sprites by Unity.

We will see the UI in another chapter, but let's start understanding why some UI elements need to be scaled differently. As you know, the game can run on different screens that usually have different resolutions and aspect ratios. As a result, the UI needs to be scaled properly depending on the screen. However, if you create a button with beautiful rounded corners, once it's scaled they will look completely different to how we had originally designed them, and not for the better.

The 9-slice technique avoids this problem by defining nine sections on the Sprite that will be scaled differently. In particular, corners will not be scaled at all: only edges along their axis and the central section will scale in all the directions. The following image should help in understanding these nine sections and how they scale:

NO SCALING	HORIZONTAL SCALING ONLY	NO SCALING
VERTICAL SCALING ONLY	HORIZONTAL AND VERTICAL SCALING	VERTICAL SCALING ONLY
NO SCALING	HORIZONTAL SCALING ONLY	NO SCALING

Let's take a UI image to learn how to do a 9-slice with the Sprite Editor of Unity. Select `ui_blank_square_icon_pink` in the `Graphics/UI` folder, and open it in the Sprite Editor. Since we didn't set its **Sprite Mode** to **Multiple**, we have only one selection around the entire image.

As we have already noticed, there are some green squares at the edges of our selection. If we drag them, we can divide the image into nine sections, and we are performing a 9-slice on that Sprite. Here is how the 9-slice should be done with a button:

You need to leave the central section as big as possible, and keep the others the right size to include corners and edges.

Now, we should know a lot about the Sprite Editor. I suggest that you practice with the Sprite Editor for a bit before moving to the next section of this book. In fact, you will need to practice the methods that we have covered so far to prepare all our assets for the game we are going to build.

Preparing the assets

In this section, you will have the chance to practice what we have learned so far. In fact, we need to prepare the assets for our game.

Let's start by selecting `Graphics/towers/cupcake_tower_sheet-01` (the same file we used before) and slice it with a 3 x 3 grid. Then, we should rename each Sprite.

In the first row, we can give them these names (from left to right):

- `Sprinkles_Cupcake_Tower_0`
- `Sprinkles_Cupcake_Tower_1`
- `Sprinkles_Cupcake_Tower_2`

In the second row, we can give them these names:

- `ChocolateChip_Cupcake_Tower_0`
- `ChocolateChip_Cupcake_Tower_1`
- `ChocolateChip_Cupcake_Tower_2`

Finally, the third row:

- `Lemon_Cupcake_Tower_0`
- `Lemon_Cupcake_Tower_1`
- `Lemon_Cupcake_Tower_2`

At the end, we should have the following in the **Project** panel:

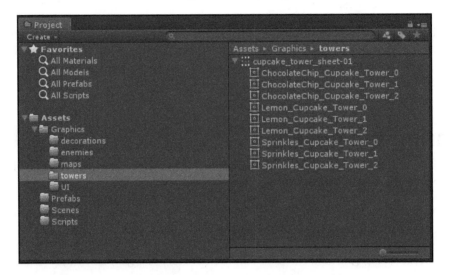

Repeat the same process with the `Graphics/enemies` and `Graphics/UI` folders by dividing the different Sprite Sheets. Don't forget to assign meaningful names. For the rest of the book, when we refer to an asset, its name will be self-explanatory. For your convenience, the original file where the Sprite has been taken will be specified.

Scenes as levels

A Unity game is made of different scenes that you can think of as levels. It's good practice to create a folder in our **Project** panel to store all the scenes. So, if we haven't done so already, right-click on the **Project** panel, then navigate to **Create | Folder**, and finally rename it `Scenes`.

In the toolbar menu, under **File**, there are options to create, save, and load scenes. Let's save the current one, even if it's empty, by navigating to **File** | **Save Scene**, as shown here:

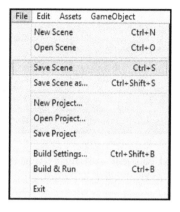

 You can also use the keyboard shortcut *Ctrl + s (Cmd + S* on Mac OS) to save the scene.

Unity will ask where to save the scene. Select the Scenes folder that we have just created and name the file Level_01. As a result, every time we save our scene, Unity will save it in this file.

Setting proportions

When building our game, we need to think about the target platform that we are intending to develop for. Of course, we would like to adapt the game to as many devices and platforms as possible. For this reason, it's an important step in the game development process to do this adaptation.

Without going into too much detail, since it is out of the scope of this book, it is important to have the screen proportion of your target platform, and develop the game accordingly. For this book, we will stick to 16:9 since it is a common proportion, and it is easy to adapt to other proportions later, and also because the package that we have downloaded has been created for 16:9 proportions.

To change the proportion in Unity, you need to select the **Game** tab. In the top-left corner, there are two drop-down menus. The first is for the displays (available from Unity 5.3) and the other one is the proportion. They are highlighted in the following screenshot:

 From Unity 5.5, next to these settings, there is also a slider that allows you to zoom in and out in the scene, by changing its scale.

If you need a custom proportion, you can select the + button at the end of the list, and a screen like the following will appear:

From here, it is possible to assign a label to this resolution and its dimensions. Once you have added a resolution, it will be shared among all of your projects.

Before we move on to the next section, remember to select **16:9** as the project's resolution.

There is more about the Unity interface

From the e-guide that I suggested to you at the beginning of the chapter, you should have learned more about the Unity interface. But, I want to share a little trick with you.

Navigate from the top-bar menu and select **Edit | Preferences...**, as shown in the following screenshot:

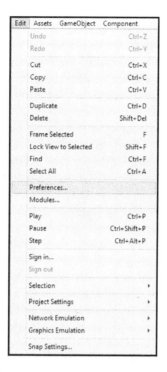

Then, from the menu that appeared, select the third tab, **Colors**, and in this screen you will have the possibility to change the color of the the main graphical elements (or Gizmos; see in the next chapter) of the scene view, such as the axis or the grid as shown in the following screenshot:.

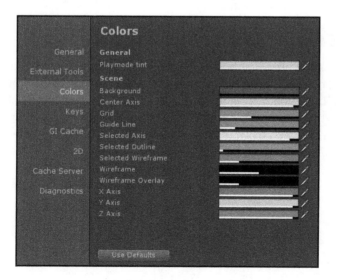

However, the trick lies in the **Playmode tint** setting. It allows you to change the overall tint of the interface when the game is running. You may not see the usefulness now, but it will be of great help when you want to modify parameters, and often you may forget to be in play mode. Personally, this little trick has helped me in many situations. Here is an example of how the Unity interface appears when it is in play mode with a blue tint:

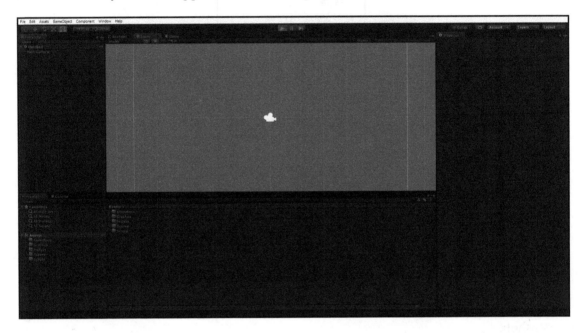

Homework

In this chapter, you have already spent some time working with the Sprite Editor, so there is no need to do more exercises about it. However, if for some reason you want to keep practicing, you can download the standard assets from the Asset Store of Unity (**Window |
Asset Store**), since it is free. Then, import the `Standard Assets/2D/Sprites` folder, and try to slice them from scratch using different modes to achieve the same result.

Summary

In this chapter, we have seen the entire pipeline for importing Sprites and preparing them to use in our game. During this process we have understood what Sprites are, how to import them, and use the Sprite Editor in different ways. Furthermore, we have explored Unity when it is set in 2D and seen an introduction to 2D game development. Finally, we have learned how to set up scenes with the right screen resolution for our target platform.

I think that we have covered a lot in this chapter and now it's time to take a break. Go grab a coffee or even a cupcake before moving on to the next chapter, where we will learn about 2D game scripting.

2
Baking Cupcake Towers

In this second chapter, we will begin to build our game. We will see how it's possible to place objects in 2D space and create templates for the most used objects. Furthermore, we will see how Unity deals with scripts, and we will write a couple of our own for our game.

In particular, we will cover the following topics:

- Placing objects in 2D space
- Setting up the map for our game
- Using tags and layers
- Creating Prefabs (templates for game objects)
- Creating new scripts
- Basic concepts of scripting in Unity
- Writing our first two scripts for our game

Like all the other chapters of this book, you will find the *Homework* section at the end. It has a range of different exercises for you to do to improve your skills and implement a range of different functionalities into your game.

So, let's get started by learning how to place 2D objects into the scene.

2D objects

In the previous chapter, we saw that 2D objects in Unity are Sprites. However, we didn't mention how to import them into the scene.

The easiest way to bring your Sprites into the scene is to drag and drop them from the **Project** panel into the **Scene view**. Unity will automatically create a new game object with the same name of the Sprite along with a Sprite Renderer attached. We have already covered this component in the previous chapter. Since we will not use Sorting Layers (as we decided in the previous chapter), we don't need to change any settings when dragging a new Sprite into the scene.

Another way to add Sprites to the scene is by right-clicking on the **Hierarchy** panel and then **2D Object | Sprite**. However, in the Sprite Renderer, you need to specify which Sprite to use.

Let's bring the `Pink_Sprinkle` Sprite into our scene (you can find it in the `Graphics/projectiles` folder within the `projectiles_sheet_01` file). It appears like this in the **Scene** view:

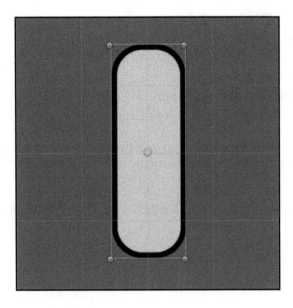

Since Sprites are also GameObjects, you can have access to their **Transform** properties, as shown here:

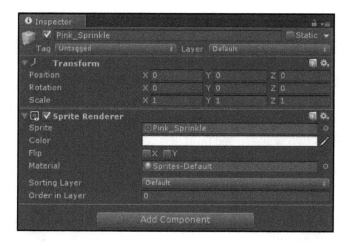

This means that you can change their position along the *x* axis and the *y* axis, as well as the scale and the rotation. Remember that the z-axis is used to determine the depth, as we discussed in the previous chapter.

By using the **Scale** parameter, it is possible to flip the Sprite. However, keep in mind that this will also flip its children. As we saw in the previous chapter, from Unity 5.3 to flip a Sprite it is preferable to use the **Flip** variable on the **Sprite Renderer**.

 You can create an empty game object by navigating to the top bar menu and select **GameObject | Create Empty**. Alternatively, on the **Hierarchy** panel, click on **Create**, then select **Create Empty**. Creating an empty game object is a very useful when we need to create containers of other game objects, or if we want to build our game object from scratch.

Parenting game objects

Each game object can have a parent. This means that the game objects will move, rotate, and scale along with its parent.

I could use many words to explain this concept, but there are things which videos can explain better than words. As such, there is a very short video explaining, *The Hierarchy and Parent-Child relationships* at:
https://unity3d.com/learn/tutorials/topics/interface-essentials/hierarchy-and-parent-child-relationships.

I recommend that you to watch it before you continue reading this book. I'll wait for you here.

Difference between world coordinates and local coordinates

Every game object in Unity has a position, but a position needs a reference frame (more about reference frames later in Chapter 5, *The Secret Ingredient Is a Dash of Physics*). In particular, Unity offers two ways to see (and set) coordinates:

- **World coordinates**: These are absolute coordinates of where the game object is located (by absolute, I mean with respect to the world frame, which is considered to be absolute in the game)
- **Local coordinates**: These are the coordinates of where the game object is with respect to its parent

You can easily switch between the two coordinates with a toggle in the upper-right part of the Unity interface, as shown in the following screenshot:

As shown in the preceding screenshot, they are both toggles, but the one to switch between world and local coordinates is the one on the left. At the moment, it is selected to be on **Global**, which means on world coordinates.

Ordering the different layers with Z-Buffering

In the previous chapter, we decided to use Z-Buffering instead of Sorting Layers. However, we need to decide which elements of our game will be in the foreground compared to the others.

In addition, it is important to keep in mind how the camera is set. Select **Main Camera**, which should be the only camera in the scene. This is what the **Inspector** should look like:

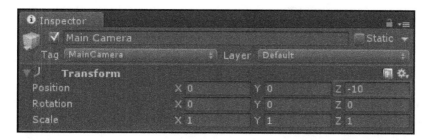

As you can see, by default, its **Z** value on the the position is set to -10. This means you cannot have any greater negative values (that means smaller than -10) in the **Z** value of a Sprite, otherwise it will not be rendered. For our purpose, -10 is perfect, and we will stick with it.

Next, we need to assign a **Z** value to all the elements that we have. We can start to place the map in the background, by assigning the lowest depth (maximum **Z** value) that we have in mind; in this case it's zero.

Then, we would like to have the enemies. Therefore, we can set their **Z** value to -1. After them, the projectiles and the towers, respectively -2 and -3. Finally, we need to add another value for the foreground. Here is a summary table:

Elements	Z value (depth)	Reasons
Map	0	The map has the lowest value, since it will be behind everything.
Enemies	-1	Enemies are rendered after the map, since they may pass behind the towers, which we would like to keep visible. Furthermore, also the projectiles should be visible on the enemies, just before they hit them.
Projectiles	-2	Projectiles are shot from the towers, so it may look odd having the projectiles on top of the tower, whereas appearing from the back appears more natural.
Towers	-3	The towers don't have any other layer on top of them, excluding the map overlay.

| Map Overlay | -9 | This is in the foreground, so it has to be rendered last. We chose -9 instead of -4 because we may add some other layers, but the foreground is always the closest one to the camera. We will see what this layer contains in the next section. |
| Main Camera | -10 | As default. |

We need to keep these values in mind when we create the Prefabs for our game elements. This is important both for this chapter and the rest of the book.

 We will discuss what a Prefab is later in the chapter.

Unfolding the map

We are finally ready to place the 2D map in our scene.

In the previous chapter, we have set the resolution to 16:9. Therefore, the maps that we will find in our packages are ready to use.

Let's start by dragging the sugar_mountain_map Sprite from the Graphics/maps folder into our scene. We need to place it in (0,0,0). Please note that the z axis is set to zero.

It is a perfect map for what we need. For example, on the left side, there is the beginning of the path that the sweet-tooth pandas will follow. At the end of the path, there is the Sugar castle that the player needs to protect. Furthermore, there is enough space at the top to implement our user interface in Chapter 3, *Communicating with the Player – the User Interface*.

The next step is to modify the camera settings. What we want to do is to fit the entire map in the **Camera** view. To achieve this, just modify the **Size** properties to 22.5 as shown here:

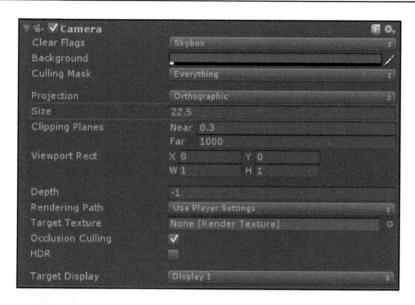

As a result, our map will be perfectly centered in the **Camera** view. This is what we should see in the **Scene** view with the camera selected:

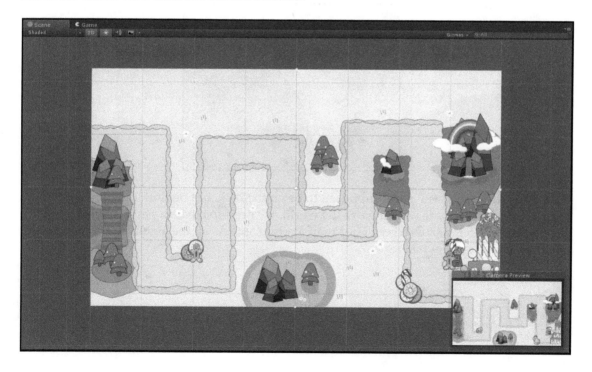

Now, let's bring in one of the cupcake tower we sliced in the previous chapter; for instance, the `ChocolateChip_Cupcake_Tower_2`. If we drag it to the beginning of the path, we have the following problem:

Or also at the bottom of the map:

In fact, the cupcake tower is not supposed to be on the rock, but behind it, due to the perspective. Since we are working in a 2D world, we need to create a perspective. Luckily, our package contains an overlay of our map. It also contains all the assets that should be in the foreground, as shown here:

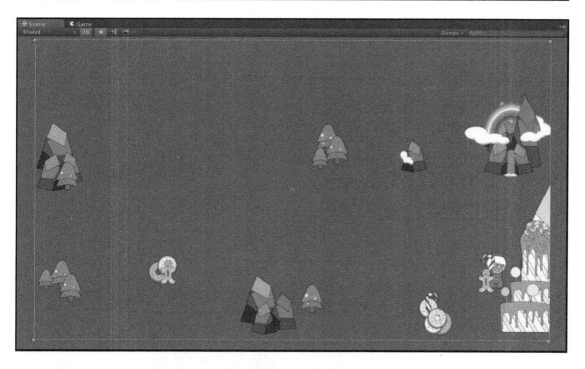

 Please note that usually, all the assets are on different levels so we can customize their positions. However, in the package they are pre-placed as for your convenience, so we don't lose time to learn amazing things!

So, let's add also this overlay to the scene. It is called `sugar_mountain_map_overlay` and can be found inside the `Graphics/maps` folder. Again, remember to set its *x* and *y* positions to zero. After we have done this, we don't see any difference, and the cupcake tower still hovers over the rock. In fact, we have decided from the previous section, that all of the *z*-axis values should be assigned to the different game elements. If you remember, the value for the map overlay is `-9`.

Once you have set the map overlay z-axis value, our cupcakes should behave as we wished:

It behaves in the right way here, as well:

The map is finally ready. One last touch; we should parent the map overlay to the map itself. Therefore, if we need to change the map, they will move and scale together.

Before we continue our journey, remember to delete the cupcake tower, since we only needed it for testing purposes.

Layers and tags

If you already have in mind what are you going to do, it's good to set everything up at the beginning. In particular, Unity has some labels that can be given to game objects. These are layers and tags. Unity uses these two properties to discriminate amongst certain kinds of game objects.

By default, some of them are already defined, but we need a few more for our project. From the toolbar menu, we can access the layers and tags settings by navigating to **Edit** | **Project Settings** | **Tags and Layers**. As a result, the **Inspector** should now look like the following screenshot:

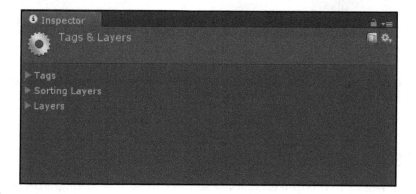

 In this menu, we also have the possibility to change the sorting layers for rendering 2D objects. However, as mentioned earlier, we will use Z-Buffering to achieve the same effect.

Let's expand the **Tags** menu, as follows:

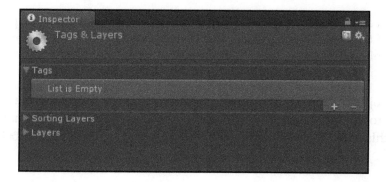

To add a new tag, just press on the + button in the bottom-right corner. We need to add two tags, respectively `Enemy` and **Projectile**, as shown in the following screenshot:

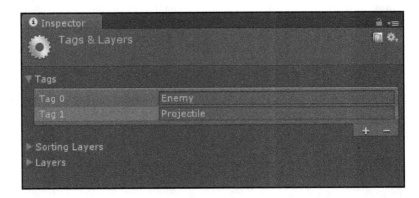

In fact, we will need these two tags later on in the development of this game. In fact, when a cupcake tower searches for surrounding objects, it needs to discriminate between enemies and projectiles.

Prefabs

When the scene begins to fill up with objects, some of these objects might become complex. By complex, I mean with a lot of components and children. If we need to use many of them in the game and maybe change all of them at once, Unity offers the possibility to create a Prefab.

As the name suggests, it is an object already assembled with all the necessary components and ready to be placed in the scene. The advantage is the possibility to reuse it often and to change all its instances quickly.

 If an object in the scene is a Prefab, its name in the **Hierarchy** panel is blue. If the name is red, instead, this means that there are some references missing.

To keep our project organized, let's create a folder named `Prefabs`, if we haven't done so yet. Inside the folder, right-click and then select `Create/Prefab`. You can name it as you want, but for this book, let's stick with `Pink_Sprinkle_Projectile_Prefab`.

We already have the sprinkle in the scene, so from the **Hierarchy** panel, drag it into the `Pink_Sprinkle_Projectile_Prefab`.

Now, we can also erase the previous sprinkle from the scene, as we don't need it anymore. For testing purposes, you can try to add as many sprinkles as you want in the scene by dragging the Prefab into the **Scene** view. Of course, remember to erase them before continuing with the rest of this chapter.

When we select an object that is an instance of a Prefab, three additional buttons appear in the **Inspector**, as shown in the following screenshot:

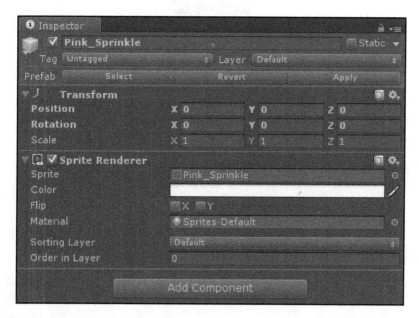

These are their functions:

- **Select**: This is a shortcut to quickly select in the **Project** panel the Prefab of the object.
- **Revert**: If we did some changes in the instance of the Prefab (the current selected object), these do not affect the Prefab. By clicking on this button, we revert all the changes to the original Prefab.
- **Apply**: If, on the other hand, you are satisfied with the changes you made to this instance of the Prefab, by clicking on this button, you can apply these changes to the Prefab. As a result, you may modify all of the other instances in the scene. So be careful when you use this function.

The game view

You should already know about the game view, but there might be some new types of functionality that you didn't know about before. So, a short recap might be useful, before we move on in our journey.

First of all, we have our three main buttons, which you should be very familiar with, as shown here:

The first is the play button, which makes your game run. The second button pauses the game, and allows you to tweak some settings. The last one makes your game run for one frame only.

In the top-left corner, we have the displays and the resolution tabs that we covered in the previous chapter. In the opposite corner (top-right), there are many different yet useful toggles, as shown in the following screenshot:

These are their functions:

- **Maximize on Play**: If this is on, every time you push the play button, the game view will be maximized to the largest window it can be. It's useful for testing the game in almost full screen; otherwise, it can be a little bit hard to tweak values without having a second monitor.
- **Mute Audio**: If this is enabled, as the name suggests, it silences all the audio sources in the game.
- **Stats**: If this is on, it provides some basic feedback about the performance of your game, as shown here:

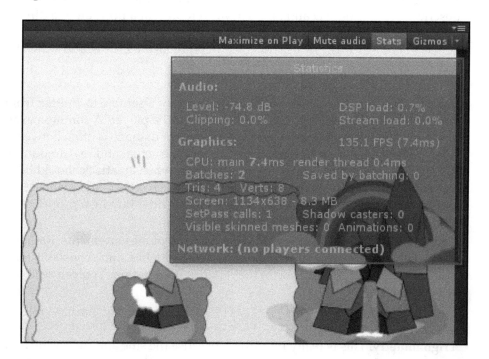

- **Gizmos**: These are used to identify objects in the scenes. However, we will see these later in Chapter 6, *Through a Sea of Sprinkles – Navigation in Artificial Intelligence*.

Math background

Either you like math or not; however, it is a fact that it is required for game development. We don't have time to go through all the math behind this game, since it is required to have a complete toolset for game development. However, this section introduces you to some basic concepts that we will need for the rest of the book. In addition, it also makes some references to the official documentation so that you can learn a bit more about it.

If you feel confident with some of the following topics, you are free to skip them:

- **Vectors**: They are really important in game development, because they are able to describe spaces (both 3D and 2D). They can represent a position or a direction. You can read more about them at `https://docs.unity3d.com/Manual/VectorCookbook.html` and watch this video: `https://unity3d.com/learn/tutorials/topics/scripting/vector-maths`.

- **Probability:** This is very important when we want a sample to emerge from our game, by including uncertainty and chances for the player. A common example is in RTS or MMORPG games, where the amount of damage is often between a range (determined by the character's stat), but the actual and real amount of damage uses random numbers. Another case is when an attack should be critical so to inflict double the damage. At the end of the chapter it is explained how to extract random numbers in Unity. However, consider buying a proper math book about probability; it might be worthwhile.

- **Radians and Degrees**: Angles can have two unit of measurements. Radians are usually used to perform calculations, but Unity has some constants that by a multiplication can convert one to the other representation. You can read more about these at `https://docs.unity3d.com/ScriptReference/Mathf.Deg2Rad.html` and `https://docs.unity3d.com/ScriptReference/Mathf.Rad2Deg.html`.

- **Trigonometry**: This is really important, because the sine and the cosine functions are often used to achieve believable behavior, since Mother Nature uses them for our world. Unluckily, there are no shortcuts. Therefore, if you really want to understand them and get into them, you should read any book about trigonometry. However, the most important notion used is that they range the value of their arguments between -1 and $+1$.

- **Quaternions**: This is a math entity that's not very intuitive, since it involves the analysis of complex numbers. However, it's not important to know them in detail (except in really specific cases) when programming in Unity. In fact, it's enough to know that Unity uses them to store rotations. Also, there are functions to convert from the Euler representations (the most intuitive of three angles). The reason of this choice is behind the scope of this book, but it's due a numerical instability of the Euler representation. You can learn more about them by watching the following video:
  `https://unity3d.com/learn/tutorials/topics/scripting/quaternions`.
- `Atan2()`: This is a function that is really important in game development, because it is able to calculate the angle of a vector. You can read more about this function at `https://docs.unity3d.com/ScriptReference/Mathf.Atan2.html`.

Scripting in Unity

In this section, we will learn one of the toughest topics in game development! However, I strongly encourage you not to be scared, but try to practice a lot. As a result, you will be able to master every single detail of your game. And that is awesome!

Creating new scripts

First of all, we need to understand how to create new scripts in Unity. The easiest way is to select a game object and in the **Inspector**, navigate to **Add Component | New Script**. In this way, you still have the possibility to rename it, but the script will be located in the `Asset` folder. Furthermore, it's not possible to create a class that cannot be attached to a game object.

A much better way is to create a folder called `Scripts` in the **Project** panel, if you haven't done so yet. Then, right-click and navigate to **Create | C# Script**. As a result, it will be in the right folder, and we don't have problems if we create a script that cannot be attached to game objects.

For the rest of this book, it will be assumed that every new script will be created in this way, and always in the `Scripts` folder.

Keeping the name of the script in mind is important, because the file should have the same name as the main class in the script. This means that if we change the name of the class later on, we need to rename the file accordingly as well. However, this may break some references in other scripts that will require correcting. So, be careful when changing names.

To open a script, you need to double-click on it. Unity will open a script editor. By default, it will be Monodevelop. However, it is possible to change this setting by navigating through **Edit | Preferences...**. In the **External Tool** tab, you can change the **External Script Editor**. Another commonly used script editor is Visual Studio, it can can be downloaded from `https://www.visualstudio.com/`.

However, if this is your first experience with Unity, I suggest that you stick with Monodevelop. In any case, for this book, we don't have any requirements (as far as you are able to edit the scripts), so feel free to choose the one you like best.

Basics about scripts

If this is your first time scripting in Unity, there is some information to know before we begin.

 Unity mainly supports two languages: C# and JavaScript. Since we created a C# script in the previous section, we are going to use this language for the rest of this book.

Variables

Variables can be public, private, or protected. We will not cover the last one, since we don't have enough time for that, and it's not really important when getting started with Unity development. Private variables can be used only within the script itself. Usually they are used to store internal data of the script that doesn't need to be shared among other components.

Public variables, instead, can be accessed from any script, so we need to pay attention where to use them. It's good practice to implement the `get` and `set` functions, when applicable. Even if we will not use them much in this book, it's worth learning what they are, which you can do at `https://msdn.microsoft.com/en-us/library/w86s7x04.aspx`.

Furthermore, public variables are visible in the **Inspector**. In fact, just for testing purposes, you can create a new script and add the following integer variable:

```
public int testVariable;
```

As a result, after you have saved the script, you are able to set its value in the **Inspector**, as shown in the following screenshot:

As a consequence, public variables don't need to be set within the script in order to be able to use them. Often, we would like to have a public variable, since it will be set from another script, but not visible on the **Inspector**. You can achieve that in Unity by using an attribute.

Attributes

Before variables and functions, Unity allows us to insert an attribute. An attribute is enclosed between [and], and can contain different parameters. Around 30 attributes exist and they really differ in functionality and usage. Since we don't have the time to go through them all, we will just cover the most commonly used ones:

- The Header attribute is formatted as [Header("string")]. It creates a header before the variables that follow it. Here is an example of adding the attribute to the variable of the test script we used earlier:

  ```
  [Header("This is a heading")]
  public int testVariable;
  ```

  The result is the following:

- The `HideInInspector` attribute is formatted as `[HideInInspector]`. It hides the variable that follows it from the **Inspector**. Here it is in use, in the previous example:

```
[HideInInspector]
public int testVariable;
```

  And this is the result:

- The `Range` attribute is formatted as `[Range(minValue, maxValue)]`. It captures the possible values of the variable in the range of numbers from `minValue` to `maxValue`. Again, we use the previous example:

```
[Range(-10, 10)]
public int testVariable;
```

  This is the result we obtain:

- Finally, The `Tooltip` attribute is formatted as `[Tooltip("string")]`. It creates a tooltip in the **Inspector** when the cursor is hovering over that variable:

```
[Tooltip("This is a tooltip")]
public int testVariable;
```

  Here is the result (when the cursor hovers):

Functions

Any script that derives from the `MonoBehaviour` class has two main functions:

- `Start()`: This function is called only once, when the game starts. It's useful to set all the variables and get the references we need within this function.
- `Update()`: This function is called every frame, and needs to compute things in real time, such as velocity or behaviors. However, since this is called so often, we need to pay attention to what we code inside, to avoid slowing down our game too often.

There are other functions that can be implemented and that will be automatically called. In actual fact, there are more than 60!

We will use some of them later on, so we will introduce them here and see them in detail in later chapters:

- `OnTriggerEnter2D()`: This is called when another object with a collider enters the trigger collider attached to the game object. We will see this better later on, when we deal with physics.
- `OnMouseDown()`: This is called when the player has pressed the mouse button while over the game object if it has a collider attached. Furthermore, it can be a `Coroutine` and works with `GUIElements` too.
- `OnEnable()`: This is called when the object becomes enabled and active.

You can find out more about them at
`https://docs.unity3d.com/ScriptReference/MonoBehaviour.html`.

Comments

As we mentioned in the previous chapter, game development is not an easy process, since it involves many stages. For this reason, it's really important to document everything that we do. This doesn't mean writing something that will be published, but just a couple of lines to remind yourself and your team what you have accomplished. In fact, human memory is great at remembering concepts, but not good for details! This is essential during the scripting stage. It is important to be able to read what the rest of your team or yourself have written a few days ago. When coding, it's easy to get lost among the many lines of code when you don't use comments!

Since Unity uses a C# compiler, it is possible to insert comments inside the code. Comments are lines that will be ignored (not compiled), and as the name suggests, they help to leave messages to those who will read the code.

There are two main ways to comment in C#. The first is to insert // at the beginning of a line. As a result, everything that comes after until the next line will be ignored. The second one is used when we have more than one line. It consists to surround the comment with an opening tag /* and the closing tag */. As a result, everything within these two tags will be ignored. Here is an example:

```
//This line is commented
This other one is not.
/*Here it is
again
commented*/
```

 Comments are also used to build automatic documentations and as markups for other things. However, this is out the scope of this book.

I strongly suggest that you always try to insert comments in your code, so it is easier to read later on. For your convenience, all the code that comes with this book is provided with comments, helping you to understand what is happening and where.

Execution order

Another important concept about scripting in Unity is the **Execution Order**. It may be fundamental that some scripts or parts of code are executed before others. As a result, this will affect how the shared resources are modified and the efficiency as well.

The standard ordering is as follows:

1. **Editor**: In particular, the Reset() function.
2. **Scene Load**: Functions such as Awake(), OnEnable(), and OnLevelWasLoaded() are called.
3. **Before the first frame update**: All the Start() functions in the scripts are called (if the object is active!).
4. **In between frames**: the OnApplicationPause() function is performed.
5. **Update**: All the different Update() functions are called.
6. **Rendering**: Specific rendering functions are performed.

7. **Coroutines**: They are executed until a yield statement is found
8. **When the object is destroyed**: The `Destroy()` function is called.
9. **When quitting**: Functions to be executed when disabling game objects or when quitting the game are called.

Of course, this is just scratching the surface to give you an idea about the execution order. If you are interested in finding out more on this topic, you can find a detailed explanation of the execution order in the official documentation, at `https://docs.unity3d.com/Manual/ExecutionOrder.html`.

Unity offers also the possibility to change the execution order within your scripts when you have specific needs. This can be done by navigating on the toolbar to, **Edit | Project Settings | Script Execution Order**. As a result, this window will appear on the **Inspector**, where it is possible to change the order:

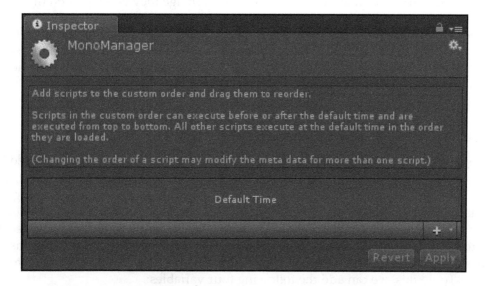

For more information about this, you can visit the following link: `https://docs.unity3d.com/Manual/class-ScriptExecution.html`. However, the execution order for scripts is for specific needs that we don't have, so we won't touch any of these settings. However, I hope that this section helped you to get a better understanding of the logic behind Unity. Saying that, I encourage you to re-read this section when you gain a better understanding of scripting in Unity.

Making sprinkles

In the *Prefabs* section, we created the Prefab for our sprinkle projectile. In this section, we will see how to make sprinkles move into the 2D space. In particular, we will learn how to create and use scripts in Unity for 2D game elements.

The projectile class

Since there might be different projectiles in our game that can be thrown against the sweet-tooth pandas, and not only sprinkles, we need to define a general class. All the different kinds of projectile will follow some general rules:

- They move in a straight line
- They carry information about how much damage they will inflict on the enemies

Whereas the first is identical for all the projectiles, the second depends on the specific kind of projectile that will be fired. So, we need to create a template. Once we attach this script to a game object, we can set some of its variables and tweak its behavior. In this specific case, we want to tweak how much damage is given and how fast.

Scripting the projectile mother class

So, to begin, let's create a new script and name it `ProjectileScript`. Next, we need to define four variables. The first is for the amount of damage, the second for its speed, and the third one, for its direction, since we need to know where the projectile is heading. The last variable stores its life duration expressed in seconds. As a consequence, it also sets, together with the speed variable, how far the projectile can reach. In fact, if the projectile misses the target, we don't want it going straight on forever, because this would consume computational resources and slow down our game. So after this duration, we need to destroy it. To do this, we can add the following four variables:

```
public float damage;        //How much damage will the enemy receive
public float speed = 1f;       //How fast the projectile moves
public Vector3 direction; //What direction the projectile is heading
public float lifeDuration = 10f; //How long the projectile lives before
   self-destructing
```

The next thing to do is to set some of these parameters in the Start() function. Since the direction will be given by the entity that will throw the projectile, we don't have a guarantee that it has a unit norm. As consequence, we need to normalize the direction. Then, we need to rotate the graphic of our projectile, which in this case is the sprinkle, towards the right direction. In order to achieve this, we need to compute the angle using the Atan2() function. After we have transformed this in degrees, we use the AngleAxis() function in the Quaternion class to rotate our game object. Finally, we need to set a timer before the game object is destroyed. As a result, this will be our Start() function:

```
void Start() {
  //Normalize the direction
  direction = direction.normalized;

  //Fix the rotation
  float angle = Mathf.Atan2(-direction.y, direction.x) * Mathf.Rad2Deg;
  transform.rotation = Quaternion.AngleAxis(angle, Vector3.forward);

  //Set the timer for self-destruction
  Destroy(gameObject, lifeDuration);
}
```

In the Update() function, we just need to move the sprinkle in that direction. If the sprinkle collides with something, such as a Panda, it's a case that we will discuss in Chapter 5, *No Longer Alone – Sweet-Toothed Pandas Strike*. So, we need to update its position according to its direction and speed, keeping it dependent on the time. So, we can write the following:

```
// Update the position of the projectile according to time and speed
void Update() {
  transform.position += direction * Time.deltaTime * speed;
}
```

At the end, save the script. There is still a lot of work to do on this script. For instance, the direction should be only on the *x* and *y*, and not on the *z*, since it is used in the Z-Buffering method. However, for now it is fine, and we will look at all these issues later on in the book.

Tons of sprinkles through Prefabs

Now that we have a general script that achieves the behavior of a projectile, we need to actually make the Prefab of our sprinkles with such behavior.

We have already created a Prefab for our sprinkle projectile, but we need to change it. So, go into the `Prefabs` folder in the **Project** panel, and select our `Pink_Sprinkle_Projectile_Prefab`. In the **Inspector**, we need to add the script that we have just created. So, navigate to **Add Component | Script | ProjectileScript**. As a result, you should see the following:

We need to tweak the values, at least for testing purposes, so that we can see our sprinkle moving. We can assign a direction such as (1, 1, 0) and any value to the **Damage** variable. At the end, we should have something like the following:

If we press the play button, we can see our sprinkle leading in the direction we specified, and be destroyed after 10 seconds.

Then, we need to assign the **Z** value on the Prefab. Since it is a projectile, we can look at the table with all the **Z** values for our objects we made earlier. Therefore, we need to assign −2 as the value. We also need to assign the tag to our projectile. We will use this tag later on, but it's better to assign it now to the Prefab.

To assign a tag, on top of the **Inspector**, just below the game object name, there is the **Tag** field, as highlighted in the following screenshot:

Once clicked, a drop-down menu appears, where it is possible to choose from the different tags, including the two we defined previously:

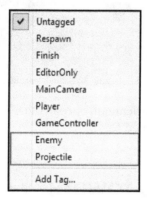

We can assign the **Projectile** tag to our Prefab, and in the end, it should look like this:

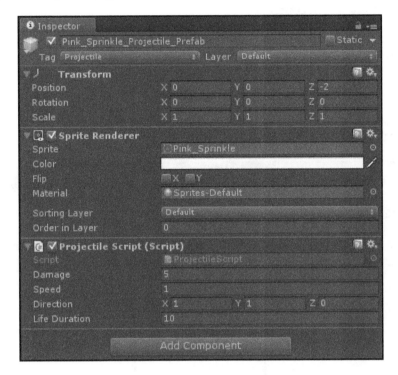

And this is all we need to do to fabricate our projectiles. In fact, we can now use this Prefab to spawn the sprinkles when we need to.

Baking cupcakes towers

In this section, we will see how to create our towers. This is not an easy task, but by doing this we will acquire a lot of scripting skills.

What a cupcake tower does

First of all, it's useful to write down what we want to achieve and define what exactly a cupcake tower is supposed to do.

The best way is to write down a list, to have clear idea of what we are trying to achieve:

- A cupcake tower is able to detect pandas within a certain range.
- A cupcake tower shoots a different kind of projectile according to its typology against the pandas within a certain range. Furthermore, within this range, it uses a policy to decide which panda to shoot.
- There is a reload time before the cupcake tower is able to shoot again.
- The cupcake tower can be upgraded (to a bigger cupcake!), increasing its stats and therefore changing its appearance.

Scripting the cupcake tower

As we have seen in the previous section, there are many things to implement. Let's start by creating a new script and naming it `CupcakeTowerScript`. As we already mentioned for the projectile script, in this chapter, we implement the main logic, but of course there is always space to improve, as we will see later in the book.

Shooting to the pandas

Even if we don't have enemies yet, we can already start to program the behavior of the cupcake towers to shoot to the enemies. In this section, we will learn a bit about using physics to detect objects within a range. However, we will see colliders in more detail in `Chapter 5`, *No Longer Alone – Sweet-Toothed Pandas Strike*.

Let's start by defining four variables. The first three are public, so we can set them in the Inspector. The last one is private, since we only need it to check how much time has elapsed. In particular, the first three variables store the parameters of our tower. There are the projectile Prefab, its range, and its reload time. We can write the following:

```
public float rangeRadius;   //Maximum distance that the Cupcake Tower
    can shoot
public float reloadTime;    //Time before the Cupcake Tower is able to
    shoot again
public GameObject projectilePrefab; //Projectile type that is fired
    from the Cupcake Tower
private float elapsedTime; //Time elapsed from the last time the
    Cupcake Tower has shot
```

Now, in the `Update()` function we need to check if enough time has elapsed in order to shoot. This can be easily done by using an if statement. In any case, at the end, the time elapsed should be increased:

```
void Update () {
   if (elapsedTime >= reloadTime) {
     //Rest of the code
   }
   elapsedTime += Time.deltaTime;
}
```

Within the `if` statement, we need to reset the elapsed time, so as to be able to shoot the next time. Then, we need to check whether there are some game objects within its range or not:

```
if (elapsedTime >= reloadTime) {
  //Reset elapsed Time
  elapsedTime = 0;
  //Find all the gameObjects with a collider within the range of the
    Cupcake Tower
  Collider2D[] hitColliders =
    Physics2D.OverlapCircleAll(transform.position, rangeRadius);
  //Check if there is at least one gameObject found
  if (hitColliders.Length != 0) {
    //Rest of the code
  }
}
```

If there are enemies within range, we need to decide a policy about which enemy the tower should be targeted. There are different ways to do this and different strategies that the tower itself could choose. Here, we are going to implement one where the nearest enemy to the tower will be the one targeted. Different policies and strategies will be discussed in the last chapter of this book.

To implement this policy, we need to loop all all the game objects that we have found in range, check if they actually are enemies, and using distances, pick the nearest one. To achieve this, write the following code inside the previous if statement:

```
if (hitColliders.Length != 0) {
  //Loop over all the gameObjects to identify the closest to the
    Cupcake Tower
  float min = int.MaxValue;
  int index = -1;

  for (int i = 0; i < hitColliders.Length; i++) {
    if (hitColliders[i].tag == "Enemy") {
      float distance =
        Vector2.Distance(hitColliders[i].transform.position,
```

```
          transform.position);
       if (distance < min) {
          index = i;
          min = distance;
       }
     }
   }
   if (index == -1)
   return;
   //Rest of the code
 }
```

Once we find the target, we need to get the direction that the tower will throw the projectile. So, let's write this:

```
//Get the direction of the target
Transform target = hitColliders[index].transform;
Vector2 direction = (target.position - transform.position).normalized;
```

Finally, we need to instantiate a new projectile, and assign to it the direction of the enemy, as follows:

```
//Create the Projectile
GameObject projectile = GameObject.Instantiate(projectilePrefab,
   transform.position, Quaternion.identity) as GameObject;
projectile.GetComponent<ProjectileScript>().direction = direction;
```

Instantiating GameObjects is usually slow, and it should be avoided. However, for learning purposes, we can live with that. In the last chapter, we will see some optimization technique to get rid of this instantiation. And that is it for shooting the enemies.

Upgrading the cupcake tower, making it even tastier

In order to create a function to upgrade the tower, we first need to define a variable to store the actual level of the tower:

```
public int upgradeLevel;   //Level of the Cupcake Tower
```

Then, we need an array with all the Sprites for the different upgrades, like this:

```
public Sprite[] upgradeSprites; //Different sprites for the different
   levels of the Cupcake Tower
```

A third variable is required to check when the cupcake tower is upgradable, so we can add:

```
//Boolean to check if the tower is upgradable
public bool isUpgradable = true;
```

Finally, we can create our upgrade function. The first thing to do is to check if the tower is actually upgradable and then increase its level. Then, we can check (based on how many different graphics we have), if the tower has reached its maximum level, and in that case is preventing the player from upgrading it anymore, by assigning the false value to the isUpgradable variable. After that, we need to upgrade the graphics, and increase the stats. Feel free to tweak these values as you prefer. However, don't forget to assign the new Sprite. In the end, you should have something like the following:

```
public void Upgrade() {
  //Check if the tower is upgradable
  if (!isUpgradable) {
    return;
  }

  //Increase the level of the tower
  upgradeLevel++;

  //Check if the tower has reached its last level
  if(upgradeLevel < upgradeSprites.Length) {
    isUpgradable = false;
  }

  //Increase the stats of the tower
  rangeRadius += 1f;
  reloadTime -= 0.5f;

  //Change graphics of the tower
  GetComponent<SpriteRenderer>().sprite = upgradeSprites[upgradeLevel];
}
```

Save the script, and for now, we are done with it. We will need to modify this function later in the book, but for now, let's create a Prefab for our cupcake.

A pre-baked cupcake tower through Prefabs

As we have done with the sprinkles, we need to do something similar for the cupcake tower. In the Prefabs folder in the **Project** panel, create a new Prefab by right-clicking and then navigating to **Create** | **Prefab**. Name it SprinklesCupcakeTower.

Now, drag and drop Sprinkles_Cupcake_Tower_0 from the Graphics/towers folder (within the cupcake_tower_sheet-01 file) in the **Scene** View. Attach CupcakeTowerScript to the object by navigating to **Add Component** | **Script** | CupcakeTowerScript. The **Inspector** should look like the following:

We need to assign `Pink_Sprinkle_Projectile_Prefab` to the **Projectile Prefab** variable. Then, we need to assign the different Sprites for the upgrades. In particular, we can use `Sprinkles_Cupcake_Tower_*` (replacing the * with the level of the cupcake tower) from the same sheet as earlier. Don't worry too much about the other parameters of the tower, such as the range radius or the reload time, since we will see how to balance the game later on. At the end, this is what we should see:

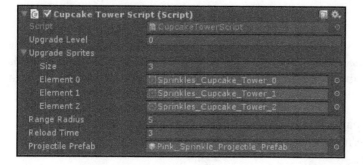

The last step is to drag this game object inside the Prefab. As a result, our cupcake tower is ready.

More about coding in Unity

Before we continue, there are few more things to learn.

Later in the book, we will use both static variables and inheritance. These are topics related with C# more than with Unity, but they are important if you want to become a good game developer. Next, you can find a very brief explanation, but I recommend that you learn them properly from a C# book.

Finally, there is probability, which is a topic of math, as we discussed previously, and it is essential in game development. However, once you know the basics of probability, you should be able to generate random numbers in Unity.

Static variables

Some classes (or components, in the case of Unity), contain variables, which eventually can be set in the Inspector or changed at runtime. However, the whole class can share a variable among all its instances. Such variables are referred to as static variables and are declared with the `static` keyword. A common use is to share a reference to another component, which all the instances of the class should refer to. We will see this better later in the book, when we will use static variables

Inheritance

If different classes share many features in common, we could give them an inheritance structure. This means, to have a parent class that holds the general and common features between these classes, and then they are implemented as children of the parent. A common example to clarify this is imagining the classes Fruit, Apple, and Banana. Fruit is the parent class, which holds all the properties of being a fruit (such as that it is edible), and the children share the same feature of the parent (since both an Apple and a Banana are fruits, and therefore edible). Then, they can implement the specific features of that fruit. For instance, the Apple is red, whereas the Banana is yellow.

Sometimes, the parent class can also have functions (such as `Eat()`) which all the children can give their own implementation. This leads to the difference between the abstract and virtual methods.

Abstract methods are so abstract that the parent class cannot give an implementation of it, but its children have to. Virtual methods, instead, can be implemented in the parent class, since it offers general functionality, but children can override it to give a better implementation of it.

We will look at inheritance in more detail, in `Chapter 7`, *Trading Cupcakes and the Ultimate Battle for the Cake – Gameplay Programming*.

Random numbers in Unity

Generating random numbers in Unity is easy since Unity provides the class `Random`, which allows us to generate random numbers. The most used function of this class is `Range()`, which generates a random number between a min and a max value. Here is an example:

```
//Generates a random number between 2 and 30
Random.Range(2, 30);
```

For more information about the `Random` class, visit the official documentation here: `https://docs.unity3d.com/ScriptReference/Random.html`.

Homework

In this chapter, we have seen how to use Prefabs to quickly replicate and clone GameObjects. So, before you continue with the next chapter, let's get good at using Prefabs.

The following two exercises are needed to have the game completed at the end:

1. **Arming the Cupcakes Towers (Part I)**: Inside `projectiles_sheet_01` in the `Graphics/projectiles` folder, there are nine different projectiles; however, we used only one, `Pink_Sprinkle`. Create the other eight Prefabs, with meaningful names. Don't forget to attach the projectile script to all of them. Do not worry too much about the values assigned inside the script, such as the damage, since we will see the balance of the game later on in the book. However, do not forget to assign the right **Z** value and the proper tag.

2. **Arming the Cupcakes Towers (Part II)**: Inside `cupcake_tower_sheet-01` in the `Graphics/towers` folder, there are three different towers with their respective upgrading levels; however, we only used the sprinkle cupcake tower. Create the other two Prefabs for the chocolate and lemon cupcake towers. Don't forget to attach the cupcake tower script to both of them and assign the respective projectiles and upgrade levels graphic. Again, don't worry much about the values, such as the range radius, because we will see the balance of the game later in the book. However, don't forget to assign the right **Z** value.

The following exercises will help you to improve your skills by familiarizing yourself with best practices:

3. **Formatting scripts for designers (Part I)**: In our scripts, we used many variables. Comments next to them help us to understand their function; however, these comments are hidden to designers. Therefore, it's good practice to add tooltips to show up in the **Inspector**. If you want, you can use the text of the comments as parameter for the tooltips.

4. **Formatting scripts for designers (Part II)**: Even if our scripts in the **Inspector** look good, they can be improved if we add some headings before groups of variables. So, assign meaningful headings and reorder the variables to fit in these headings.

5. **Formatting scripts for designers (Part III)**: The `direction` variable inside the projectile script must be set to public since it is changed from the cupcake tower script. However, it should be visible in the **Inspector**. Use attributes to hide it from the **Inspector**.

6. **Formatting scripts for designers (Part IV)**: Some variables in our scripts are better to show with a slider rather than a numeric input field, especially those that cannot assume negative numbers. For these, transform their appearance to a slider and don't allow negative values for them.

7. **Best Practices (Part I)**: Inside the cupcake tower script there is the `Upgrade Level` variable, which is private. However, it might be useful to create a get function to retrieve its value. By following the guidelines in the link shown in the *Variables* section of this chapter, implement the respective get function.

8. **Best Practices (Part II)**: Again inside the cupcake tower script, inside the `Upgrade()` function, the `GetComponent()` function is called to get the `SpriteRenderer`. Best practice suggests to call this function only once and store the reference inside a variable. Create a new variable to store the `SpriteRenderer` component attached to the cupcake tower game object. Assign its value inside the `Start()` function by using the `GetComponent()` function. Then, use this variable in the `Upgrade()` function to update the graphic of the cupcake tower.

9. **Best Practices (Part III)**: We didn't define a tag for the cupcake towers because we don't need to distinguish between them. However, it's good practice to assign a tag to them. This is because it might be needed later on when we would like to extend our game (for example, enemies that try to avoid cupcake towers within their limits). Therefore, create a new cupcake tower tag and assign it to all the cupcake tower Prefabs (there should be three, also counting the one created in the first exercise of this section).

Summary

In this chapter, we have seen how to use Prefabs to quickly replicate and clone game objects. We also learned how to place 2D objects, order them with the Z-Buffering method, as well as how to set up tags and layers in Unity. Then, we created a couple of scripts, and learned along the way how to code complex behaviors with just a few lines. In fact, we explored how Unity handles scripts, their main functions and attributes, and the general execution order.

However, we will improve the scripts written in this chapter later on in the book, to improve the gameplay. In fact, the goal of this chapter was to get used to scripts, and to write down the main logic. Therefore, improving and tweaking is left for later.

In the next chapter, we will dive into the UI world, and integrate it into our game.

3
Communicating with the Player – the User Interface

User interfaces, often referred to as UIs for short, play a vital role in a game, since it's one of the main way to exchange information with the player. Usually, the game provides information, status, or stats of the game and the player interacts with the game with input through the UI.

This chapter will explain why UIs play such an important role in games and about the different things that we need to take into consideration when we design and/or implement UIs. Of course, this chapter will focus on the Unity framework to build UIs, and explains how to use it.

In the last part of the chapter, we will see how to start with UI programming from a practical point of view by implementing two important game play elements within the UI of our game. However, we will see more about UI programming in Chapter 5, *The Secret Ingredient Is a Dash of Physics*, where we will polish the game and implement the whole gameplay based on the elements built in the previous chapters.

Lastly, you should definitely consider buying a book that is specifically about UI. Before writing this book, I wrote another book year: *Unity UI Cookbook, Packt publishing*. It has a perfect set of recipes ready to use. There you will find all the concepts mentioned here and much more, such as different tips and tricks. You can find it at https://www.packtpub.com/game-development/unity-ui-cookbook.

Therefore, in this chapter, we will learn how the UIs are designed and how to implement them in Unity:

- Designing UIs
- Understanding the Unity framework to build UIs by looking in detail at each of its components
- Manipulating and placing UI elements
- Designing the UI for our tower defense game
- Implementing a health bar within our game
- Implementing a sugar meter within our game

Like all the other chapters of this book, you will find the *Homework* section at the end. It has a range of different exercises for you to do to improve your skills and implement a range of different functionalities into your game. So, let's get ready to learn a lot about UIs.

Getting ready

We will use the graphics from the same package of the previous chapter to build our UI as well. Therefore, be sure to have it imported and have the images imported as Sprites in order to use them in the UI.

Designing the user interface

Think about when you are reading a book, the text or images are on the center of the page, the page number is located, usually, in a corner, and the pages are numbered consecutively. The whole process is pretty straightforward and hassle free. Players expect the same experience, not only with gameplay, but also with other on-screen elements such as the UI. The design of a UI requires considerations of a number of things. For example, the platform that you are designing for has limitations, such as screen size, and the types of interaction that it can afford (does it use touch or a mouse pointer?). But physiological reactions that the interface might give to the player need to be considered, since he or she will be the final consumer. In fact, another thing to keep in mind is that some people read from right to left in their native languages, and the UI should reflect this as well.

Another thing to keep in mind is that if you are designing for multiple devices, try to keep the experience the same. With many applications being multi-platform, you don't want the user getting used to an experience on a mobile that is presented in one way, and then to log on to the computer version, and it's completely different. Therefore, while you are designing the UI, determine how it will look on each device. Is the home icon too small on a mobile to understand what it is? Is the navigation menu too large for a desktop version? Making sure that the UI is optimized will ensure that users who use your application across multiple devices will have a seamless transition and won't have to try to figure out how to access features all over again.

Just like our book example, players or users of applications are used to certain conventions and formats. For example, a house icon usually indicates home or the main screen, an e-mail icon usually indicates contact, and an arrow pointing right, usually indicates that it will continue to the next item in the list, or the next question, and so on. Therefore, to improve ease of use and navigation, it is ideal to stick to these or to at least keep these in mind during the design process. In addition to this, how the user navigates through the application is important. If there is only way to get from the home screen to an option, and it's via a whole bunch of screens, the whole experience is going to be tiresome. Therefore, be sure to create navigation maps early on to determine the route for each part of the experience. If a user has to navigate through six screens before they can reach a certain page, then they won't be doing it for very long.

Loud noises can immediately get people's attention. So can UI elements. Therefore, you want to make you more important elements the focal point. The key here is to have fewer elements, if not only a single element, the focal point to reduce the player from feeling overwhelmed. For example, in a game, you may want the health bar to be the main item of focus. Therefore, place it somewhere where it will be noticed and not in the corner in the player's peripheral view. One way to achieve this is to have the UI elements contrast the environment, ideally within the same color palette so that they stand out, but not draw so much attention that they are distracting.

A great website to create great color schemes is Adobe Color (https://color.adobe.com/). An example of it can be seen in the following screenshot:

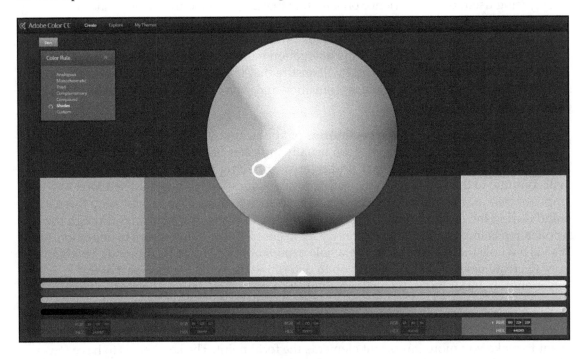

In saying all of this, don't let the design over take the practicality of the user's experience. For example, you may have a beautiful UI but it makes it really hard to play the game or it causes too much confusion. Particularly during fast-paced gameplay, you don't want the player to have to sift through twenty different on-screen elements to find what they are looking for. You want the level mastery focused on the gameplay rather than understanding the UI. One way to also limit the amount of UI elements present at any one time is to have sliding windows or pop-up windows that have other UI elements present. For example, if your player has the option to unlock many different types of ability but they are only able to use one or two of them at any single moment during gameplay, there is no point in displaying them all. Therefore, having a UI element for them to click that then displays all of the other abilities, which they can swap for the existing ones, is one way to minimize the UI design. Of course, you don't want to have multiple pop-up windows, otherwise it becomes a quest in itself to change settings in-game.

One thing that a UI can offer is feedback. Feedback is not necessarily a pop-up screen that is displayed in the center of the screen; it can be something as simple as a meter increasing/decreasing, such as a health bar, or a player's avatar changing over time; for example, they begin to age as the player progresses through the game. The next thing about adding feedback is how you are going to alert the player to changes in the UI. In some instances, it is not necessarily to alert the player, it's just a natural part of the process; in others, they need to know that changes have occurred or are occurring. One way to indicate changes to a player is to animate the UI element in question. This can be as simple as a glowing effect; for example, each time the player is attacked their health meter glows or pulsates as it decreases. Another option is to indicate that changes are occurring in the UI with sound; for example, each time the player's currency increases, a soft chime sound plays. Audio can be just as effective as an animation, but also keep in mind that feedback that is based on audio won't always be heard. For example, sometimes, players opt to disable the sound if they are in a public place and do not have headphones, so keep this in mind if you are using sound as the only way to indicate a change in the UI to the player. In addition to the types of feedback, each action needs a reaction, and if the player does something that they are not supposed to do, they need to be notified. So each time that a player provides input, clicks a button, or interacts with the UI, something should happen. How prominent it is is up to you; just make sure that it is clear and not over the top.

This section gave you an introduction into the issues behind designing a good UI. There are so many other factors to take into account that specific books just about UIs have been written. For instance, one of these is localization, which is so vast that a whole chapter is needed to describe it (you can find a brief introduction to Localization in `Chapter 8`, *What Is beyond the Cake?*).

However, before moving on, I just want to point out a technical term about UIs, since it also appears in the official documentation of Unity. Some UIs are not fixed on the screen, but actually have a physical space within the game environment. Some designers call these UIs *diegetic*, as opposed to classical interfaces that are *non-diegetic*. It is a term that has been borrowed from other disciplines, and therefore is not unanimously accepted for UIs. In fact, it might even cause a little confusion. Just to provide you with a bit more of a historical background, the term derives from the word *diegesis*. We can see its definition in the Merriam-Webster dictionary:

> *"the telling of a story by a narrator who summarizes events in the plot and comments on the conversations, thoughts, etc., of the characters."*

An example of a diegetic interface, or just for simplicity an UI placed within the game word, is the minimap of the game *Dead Space* (Visceral Games, former EA Redwood Shores), which we can see in the following screenshot:

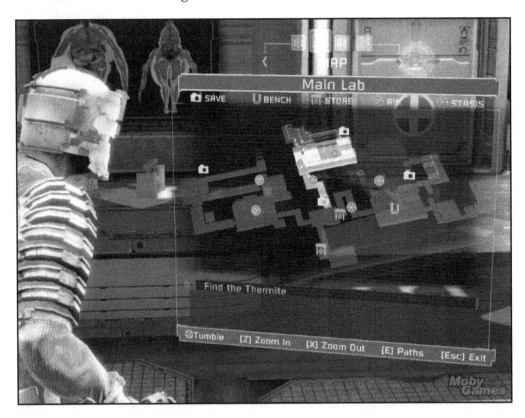

Programming the user interface

As we have seen in the previous section, designing UI can be tough, and requires experience to get into, especially if you take into consideration all the elements you should, such as the psychology of your audience. However, this is just half way through. In fact, designing is one thing, making it work is another. Usually, in large teams, there are artists who design the UI and programmers who implement it.

Is UI programming that different? Well, the answer is no, programming is still programming; however, it's quite an interesting branch of the field of programming. If you are building your game engine from scratch, implementing an entire system that handles input is not something you can create just with a couple of hours of work. Catching all of the events that the player does in the game and in the UI is not easy to implement, and requires a lot of practice. Luckily, in the context of Unity, most of this backend for UIs is already done. Furthermore, as we will see in the next section, Unity provides a solid framework to work also on the frontend for UIs. This framework includes different components that can be easily used without knowing anything about programming. But if we are really interested in unlocking the potentiality of Unity framework for the UIs, we not only need to understand it, but also program within it.

Even with a solid framework, such as the one in Unity, UI programming still needs to take into consideration many factors, enough to have a specific role for this in large teams. Achieving exactly what designers have in mind, and possible without hitting the performances too much, is most of the job of an UI programmer (at least using Unity).

Mastering these skills requires time and patience, and this chapter is just an introduction to this world. I hope you will enjoy reading this chapter.

User interface system

Now that we have acquired a basic knowledge about how to design UIs, it's time to learn how Unity handles all of this. From Unity 4.6, it is possible to use a dedicated UI system called UI. The goal of this section is understand how it works.

It is worth mentioning that, before version 4.6, Unity used an old system called GUI. Recently, Unity developer didn't completely dismiss the system, but slightly changed it and renamed it **IMGUI**, which stands for **Immediate Mode GUI**. As we can see in the official documentation, it is not intended to be used in game, but rather for programmers to quickly debug. Moreover, it is also used to create windows or a custom Inspector when Unity is extended through scripts, a topic that is definitely out of the scope of this introductory book. However, if you are interested in learning more, I invite you to read the official documentation:
`https://docs.unity3d.com/Manual/ExtendingTheEditor.html` Also, follow this video tutorial:
`https://unity3d.com/learn/tutorials/topics/interface-essentials/building-custom-inspector?playlist=17090.`

However, you might find this section a little bit encyclopedic. In fact, you can use this section as a quick reference to the UI elements you need. Therefore, feel free to skip part of it, if you already have a certain knowledge about Unity UIs.

Moreover, this section is structured in such a way that the fundamental things are at the beginning, and progressively deals with more complicated topics, up to arrive out of the scope of this book. In fact, we you have reached this level, where it is really just matter of fine tuning, or achieving a really specific effect, this section will give you a general idea of how it works, so to have a ground from which to further extend your knowledge, especially with the official documentation.

Canvas

If you are wondering what a Canvas is, let's begin with some background information. From the Merriam -Webster dictionary, a canvas is considered to be the following:

> *"A firm closely woven cloth usually of linen, hemp, or cotton used for clothing and formerly much used for tents and sails."*

But probably the definition that is closer to what Unity means is this, also from the Merriam-Webster dictionary:

> *"A piece of cloth backed or framed as a surface for a painting; also: the painting on such a surface."*

In computer graphics, a canvas is something slightly different, and we can see its definition on Wikipedia:

> *"In computer science and visualization, a canvas is a container that holds various drawing elements (lines, shapes, text, frames containing other elements, etc.). It takes its name from the canvas used in visual arts. It is sometimes called a scene graph because it arranges the logical representation of a user interface or graphical scene. Some implementations also define the spatial representation and allow the user to interact with the elements via a graphical user interface."*

In Unity, a Canvas is an important component of the UI system. Since the UI is internally rendered by Unity in a different way than the rest of the scene, we need to specify which elements within our scene belong to the UI. In particular, all the UI elements should be children of a Canvas, which is a Game Object with a Canvas component attached on it. We can create a Canvas by right-clicking on the **Hierarchy** panel and then navigate to **UI |** **Canvas**.

As a result, two objects will be created in our scene, as we can see in the following screenshot:

However, at the moment let's just focus on the Canvas, leaving the **EventSystem** for later.

 Creating a new UI element, such as an image, for instance by right-clicking on the **Hierarchy** and then **UI | Image**, automatically creates a Canvas (and an EventSystem as well), if there isn't already a **Canvas** in the scene. The UI element is created as a child of this Canvas.

The Canvas is represented in the scene as a white rectangular. This helps us to edit the UI without switching back and forth from the Game View.

If the **Scene** view is not set in 2D, for instance we are working in on a 3D game, the Canvas appears distorted, as shown here:

Since UI will be rendered orthographically, a rule of thumb of working with UIs is to switch the Scene View to 2D (as we learnt in Chapter 1, *A Flat World in Unity*), to have something like the following:

If we select the Canvas, we should be able to see the following in the **Inspector**:

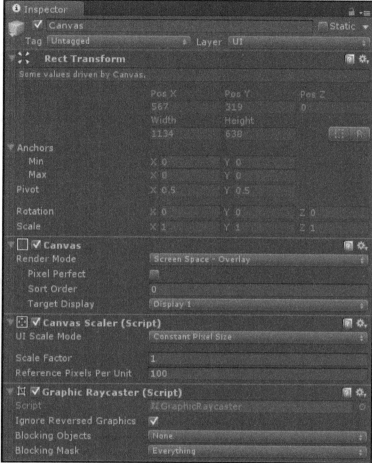

The main setting is the **Render Mode**, which allows us to specify how we intend to use our UI. Let's take a closer look at these options.

Screen space – Overlay

This render mode is the most used. In fact, it places UI elements on the screen by rendering them on top of the scene, as in many games. This means that UI elements are rendered perfectly orthographically.

Furthermore, if the screen changes resolution or is resized, the Canvas will change size to automatically fit the new ratio.

Screen space – Camera

This render mode, instead, is linked to a specific Camera where the UI will be render on top of it. This means that the Canvas is placed at a given distance in front of the selected Camera. As a result, the UI elements will be affected by all the camera parameters and effects. This includes the perspective distortion, if the **Camera** is set to **Perspective**, which is regulated by the **Camera Field of View** parameter.

Like previously, the Canvas may change size based on the resolution of the screen as well as the camera frustum.

If you are wondering what the camera frustum is, keep reading this info box. When you select a camera, you will see a trunked pyramid (if the camera is in perspective mode, otherwise it has a Parallelepiped as shape), like the one in the following screenshot:

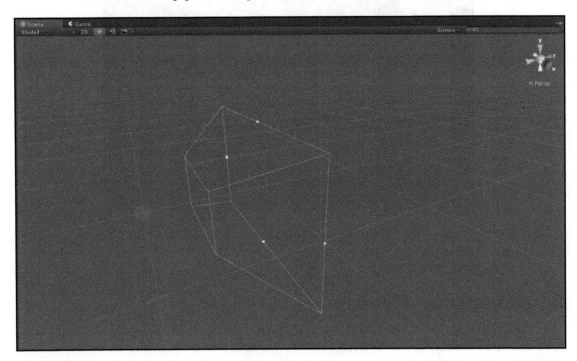

This is the camera frustum, and everything that is inside it will be rendered by the camera. The plane that is closer to the camera is called **near clipping plane**, whereas the far one is called the **far clipping plane**.

Understanding why a perspective camera has this shape is not hard, but it's out of the scope of this book. However, in the documentation, you can find two interesting pages that talk about this. They are easy to understand, and as for your convenience, here are the links: `https://docs.unity3d.com/Manual/UnderstandingFrustum.html` and `https://docs.unity3d.com/Manual/FrustumSizeAtDistance.html`.

World space

This render mode will make the Canvas behave like any other game object in the scene. This means that the Canvas has a precise position in the world (from here the name, since it is placed in the world space). As a result, the UI can be occluded by other objects in the scene. Its dimensions are set manually using the Rect Transform component (see some paragraphs ahead). This mode is useful for UIs that are meant to be a part of the world. As we have discussed previously, this is also known as a **diegetic interface**.

Draw order of UI elements

As we will see in the next paragraphs, UI elements will be images or text that is rendered on the screen. However, what happens when two of these components overlap? There is an order, so that the UI elements in the Canvas are drawn in the same order they appear in the hierarchy. This means that the first child is drawn first, the second child next, and so on. Therefore, when two UI elements overlap, the later one, in the Hierarchy, will appear on top of the earlier one.

To change which element appear on top of other elements, it's just matter of reordering the elements in the **Hierarchy** by dragging them.

To better understand this, look at the following screenshot, which represents two different situations with two images. For your convenience, the respective **Hierarchy** panel has been superimposed next to the images.

The Lemon Cupcake is rendered on top of the chocolate one because the Lemon Cupcake is the last child of the Canvas

The order can also be controlled from scripting by using these methods on the Transform component:

- **SetAsFirstSibling()**: Place the game object as the first child of its parent. As a result, it will be rendered for first (with respect to its siblings), and therefore sent to the back (all other UI elements will be on top of it).
- **SetAsLastSibling()**: Place the game object as the last child of its parent. As a result, it will be rendered last (with respect to its siblings), and therefore brought to the front (all other UI elements will be behind it).
- **SetSiblingIndex()**: Place the game object to a specific index, allowing to decide at which point of the rendering hierarchy this game object will be.

Visual components

The Unity UI comes with different premade components to build our UI. The most commonly used are the visual components, which allow rendering custom content on the screen.

The Image component

The Image component, as the name suggests, allows us to render an image on the screen. In fact, we need to specify a **Source Image**, which is the image we want to render. An example of this can be seen in the following screenshot:

 As for Sprites, the image assets we intend to use for the UI in our project must be set to Sprite (2D and UI), as Chapter 1, *A Flat World in Unity* explained.

Then, we can adjust the color, which is a multiplier of the Sprite, as well as assign a material, if we need to.

Once a **Source Image** has been set, we can define how the Sprite will appear by selecting the **Image Type**. The options are as follows:

- **Simple**: just scales the image or Sprite equally.
- **Sliced**: if the Sprite has been 9-sliced (as Chapter 1, *A Flat World in Unity* explained), the nine different parts of the image will be scaled differently.
- **Tiled**: this is similar to the previous one, but the central part of the 9-slicing is tiled instead of stretched.

- **Filled**: this is similar to Simple, but allows us to show part of the image as it would be filled. This is controlled by parameters such as the Origin of the Filling, as well as the method and the amount. We will use this feature later in the chapter, and we will find out that is really useful for creating bars in video games:

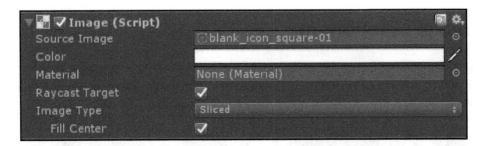

 Some advanced bars, such as the health bar in Kingdom Hearts style, can be found in the book pointed out previously: *Unity UI Cookbook*, *Packt publishing* towards the end of *Chapter 2, Implementing Counters and Health Bars*.

Furthermore, when the image is **Simple** or **Filled**, the button **Set Native Size** is visible. It just restores the original size of the image. This is really useful when you assign a new **Source Image**, and you can restore the original ratio by using this button as well, before scaling to the right size for your UI.

The Text component

The Text component, as the name suggests, allows us to render any text on the screen. Sometimes, in some books, it is referred to as label, since usually it is used to give a label to other UI components. An example of this can be seen in the following screenshot:

It contains a text area, which can be extended using the Rect Tool (see the next paragraph). Within the component, you can find all the basic **Text** transformations, such as setting the font, the font style, and the font size. Furthermore, it is possible to enable or disable the rich text capability, which is enabled by default.

If you a wondering what rich text capability is, keep reading this info box. Rich text capability allows us to place some HTML tags within the text to change only specific part of the text. In non-technical terms, you can change the color of a single word or change its font style to italic. For instance, you can have something like *This book is really amazing* in the **Text** area, but in the text component, it is written as `This book <b>is really</b> amazing`.

Since they are HTML tags, they must be placed at the beginning, specifying the settings, and at the end of the part of text where you want to apply the change.

These are the main tags supported from unity:

`<b>The text between these tags will be in bold</b>`
`<i>The text between these tags will be in italic</i>`
`<size=50>The text between these tags will have a size of 50, and you can change the number to any number</size>`
`<color= #rrggbbaa>This text between these tags will be colored with the hex color specified at the beginning</color>`

If you don't know what a hex color is, it is just a hex number (therefore, it contains also some letters) that represents a color; you can learn more about them on the Wikipedia page here:

`https://en.wikipedia.org/wiki/Web_colors`.

However, keep in mind that you don't need to know all the detailed theory behind the Wikipedia page to use these colors. In fact, there are plenty of online color pickers that give you the hex number of a specific color. Then, you just need to copy and paste the code into your text in Unity. Furthermore, you don't need necessarily to use the hex code for the color, but there are some presets in Unity. In fact, you can just use This `<color=red>word</color>` is red to make the word red, without specifying the whole hex code. The list of all these color shortcuts can be found by following the link at the end of this info box. Alternative, you could also select hex colors from online tools, such as: `http://www.w3scho` `ols.com/colors/colors_picker.asp` or `http://htmlcolorcodes.com`. There are a couple of special tags, material and quad, which have a really specific use. If you want to learn more, follow the link at the end of this info box.

Another cool feature of these tags is that you can nest them! This means you can use more than one at the same time. For instance, you can have part of the text that is blue, bold, and italic. However, they must be closed in reverse order, otherwise they won't work.

If you want to learn more, follow this link:

`https://docs.unity3d.com/Manual/StyledText.html`.

In addition, you can find options to change the alignment of the text as well as for vertical and horizontal overflow, which means to control what happens when the text is larger than the text area. The **Best Fit** option rescales the text to fit the available space of the text area.

Basic transformations

We have seen some basic UI elements, but how can we place and manipulate them? We will learn various different forms of implementing transformations in the next sections.

The Rect Tool

Since UI elements are similar to Sprites (both are 2D), the best way to quickly manipulate them is by using the Rect Tool.

A fast recap, you can find the Rect Tool in the top-left corner of the Unity Editor, and it is the last one on the right, as shown here:

A border around our Sprite or UI elements should appear. As a result, we can transform it in the following ways:

- If we click and drag within the rectangle, we can move the object, as in the following picture (for learning purposes, a tasty cupcake has been used in an Image component):

- If we click on the blue dot in the middle, which is the pivot point, we can change its position (in this book we will not change any pivot points, since we won't need this):

- If we click and drag an edge we can scale along that direction, as we can see here:

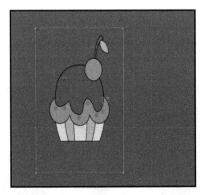

- If we click and drag a corner, instead, we can scale freely along both directions. Furthermore, if you press Shift while dragging, the scale will be uniform, which means it will increase in size by the same quantity on both axes by keeping the ratio of the object constant:

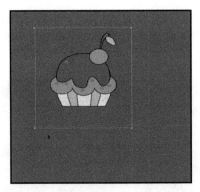

- Finally, if we place the cursor next to a corner that is, outside of the rectangle, a little rotation icon appears. By clicking and dragging it is possible to rotate the object around its pivot point:

And this is all for the Rect Tool.

The Rect Transform

There is a major difference in how Unity handles Sprites and UI elements. In fact, Sprites have the usual Transform component, to indicate position, rotation, and Scale. UI elements, instead, have a Rect Transform (the 2D layout counterpart), which is much more complex and store more information. In fact, the Transform represents a single point in the space, whereas the Rect Transform represent a rectangle in which a UI element can be placed. An example of this can be seen in the following screenshot:

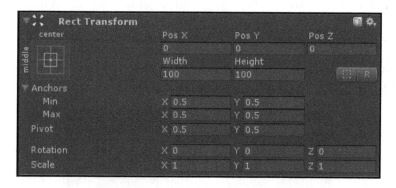

Unity performs all the calculations of the positions of the different Rect Transform at the end of the frame to ensure having up-to-date values with respect to the rest of the frame. As a result, these values of the Rect Transform might not be correct when you use the `Start()` function. To overcome this problem, you can force the update of the canvas by calling the `Canvas.ForceUpdateCanvases()` function.

Furthermore, if the parent of a Rect Transform is also a Rect Transform, the child Rect Transform can also specify how it should be positioned and sized relative to the parent rectangle. This hierarchical structure is what makes Rect Transform so powerful, especially when you need to design for multiple resolutions.

Other than scaling, a Rect Transform can be resized. They are similar operations, but the difference lies that resizing leaves invariant the local scale, and change the height and the width. As a result, font sizes, borders on sliced images, and so on, won't be affected from resizing, whereas they are in the case of scaling.

Similar to 2D Sprites, the Rect transform applies scaling, rotation, and resizing by the pivot point of the UI element. However, it is possible to change it directly inside the Scene View, by dragging it (the little blue circle) within the UI element.

One of the most import concepts about this component is the Anchors, which allow us to specify the relation of the UI element with respect to the Canvas and its parent. They are displayed as four small triangular handles in the Scene View. The information related to these anchors is shown in the Rect Transform component in the Inspector.

Unfortunately, there is no a simple way to explain Anchors without seeing the effects in motion, such as in a video or in an animated gif. Since this is a book, it cannot contain such animated media, which would clarify the concept immediately to you. Therefore, instead of losing time in a complicated explanation of anchors, which may not be fully understandable, I invite you to visit the official documentation here, in the anchors section: `https://docs.unity3d.com/Manual/UIBasicLayout.html`. Don't worry, I'll still be here when you come back from the webpage.

If you have read the webpages, other than seeing the animated gif, you also have seen the Anchor presets, which are shown in the following screenshot:

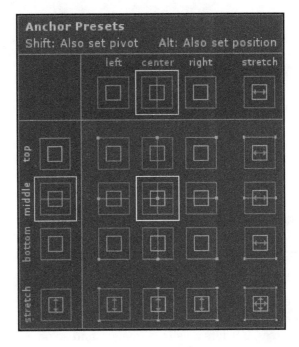

These are useful shortcuts to quickly correctly anchor UI elements. Of course, I invite you to manually change this configuration in your game, when needed.

Layout components

In the previous section we saw how it is possible to place UI elements in the screen. However, sometimes, it's really useful to automatically place them in the screen within a certain criteria, especially when the number of UI elements is not known a priori, and changes at runtime. This can be manually scripted, but Unity comes with a series of layout components that helps with basic layout placement.

The auto-layout system is composed of two different kinds of elements: layout elements and layout controllers. To understand the former, note that every game object that has a Rect Transform, and eventually other components, is a layout element. These types have certain knowledge about what size they should be of, but they do not control it directly. Layout controllers, instead, are components that control sizes and also positions of one or more layout elements. They can control their own layout element or child Layout Elements of the game object to which they are attached.

Layout controllers change the Rect transforms in such a way that it's hard to restore the previous status. Therefore, before to even add a layout controllers and/or modify one, be sure to be in Play mode in order to make changes without causing any unwanted layout change to your UI. Once you are happy with the changes, stop Play mode, and insert the values that you have found that fit your needs.

The layout controllers are divided into Fitters and layout groups.

Fitters

The Fitters only control the size of its own layout element. When resizing UI elements, keep in mind that it happens around the pivot point, as we discussed in the previous section. Therefore, you can use it also to align UI elements. For instance, if the pivot is in the center, the element will scale equally in all the directions, whereas if it is placed in a corner, such as the top-left, the element will scale down and to the right. All other positions will give different weighs along the four directions where the element will scale.

With this said, let's take a look at the Fitters controllers:

- **Content Size Fitter**: controls the size of its own layout element. The size is determined by the minimum or preferred sizes provided by layout element components on the Game Object. Such layout elements can be Image or Text components, layout groups, or a Layout Element component:

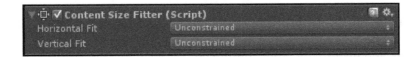

- **Aspect Ratio Fitter**: can adjust the height to fit the width or vice versa, or it can make the element fit inside its parent or envelope its parent. The Aspect Ratio Fitter does not take layout information into account, such as minimum size and preferred size:

Layout groups

The layout groups, instead, control the layout elements of their children, and not their own. They are used to orderly place the UI elements. They have different options to control the spacing between the children and define the preferred heights and/or widths. Other options include the possibility to force the expansion of the children so to fit the space available or to decide what happens when they are bigger than the space available. They are as follows:

- **Vertical Layout Group**: allows us to stack the children along a vertical axis, and place them on top of each other:

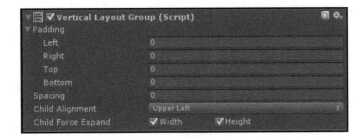

- **Horizontal Layout Group**: allows us to stack the children along a horizontal axis, and place them next to each other:

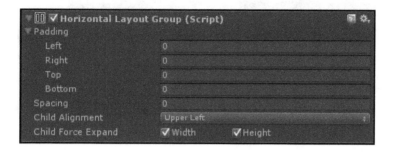

- **Grid Layout Group**: this allows us to stack the children in a grid, both vertically and horizontally:

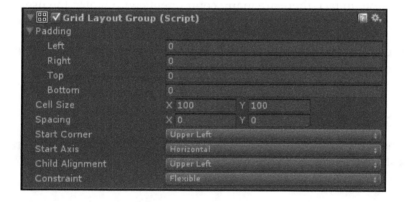

The layout element component

There is one more component, which is the **Layout Element** component. As the name suggests, it is not a controller, but rather allows us to change the layout element settings from the Rect Transform. In fact, when placed on a layout element, it allows us to override the settings, such as min, preferred, and flexible both for height and width. Furthermore, it has a flag to ignore the controllers. So, imagine having a label inside a grid layout component, you don't want the label to be stacked in the grid along all the other elements, but rather on the top, defining what the grid is about. In this case, ignoring the controller is useful to place the label outside the grid, and yet be a children of the grid, so to move it as a unique block, without replacing the label every time.

Here is a picture of what this component looks like:

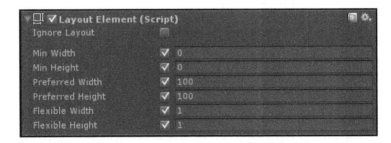

Interaction components

Unity UI comes with more powerful premade components than the one seen in the visual components section. In fact, there are many components with which the user can interact. These interaction can be mouse or touch/tap events as well as keyboard or controller events.

However, this components are not visible on their own, and must be combined with one or more visual components in order to work correctly.

The selectable base class

Before seeing how the single interaction components work, we need to understand some basic settings shared among all of them. In particular, these settings derive from the Selectable base class, which has transition and navigation options.

Interactable option

This is just a flag that determines if an interaction component is enable for interaction or not. When checked, the interaction component will be in the **Disable** state (see the next section).

Transition options

Usually, interaction components needs to send some feedback to the player, so he or she can understand if the action has been performed.

In this implementation of Unity, there are four states in which an interaction component could be. They are as follows:

- **Normal**: the interaction component is untouched
- **Highlighted**: when the pointer is on the interaction component, but a click (or a touch/tap in the case of touch-screens) hasn't been performed yet
- **Pressed**: when the click (or touch/tap) is happening on the interaction component
- **Disable**: when the interaction component is not interactable

They transitions and the specifications of these states can happen in four different ways:

- **None**: The interaction component doesn't change state. This is really useful when we want to implement the kind of interaction with the component in a custom way:

- **Color Tint**: this option is selected by default and defines a color tint for each of the preceding states. Furthermore, it contains a **Fade Duration** to regulate how fast the component should change from one color to another, and a **Color Multiplier**. As a result, the interaction component will smoothly change color for each of the four states:

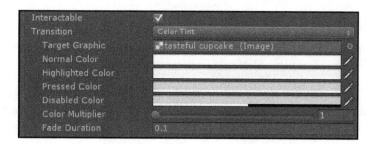

- **Sprite Swap**: Usually, the interaction components have also an Image component attached to them, which defines the basic graphics. In this transition mode, instead of changing color, there is a different Sprite for each one of the four states. This is useful when you have custom graphics for each one of the states:

- **Animation**: This is the most versatile transition mode, since it allows you to have a custom animation for each one of the states (we will talk more about animations in the upcoming chapters):

Navigation options

The navigation options determine how the player can navigate through the UI elements during play mode. These are the different options available:

- **None**: No keyboard navigation. This is useful when you want to implement your own navigation system within the game. Furthermore, the interaction component that is set in this mode will not receive focus from clicking (or tapping) on it.
- **Horizontal**: navigates horizontally.
- **Vertical**: navigates vertically.
- **Automatic**: Unity will try to guess which is the right navigation based on the positions of the UI elements.

- **Explicit**: In this mode, you can specify the next UI element to select for each arrow key. This allows fine navigation control:

Furthermore, the **Visualize** button allows to visualize the navigation scheme within the **Scene View**. An example of this visualization is presented in the following screenshot:

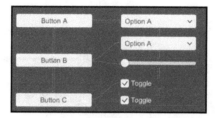

Button

This is the classical interaction component that can be found in any game. It contains only one event, OnClick(), which is triggered when the button is clicked/tapped. Of course, you can link any action to the event. An example of this can be seen in the following screenshot:

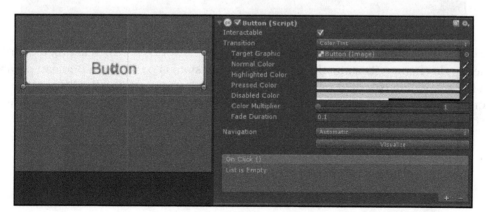

Keep in mind that if the pointer is moved away from the button before the click/tap is released, the action doesn't take place. You can find an exercise on this in the *Homework* section.

Toggle and Toggle Group

The Toggle component allows the player to turn off and on an option. An example of this can be seen in the following screenshot:

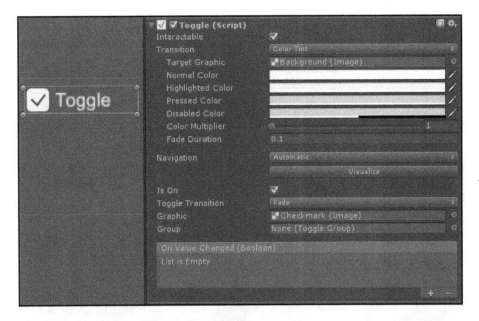

As the button, the toggle has a single event OnValueChanged(), which is called every time that the toggle changes its state; the value of the new state is passed as a Boolean parameter within the event data (see next paragraph). This component works well with another component, called Toggle Group, which controls whether there is only one option among a group of toggles to be turned on, as shown in the following screenshot:

You can set up a toggle group by just add it to the **Group** property of all the toggles you wish in to be in the group. This is, for instance, really useful for mutually exclusive choices, such as character or class selection. Other common use is tuning the game settings, such as game speed, difficulty, or color scheme. Of course, you can use more than one toggle group per time within your scenes; however, a toggle can only belong to one group.

Slider

As the name suggests, a slider is a bar with a handle along it, which can slide from the beginning, which is considered the **Min Value**, to the end, which is considered the **Max Value**. All the values in between are in proportion to the position of the handle along the bar. By default, the handle increases its value from left to right, but by tweaking the **Direction** property, it's possible to change in other directions, so not only from right to left but also along the vertical axis. An example of this can be seen in the following screenshot:

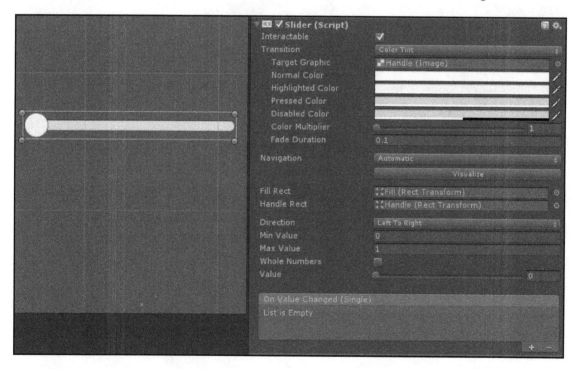

The slider has a single event, OnValueChanged(), which is triggered when the handle is dragged, and the new value of the slider is passed as a float to the triggered action.

Scrollbar

This component is very similar to a slider, since it has a handle along a bar, and the minimum value is always 0.0 and the maximum is 1.0. All the values in between represents the different percentage of where the handle will be. Again, the scrollbar can be orientated by tweaking the **Direction** property. An example of this can be seen in the following screenshot:

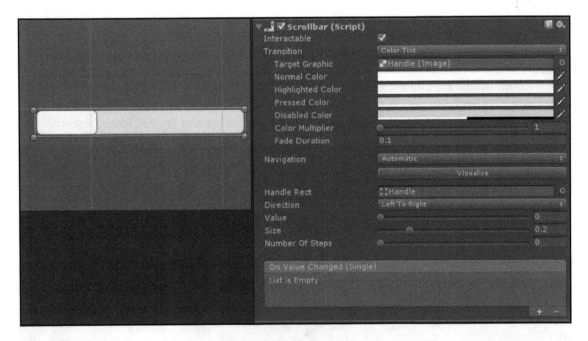

The difference between this and the slider is the possibility to stretch the handle of the scrollbar depending on some content, such as text areas. When the text increases, the handle becomes smaller to slide among more content, which represents the amount of scrolling available. On the other hand, when the content is not large, the handle increases its dimensions to completely fill the bar and not allow scrolling.

The scrollbar has a single event, called `OnValueChanged()`, and it works exactly the same way as the homonymous event on the slider.

Dropdown

The **Dropdown** is a relatively new component in the Unity UI, since it has been released/implemented since Unity 5.2. This component allows the player to select among a list of options. The component shows the current selected option only, and when the player clicks/taps on it, the full list appears. Once another item from the list is selected, the list closes and the new item is picked. Furthermore, the player can close the list without changing the item if he or she clicks somewhere else outside the component. An example of this can be seen in the following screenshot:

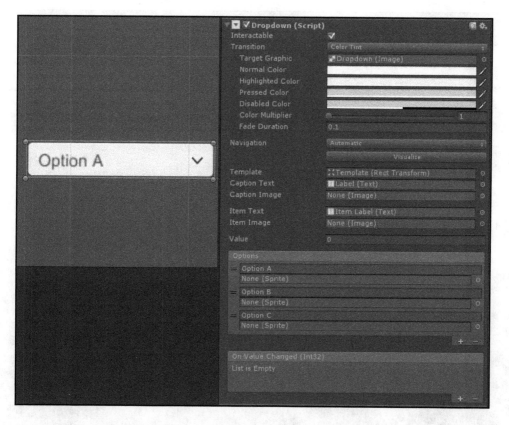

Using the dropdown in the inspector is quite intuitive, even if you need to get used to the template in the hierarchy if you want to change its appearance. Unfortunately, we don't have time to go into detail about how this component works, but I'm sure you can easily understand it by visiting the official documentation here:

https://docs.unity3d.com/Manual/script-Dropdown.html.

In any case, we won't use this component for our game, but in the *Homework* section you can challenge yourself to understand this component better.

Input Field

The **Input Field** component allows the player to type text in the game, specifically within a text area. Of course, you need to use it in conjunction with a Text component, and/or other visual elements. An example of this can be seen in the following screenshot:

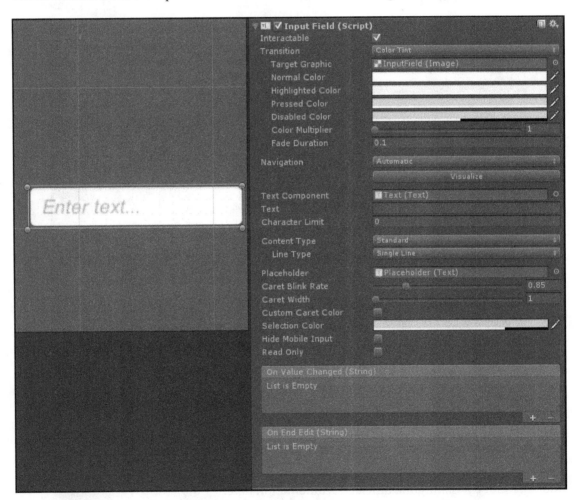

The **Input Field** can be added also to an already existing **Text** component to make it editable. In order to do so, select the **Text** component in the **Hierarchy** panel and navigate to **Add Component** | **UI** | **Input Field** in the **Inspector**. Then, drag the **Text** component (also the game object itself will work) inside the **Text** component variable of the **Input Field**. Furthermore, you may want to add a placeholder as well. As such, I suggest that you create an **Input Field** and study how it works with its original structure, and then add existing text areas.

When the player is typing, the **Text** property of the **Text** component will change, and it can be retrieved from the script.

Moreover, the **Input Field** has different options to define the kind of characters that are allowed, whether they should be masked (for instance, if it is a password or a pin), whether there is a limit to the number, or whether multi-line editing is allowed. You can learn more about these additional features in the official documentation:
`https://docs.unity3d.com/Manual/script-InputField.html`.

The **Input Field** component has two events: `OnValueChanged()`, which is triggered every time the player types something, and `OnEndEdit()`, which is triggered only when the player has stopped typing. In both the cases, the whole text in the **Text** component is passed to the action function through a string parameter.

Keep in mind that **Rich Text** is turned off by default. You can enable it, but it is not well supported for the **Input Field** because the navigation in the text includes markup, whereas the visual doesn't. As a result, it is really confusing for whoever is going to type there. Usually, you don't need **Rich Text** capability for editable texts; therefore, as a rule of thumb, just keep **Rich Text** turned off.

Scroll Rect

This component is used when your content is larger than the area it should occupy. Scroll Rect allows us to make a content scrollable inside a rectangle, and display all the content in a relatively small area. Usually, this component is used with the **Mask** component; in this way all the content outside the rectangle will not be visible, and you will have achieved a scroll view. An example of this can be seen in the following screenshot:

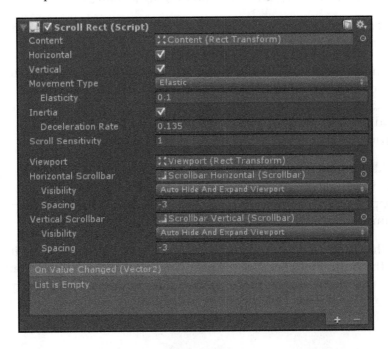

Furthermore, you can assign scrollbars (both on the horizontal and the vertical axes) to easily scroll through the content. You can find more options to tweak in the component, and if you really want to understand them, I invite you to consult the official documentation: `https://docs.unity3d.com/Manual/script-ScrollRect.html`.

Finally, the Scroll Rect has only one event, `OnValueChanged()`, which is triggered when the position of the Scroll Rect is changed, signifying that the player scrolled.

More about UI rendering

We have seen a lot about UI, yet it's not everything. This section presents some relative advanced topics in the UI of Unity. Feel free to skip this section, or read without focus to completely understand what's written, You can always come back here later.

The canvas renderer

The careful reader has noticed that in all the UI elements there is always attached a Canvas Renderer, such as the one in the following screenshot:

What is this component that doesn't allow us to change any options? It allows Unity to know that that specific UI element should be rendered in a Canvas. In very particular cases, when an UI element is built from scratch, we need to manually add this component. However, if you are not planning to build custom UI elements from scratch, but just using the ones that Unity provides (which are more than enough to build really complex UIs), you can forget about this component. In fact, it is automatically created every time we create an UI element.

Even if the **Canvas Renderer** doesn't have any options in the inspector, it has some properties that can be accessed through script. For such functions and variables, you can find details here: `https://docs.unity3d.com/ScriptReference/CanvasRenderer.html`.

More visual components

We have analyzed the main visual components; however, there are more visual components, which are used rarely in special situations:

The most common is the **Mask** component. It is used to create a scroll view in conjunction with the **Scroll Rect**. It forces the children to have the shape of the parent. However, it doesn't support alpha channels. This means that part of the children will be either visible or not, without having any kind of opacity specified in the mask.

If you are interested in knowing why the alpha channel is not supported, we need to mention implementation of Mask beneath Unity.

When you program with a GPU, you are constrained to use certain buffers to render things. Modern GPUs have a buffer called Stencil Buffer, used together with the **Color Buffer** and the **Depth Buffer**, which can only assume integer values and work on a pixel base. Usually, it is used to avoid rendering certain parts of the screen, and improve performance overall, and this is the case with Unity. Advanced uses of this may include changing it dynamically based on the Depth Buffer. However, Unity just uses this buffer to not render the part of the screen not covered by the mask, in particular, assigning the value of 1 to the pixel that should be rendered.

Furthermore, Unity allows nested masks, in particular, using the AND (&) operation on them. As a result, a pixel will be rendered if and only if it is within all the nested masks. You can easily imagine this by overlapping different paper masks to a drawing, which is visible only in the parts that all the paper masks overlap.

Recently, Unity has introduced also another kind of Mask, **Rect Mask 2D**:

It has some limitations with respect of the previous mask component, such as the fact that it only works in a 2D environment and with coplanar elements (non-coplanar is still possible, but the component might not work as it should). However, this approach brings some advantages, such as not needing to use the Stencil Buffer (see the preceding info box) with consequent performance improvements since there are no extra draw calls.

Another very special visual component is the **Raw Image**. It has some limitations with respect to the **Image** component, but has other features. In fact, the **Raw Image** doesn't have the option to animate an image. However, it works directly with bytes, as the name suggests. As a result, it is able to display not only Sprites as the image, but also textures. To understand why this is useful, imagine that a texture is just an array of bytes, and as such, they can change at runtime. This means that you may download a texture from a URL during runtime, and show it on within a **Raw Image**. Other uses might be the use of **Render Textures** (from Unity 5.x, they are also available in the personal edition, and not only in the Pro version), and stream what another camera in the game world is seeing. This might be used, for instance, to quickly create a minimap in the game. You can find this process described in detail in the last chapter of the *Unity UI Cookbook* suggested at the beginning of this chapter. One more thing about raw images: they have a **UV Rect** option. This means you can scale and zoom the image/texture they have as you like, without changing the texture itself.

UI effect components

In addition to the visual components and the interaction ones, Unity has special classes of components called effect components. In some books, and in the documentation itself, you might find them as a subclass of the visual components.

These components are as follows:

- **Shadow**: This allows us to add a shadow effect to an image or text component. It must be attached to the same game object of the text or image component. Its options change the distance of the shadow and the color. Furthermore, in the case of an image, a Boolean controls if the component in creating the shadow should use also the alpha channel of image:

- **Outline**: This works similarly to the shadow component, but instead of a shadow, it adds an outline. The control options are the same as the shadow component:

- **Position as UV1**: When this is on an Image component, Unity passes the canvas position through to the first UV channel. This means that if you have a custom shader, you can use this to create refraction or an UV offset sampling.

UI and lights

In addition to all that we have discovered about UI, you can use lights on the UI. They are used to make them feel more realistic, especially when the UI is place within the 3D world, or when it has a kind of perspective. However, keep in mind that adding a light might decrease performance.

If the UI is in a 3D world, you may want it to be affected by the world lights, but if it has a perspective, such as in the case of the **Screen Space – Camera** of the Canvas, you may want it to just be affected by certain lights. As such, you need to create some layers to filter which lights will affect the UI.

However, it is not so simple as placing a light in the scene to make a UI component affected by light, since you need a material that responds to light. In this case, Unity provides specific shaders for UIs. In any case, this is out of the scope of the book, since it deals more with 3D game development, rather than 2D. But if you are interested in knowing more, in the *Unity UI cookbook*, in *Chapter 2, Creating Panels for Menus*, you'll find a recipe that deals with lights in the UI. That is a good start to play with lights within the UI.

The canvas components

At the beginning of the chapter, we talked about the Canvas, and its main property about the **Render Mode**. However, if we look at the Canvas in the Inspector, we can see that it actually has three different components, which usually are used all together to make a Canvas. For your convenience, the following screenshot shows them in the Inspector:

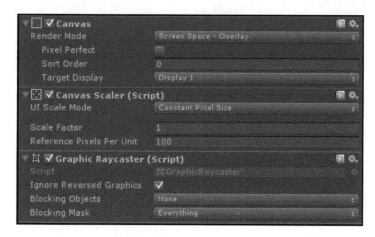

Let's take a general look at their functionalities:

- **Canvas**: This is main component, which actually create the canvas, so Unity knows that everything inside it should be rendered as UI.
- **Canvas Scaler**: This controls the overall scale and pixel density of UI elements within the Canvas. This scaling affects everything on the Canvas, including font sizes and image borders. There's more information in the official documentation here: `https://docs.unity3d.com/Manual/script-CanvasScaler.html`.
- **Graphic Raycaster**: This component belongs to the event system and allows us to detect mouse or touch events with respect to graphics. For more information about this component, you can look at the official documentation here: `https://docs.unity3d.com/Manual/script-GraphicRaycaster.html`.

If you are going to face this topic, I suggest that you study the whole Event System framework that Unity provides (see the next section).

Canvas group

In addition to the UI components we already have seen, there is another one called **Canvas Group**. It allows us to define a group, or if you prefer, a subset of the UI elements within a Canvas. This is what it looks like in the Inspector:

Furthermore, it provides some general functions to apply to all the elements belonging to the group. These may include alpha, if, for instance, you want to smoothly make part of the interface appear or disappear, or if it is interactable (or disabled).

Another common use for **Canvas Group** is to not block mouse events in certain areas of the UI, which means the player can click on a button that lies under an Image belonging to a **Canvas Group** with the **Blocks Raycast**s property set to false.

Event system

As we pointed out in the *Canvas* section, every time we create a Canvas in new scene, an even system is also created. In fact, game objects contain a series of components that allow us to exchange messages between different parts of your game. In the case of the UI, the messages that are exchanged are the inputs from the user and the UI itself. Without this event system, the interaction components will not work. This is what the event system looks like in the **Inspector**:

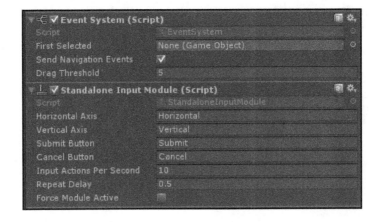

As you can see, it is divided into modules (this might change with respect to the platform your game is addressed; there's more about this in Chapter 6, *Through a Sea of Sprinkles – Navigation in Artificial Intelligence*). The basic functionalities exposed here allow you, for instance, to define which ones are the main interaction buttons/events (in the case of a standalone game).

However, for our purposes, we don't need to extensively know how the Even System works, how to change its settings, or how to set up a custom message. For that, I suggest you read the official documentation here: https://docs.unity3d.com/Manual/EventSyste m.html.

As far as we're concerned, we just leave the default settings, and every time we use the event system in our scripts, we will just use its basic functionalities, and will be explained when we encounter them.

With this said, we have covered a lot about UI, especially if you have been reading this whole section in one go. If so, I suggest you to take a little break before moving on to the next sections, which will guide us through practically using the UI interface in our game.

Scripting user interfaces

Before moving into our game, let's mention general UI programming in Unity. Each of the elements we have met in the previous section has a class that exposes some variables and some functions that we can use within our scripts. However, all of these classes are in a different namespace. As such, every time we want to use these classes, we need to add the following line of code at the beginning of our script:

```
using UnityEngine.UI;
```

Actually, we can still use the classes without the using statement by explicitly call the namespace every time. However, this approach is fine only if we need to use the namespace few times. Since we are programming with UI, it is good practice to import the namespace by adding the line of code shown previously.

Designing the interface for our game

The next step is to begin designing the layout for our game. You can do this on paper or on the computer; it depends on how you feel most comfortable.

In tower defense games, the UI often provides the way to interact with the game. Through the UI it is possible to build towers, sell them, or upgrade them. Furthermore, the UI is also used to visualize stats such as money and lives.

Here is a preliminary sketch for designing the UI for our cupcakes tower defense game:

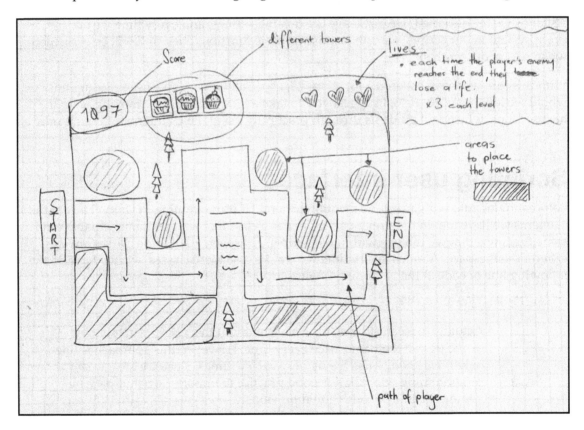

As you can see, a number of key components have been mapped out. These are primarily around the player's interaction, as well as the way that their opponents, the pandas, will move and be targeted on the map. For example, areas where players can place towers are roughly indicated, and the direction that the player can head in is also displayed. The UI elements, such as health, points, and tower upgrades, are also included.

Of course, at this stage, it is all about experimenting with what feels better from an interactive point of view and what looks better. By *feels better*, it is not directly referring to the aesthetics but also the layout of the UI. Too many UI elements in one place can make the screen feel overwhelming, especially if they aren't explained properly. Now, this is not to say that you cannot have a lot of UI elements. In some instances, games (such as *MMORPGs*) can have a large amount of UI elements, but they need to be placed in a way that is meaningful and logical. There is no sense in having a purchase tower button on one side, then an upgrade button on the other side. The simplest way to consider UI is based on routine. If first you buy a tower and then upgrade it, then you need to follow that process in the UI.

As you can see, we have placed all of the key components at the top of the screen. That way, the focus is on the map. The health is indicated with large hearts, the score is indicated with large text, and the cupcake towers are in the center of the screen. However, what is missing is some labels about what is what, such as the score and buy options for the towers. In the following screenshot, you can see the final version, where these, as well as few UI adjustments, have been made:

As you can see, the lives became a health bar, since it does make more sense for a strategy game (whereas for a platform, maybe lives could have suited better). Since we are targeting an occidental audience, we started to place the important elements on the left. (I apologize to readers who read from right to left, but for learning purposes I had to pick one choice. On the other hand, if you are reading this book, that means your understanding of English and languages that read from left to right is high enough to justify this interface we are developing).

Furthermore, the amount of sugar is the currency with which the player can upgrade and buy new towers. It is another important resource, and therefore has been placed below the health bar.

Next, you can find a section of the UI where the player is able to buy a tower from the three available. The following box, instead, is specific to a single tower, and it appears when the player selects a tower. It allows the player to sell and upgrade the cupcake tower.

Finally, on the right, there is the level name, which is information that the player will want to take into consideration, but not as often as health and sugar.

With this said, we have a UI design for our game, so let's start to implement it in the next sections.

Preparing the scene for the UI

Now that we have a good understanding of the UI system, it's time to implement something within our game to practice a little bit. But the most important outcome from the rest of the chapter is to understand how to program UI within the framework of Unity.

First of all, we need to create a Canvas in our scene, and as a consequence, an event system will also be created. You can do it by right-clicking on the **Hierarchy** panel and then navigating to **UI | Canvas**. Select the **Canvas** object from the **Inspector** and tweak the options in the Inspector based on your needs. This really depends on your target platform (more on this in the last chapter of this book), and the best way to understand which of these options suit your needs is to test and test and test again.

The next step is to have a nice background for our interface. We got a really nice blue bar in our package that you can find in the `Graphics/UI` folder. In order to place it within our interface, let's create a new image.

Right-click on the **Hierarchy** panel and navigate to **UI | Image**. We can rename the object `UI_Background`. Drag and drop `ui_blue_top_with_text` from the project panel into the Sprite variable of the Image component. Since our package is already in proportion with respect to the resolution we decided in `Chapter 1`, *A Flat World in Unity*, we can just press the **Set Native Size** button to restore the original ratio. Then, scale the bar and place it as shown in the following screenshot:

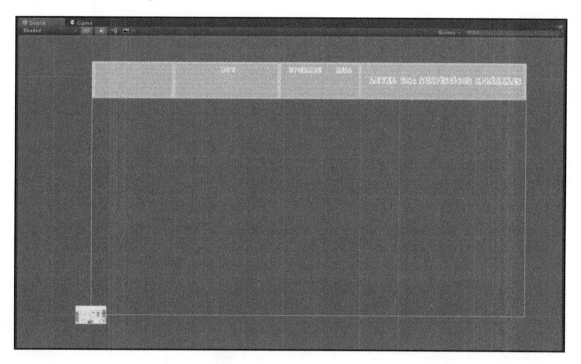

In the game view, it will look like this:

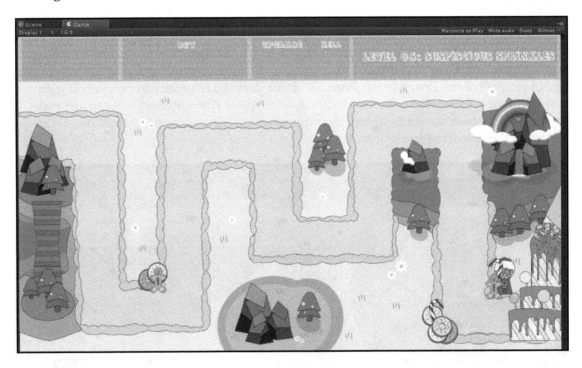

As for your convenience, the package contains an instance of the UI, which has already placed labels on it. This will allow us to save some time. However, if you want to create your UI, remember to place labels and format them with the right font.

As a result, we have got a place to start developing our UI as we designed it in the previous section.

Creating a health bar

In our game world, the terrible sweet-tooth pandas make a lot of trouble for our player, especially when they reach the longed-awaited cake. As such, with every bite they take, the player will lose some life. However, the player needs a way, and so does the game, to keep track of his or her life. In our design, we chose a health bar, which we are going to implement in this section.

Creating and placing the health bar

Within the UI_Background we created before, let's create another image by selecting **UI |
Image** (you can right-click directly on UI_Background to parent already the new image to it). Then, rename it Health_Bar.

Assign ui_health_bar_frame as a Sprite in the Graphics/UI folder. Again, scale it properly (and if you wish use also the **Set Native Size** button, like we did for the bar) and place it as in the following screenshot:

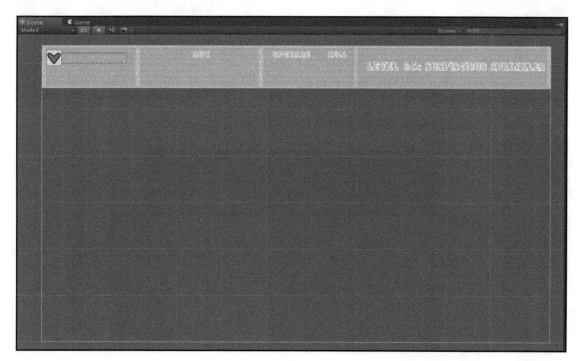

Now, we need to create the health bar filling. Create a new image and name it
Health_Bar_Filling. Assign ui_health_bar_filling to the image Sprite, and place in
the scene as follows:

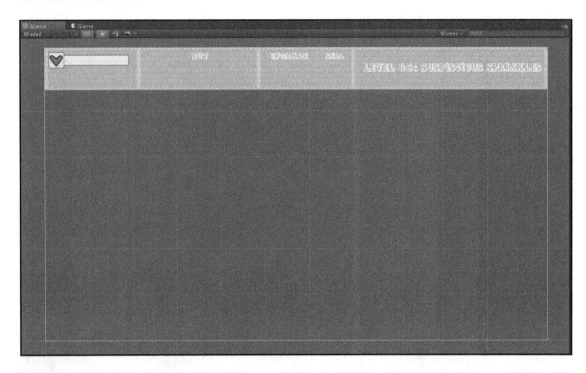

At the end, you should have the following in the **Hierarchy** panel:

Now, in the **Inspector**, we need to set the **Image Type** of Health_Bar_Filling to **Filled**. Then, set **Fill** Method to **Horizontal** and **Fill Origin** to **Left**, as shown here:

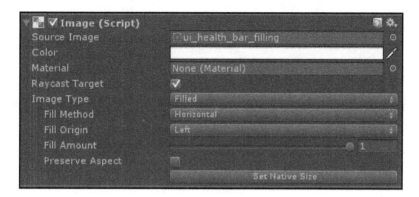

As a result, if we change the amount variable (you can play with in in the Inspector with the slider), the bar will be more or less filled, as a health bar should be.

Now we are ready to actual make the health bar work by using a specific script.

Scripting the health bar

Finally, after many pages about UI, we start to see some code in this chapter. Again, as we said in the last chapter, don't be afraid of code, but try hard to understand why it works in that specific way, and you will be rewarded with the ability to program a game, which in my opinion is not bad.

Okay, let's start to create a new Script within the Script folder. If you prefer, you can also create a sub-folder named UI_Scripts, but this is up to you. We can name the script HealthbarScript.

Let's open the script by double-clicking on it. In order to use the UI classes, we need to import the namespace. This can be done by adding the following line at the beginning of our code, as we already pointed out:

```
using UnityEngine.UI;
```

Now that we can use also the UI classes, we need three variables. One is a public variable that allows us to decide the maximum amount of health that the player can have. The other two are private to keep track of the Image component attached to Health_Bar_Filling, in order to change the bar filling, and the current amount of health that the player possesses:

```
public int maxHealth; //The maximum amount of health that the player can
possess
private Image fillingImage; //The reference to "Health_Bar_Filling" Image
component
private int health;   //The current amount of health of the player
```

Next, we have to set a couple of variables in our Start() function, in particular, the reference to the UI Image of Health_Bar_Filling by using the GetComponentInChildren() function. We also need to set the current amount of health to the maximum. In this way, the player will start with the maximum amount of health, and this makes sense. Finally, we call a function to update the graphic of the health bar, which we will implement in a few steps:

```
void Start () {
    //Get the reference to the filling image
    fillingImage = GetComponentInChildren<Image>();

    //set the health to the maximum
    health = maxHealth;

    //Update the graphics of the Health Bar
    updateHealthBar();
}
```

Then, we need to expose a public method to reduce the amount of health the player possesses, based on an integer parameter we pass to it. This function will be called when one of the sweet-tooth pandas bites the cake, or in the worst-case scenario, it will dive into the cake. At the same time, the function should also check if the amount of health has reached zero. In this case, for the player, the game is over. As such, this function will return a Boolean value, which if true, means there is no more cake: the sweet-tooth pandas have eaten it all! Of course, we also need to update the graphic of the health bar when we change the health amount. Furthermore, to make the code slightly more robust. When the amount of health reaches zero or below, the current health is just set to zero and not to negative values. Therefore, we can write the following:

```
//Function to apply damage to the player
public bool ApplyDamage(int value) {
    //Apply damage to the player
    health -= value;
```

```
//Check if the player has still health and update the Health Bar
if(health > 0) {
  updateHealthBar();
  return false;
}

//In case the player has no health left, set health to zero and
  return true
health = 0;
updateHealthBar();
return true;
}
```

Finally, we need to write the function to update the Health Bar graphic, the one we have called in the previous functions. First, based on the current amount of health and the maximum available, the function computes the percentage (from 0% to 100%) of the amount of health of the player as a float between 0.0 and 1.0. Note that *1f is a fast way to convert the number into a float, and therefore make a division between floats, instead of integers. Then, the function assigns this percentage to the fillingAmount of the image component:

```
//Function to update the Health Bar Graphic
void updateHealthBar() {
  //Calculate the percentage (from 0% to 100%) of the current amount of
    health of the player
  float percentage = health * 1f / maxHealth;
  //Assign the percentage to the fillingAmount variable of the
    "Health_Bar_Filling"
  fillingImage.fillAmount = percentage;
}
```

After we have saved the script, it is ready to go. Also, remember to assign the maximum amount of health in the Inspector. For the purpose of our game, we set it to 100. At the end, our script will be like the following in the **Inspector**:

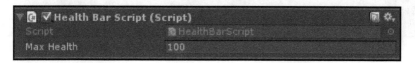

Now that the player has a health, we need to focus on storing and displaying the amount of sugar that the player collects.

Implementing the sugar meter

If in the previous section we have seen how the sweet-tooth pandas can defeat the player, now it's time to give the player a way to stop them. The first step is to have enough sugar to build cupcakes towers. As such, we need a sugar meter to keep track of the amount of sugar that the player possesses.

As we have seen in our design, this will be a number, and not a bar like the health. Therefore, even if the concepts are similar, the implementation is slightly different.

Creating and place

The process for creating the sugar meter is similar to the health bar, so let's start to create a new Image, parented with the Canvas, named `Sugar_Meter`. As a Sprite, you can use the `ui_sugar_meter` file in the `Graphic/UI` folder. Place it, and scale it if necessary, in the scene to match the following screenshot:

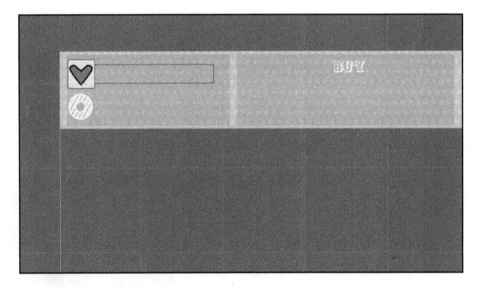

Next, create a Text component, parent it to Sugar_Meter, and name it Sugar_Meter_Text. You can set the font and the color that you prefer. At the end you should have something similar to this:

At the end, we should have the following in the **Hierarchy** panel:

```
▼ Canvas
  ▼ UI_Background
    ▼ Health_Bar
        Health_Bar_Filling
    ▼ Sugar_Meter
        Sugar_Meter_Text
```

Now, let's make it work with a script.

Scripting the sugar meter

The script for the sugar meter works similarly to the script for the health bar. Let's import the namespace in order to use UI classes by adding the following line at the beginning of our script:

```
using UnityEngine.UI;
```

We need two private variables to store the reference to Sugar_Meter_Text and the actual amount of sugar possessed by the player. As you can see, we don't have a maximum, because in theory the player can accumulate an infinite amount of sugar:

```
private Text sugarMeter; //Reference to the Text component
private int sugar; //Amount of sugar that the player possesses
```

In the Start() function, just get the reference to the UI text and update the graphic through a function, which we will implement in few steps:

```
void Start () {
    //Get the reference to the Sugar_Meter_Text
    sugarMeter = GetComponentInChildren<Text>();
    //Update the Sugar Meter graphic
    updateSugarMeter();
}
```

Now we need a generic function to increase or decrease player's sugar by an arbitrary amount the. We also need to take into account that it is not possible to have a negative amount of sugar. This is more for code robustness rather than a real need for the game. In fact, the only way to decrease the sugar is if the player buys cupcake towers (or upgrades their towers), but he or she won't if he or she doesn't have enough sugar. One last thing to do is to update the graphic of the Sugar Meter as well:

```
//Function to increase or decrease the amount of sugar
public void ChangeSugar(int value) {
    //Increase (or decrease, if value is negative) the amount of sugar
    sugar += value;
    //Check if the amount of sugur is negative, is so set it to zero
    if(sugar < 0) {
        sugar = 0;
    }
    //Update the Sugar Meter graphic
    updateSugarMeter();
}
```

Since we will need to retrieve the amount of the sugar that the player has in the upcoming chapters, mainly to check if he or she has enough to buy an upgrade or a tower, we need a function to retrieve this value. The reason to create this function is that the sugar amount is a private variable, and we don't want to make it public, since for robustness we want it to change only with the ChangeSugar() function, which updates the graphic too:

```
//Function to return the amount of sugur, since it is a private
  variable
public int getSugarAmount() {
  return sugar;
}
```

Finally, we need the function to update the graphic. This function converts the amount of sugar possessed by the player into a string, and assigns the string to the **Text** component of Sugar_Meter_Text:

```
//Function to update the Sugar Meter graphic
void updateSugarMeter() {
  //Assign the amount of sugar converted to a string to the text in the
    Sugar Meter
  sugarMeter.text = sugar.ToString();
}
```

Once the script is saved, we don't have any parameters to set in the **Inspector**. Therefore, our sugar meter is ready to measure the amount of sugar.

More about UI scripting – handlers

There is one last topic that we need to cover, since we will be using this technique later on in Chapter 7, *Trading Cupcakes and the Ultimate Battle for the Cake – Gameplay Programming*.

Imagine that you want to create an UI component that does something when it is clicked. We could create a script with a public function, then attach a button component to the game object. Finally, we should create a new OnClick() event on the button component to trigger the function we have written before. It's fine, but isn't a bit laborious?

Another example is, suppose you need to drag a UI component around because it is a floating window. How are you going to do it? For what we have seen so far, this appears to be an hard task; but there is an easy solution.

In fact, in our scripts, we can directly include directly the event systems, by using this line of code:

```
using UnityEngine.EventSystems;
```

As a result, you will be able to extend your script with some (C#) interfaces.

 In case you don't know what a C# interface is or don't know how to use it, you can check any C# manual. However, I recommend this video from the official Documentation of Unity, since it applies interfaces directly to Unity: `https://unity3d.com/learn/tutorials/topics/scripting/int` `erfaces`.

These interfaces allow you to create a function within your script that is triggered whenever the specific event you chose occurs. Moreover, this function provides some information about that specific event as a parameter within the `PointerEventData` class. For instance, to implement our dragging behavior from before, we need to add a handler/interface for the drag event next to the class declaration, like as follows:

```
public class DragTest : MonoBehaviour, IDragHandler {
```

Then, you need to implement the interface with its specific function. In this case we have:

```
public void OnDrag(PointerEventData eventData) {
}
```

 In case you are using Visual Studio as your code editor, you can right-click on the name of the interface and from the quick action menu select **Implement interface** to automatically create that the function we need to implement.

At this stage, implementing the drag behavior is simple, since within the `eventData` variable, we have all the data regarding the event, such as the mouse position. Therefore, we can write the following line of code:

```
transform.position = eventData.position;
```

 Alternatively, you can also use the `Input` class, as shown here: `transform.position = Input.mousePosition;`

For a complete list of events you can consult the official documentation here: `https://docs` `.unity3d.com/ScriptReference/EventSystems.EventTrigger.html`.

For details about the `PointerEventData` class and which kind of information of an event it holds, here is the link to the official documentation: `https://docs.unity3d.com/ScriptRe` `ference/EventSystems.PointerEventData.html`.

What about all the rest?

What about all the cool menu interfaces, and all the gameplay interface to buy/sell towers that the book promised? Well, don't you think we have learned a lot in this chapter?

In fact, this chapter provided a lot of information about UIs, and I suggest you take your time to get familiar with all the concepts, as well as doing the exercises in the next section. Then, we will come back to implementing all of this when we will build the gameplay in `Chapter 5`, *The Secret Ingredient Is a Dash of Physics*.

Homework

In this chapter, we looked at many aspects of UIs in the first part, whereas we got handy with it in the second part, by implementing a UI within our game. However, before going on to the next chapter, I invite you to take a look at these exercises to improve your UI designing/programming skills. They are divided, for your convenience, into two parts: the first to improve your designing skills, and the second to improve your programming skills.

Improving UI designing skills:

1. **A great exercise**: A great exercise is to find around three examples of games that you like, which are all different. For example, choose a strategy, adventure, and puzzle game. Next, for each of them, write down, or draw and annotate, each of the UI elements, what their function is, and what happens when a user interacts with it. For example, if the user presses the next button, what happens? Do they go to a new screen, or does a pop-up appear? You don't have to do this for the entire game, but enough to get a feel for how the UI works, and to understand how the placement of icons impact the user's experience. Next, try to experiment with changing the way that the UI is positioned and even the types of UI element. For example, if there is a health bar on the left, move it to the right or substitute the bar with text and see how it changes the feel. The main purpose of this exercise is to keep experimenting with different approaches to the UI. This is

especially useful when you may have too many elements on screen, and as a result you need to remove some. In this way, you will have begun to develop different ideas and approaches to modifying the UI to achieve different types of interaction. Finally, document what you have done, and feel gratified by what you have accomplished and learned.

2. **A frame interface (part I)**: Take the map provided in the package of this book (or the one you are currently using). Now imagine that, instead of having only a bar at the top for the UI, you have also a right lateral bar. Furthermore, imagine to have more than 20 kinds of cupcakes tower, two kinds of sugar that the player can collect, brown and white, and that for each tower the player can decide two different upgrades other than selling. In this scenario, design an interface that easily display to the player all what he or she needs. In particular, ensure that the interface is intuitive, and could be used even without an explanation. At the end, ask to your friends to take a look at the paper prototype of your interface and check if it really achieves what you had in mind. Little tip: it's impossible to fit 20 kinds of tower all at once in the interface; therefore, you may want to divide them into categories, or have a scrollable area with all the towers.

3. **A frame interface (part II)**: Once you have designed the interface of the previous exercise, look carefully at the colors of the map provided into our package (or the one you are currently using). Now, choose the color palette carefully for your UI so that there is enough contrast to be able to read the interface without much effort, but at the same time it is pleasant to look at, since it is in harmony with the colors of the map.

4. **A frame interface (part III)**: Now it's time to create all the graphics necessary for the design you have created in the last two exercise. You can create the graphics from scratch, or take part of the graphics from the package of this book. Once created, import them into Unity, including slicing, dividing into Sprites, and so on.

Improving your UI programming skills:

5. **An evil button**: We have seen that the event on the button is triggered only when the pointer is released and still within the button. In fact, if the player moves the pointer out the component, the event won't be triggered. In the case of an evil button, once the player has clicked it, it's done, the action will be executed. However, in the case of the button, the action is not executed when the player clicks, but when released. Implement an evil button so that even if the player moves the pointer away from the button and release, the button will still trigger the action.

6. **The selected toggle**: Unfortunately, at the moment, Unity doesn't have any functions to retrieve the toggle that is selected from a toggle group. If by the time you are reading this book, a new version of Unity releases this function, you can still improve your skills by doing this exercise and ignoring the new pre-made function of Unity. In fact, having the ability to retrieve the active toggle is really handy in many situations and in many of your games. As such, implement a script that given a toggle group with an arbitrary number of toggles is able to retrieve and return the selected one (if any; in fact, there might be none).

7. **Runtime dropdown (part I)**: Read the official documentation of the drop-down component carefully, and implement one that can change the number of options at runtime. In particular, place a toggle group that allows the player to pick a set. Every set contains different options for the drop-down menu. Once the player choses a set, the options of the set are loaded into the drop-down menu (there should be only one drop-down menu in the scene, and you need to dynamically load the new options). Little tip: since the number of options in each set is variable, the easiest way to do this is to clear all the previous options of the drop-down menu and load the new ones.

8. **Runtime dropdown (part II)**: If you want to go further, take the previous exercise and through a Input Field and a button allow the player to add an option to the current selected set.

9. **Runtime dropdown (part III)**: If you felt confident doing the previous exercise, keep going by implementing the possibility to remove an option from the set.

10. **The lighting pointer**: If you have read the UI effect component section, you will know about the existence of a special component that creates shadows. Place a text in the middle of your scene and apply the shadow component. Play a little bit with its values to understand how they work, and how to simulate the light coming from different directions. Now, implement a script that, based on the pointer positions, changes the shadow component so that it seems that the pointer has a kind of light on the text. Therefore, if the pointer is above the text, the shadow will be below, whereas if the pointer is on the left, the shadow will be on the right. By the way, I warn you that a possible consequence of doing this exercise is to create something that you will spend a fairly large amount of time to play with, because playing with it can become addictive!

11. **Again Prefabs**: We faced prefabs in the previous section, in game development they are always really useful, particularly when you have multiple scenes and we don't want to implement the whole UI again for each level. Since we are going to create different levels in the last chapter, it's a good idea and good practice to create a prefab for each of the main UI functionalities. As such, create a prefab for the health bar, one for the sugar meter, one for the buy section of the UI and another one for the upgrade/selling section of the UI. Furthermore, create one last prefab containing all the UI (basically the canvas along with all its children). In this way, we can just place this last prefab in the scene in the next levels. However, remember to then add an Event System manually in the new scene.

12. **A frame interface (part IV)**: If you have done at least the part 1 of this exercise, you have designed an interface. Scale the map so that you can create the frame described in part 1. Then, implement the interface. Afterwards, test the interface again with your friends to check if it feels right now that it is digital. Eventually, modify it based on the suggestions of your friends, and don't forget to share your work, also with me if you want. If you also quote the book, I'd be pleased.

13. **A negative damage**: When we created our health bar script, we wrote a function to apply damage, and it checks if the health has reached zero. However, what about a negative damage? In that case, the health of the player increases, and it shouldn't. Therefore, add a control to avoid a negative damage, such as setting the damage to zero if it's below zero.

14. **Healing the player**: If you have done the previous exercise, it's not because we are sadistic against the player, but because that function should only apply damage. To heal the player instead, create another function that takes as a parameter an amount to cure the player, and checks if the health is no more than the maximum amount. If so, it just caps the health to the maximum.

15. **Warning the player I**: When the health goes below 30% means that the sweet-tooth pandas are devouring the cake, and the player should be warned. Warn the player by showing a pop-up that appears on the screen only once, when the health is below 30%.

16. **Warning the Player II**: In the same vein as the previous exercise, a pop up menu could disturb the gameplay. Therefore, warn the player in this way: change the color of the health bar to yellow when the health is between 20% and 40%, and to red when it is below 20%. Of course, restore the green color once the health is above 40%.

Summary

The chapter began with an introduction to UI designing and programming, in order to understand the main complications behind UIs and why they are so important. Then, in the first part of the chapter, we saw in detail how the Unity UI system works. In particular, we analyzed every component of the Unity framework and learned their use and functionality. In addition, a section explained some special components present in the framework, but that we won't need for this book.

You can find more about UI designing and programming (although with a major focus on gamification), including also how to use Illustrator to create your own graphic, in *Gamification with Unity 5.x* by *Lauren S. Ferro, Packt publishing*. You can find the book here: `https://www.packtpub.com/game-development/gamification-unity-5x`.

In the second part, we started to create the UI for the tower defense game. In particular, we implemented the logic for a health bar as well as for a sugar meter. However, we will implement more in `Chapter 5`, *The Secret Ingredient Is a Dash of Physics*.

In the next chapter, we are not going to be alone anymore. In fact, we will finally meet the terrible sweet-tooth pandas we have so anticipated.

4
No Longer Alone – Sweet-Toothed Pandas Strike

"They are angry and they are hungry. Beware, the sweet-tooth pandas are getting closer for your delicious cake!

Animations and artificial intelligence are at the core of giving life to an **Non-Playing Characters** (**NPCs**) or complex objects in games. The former makes NPCs appear dynamic and not static; the latter gives them an intelligence, with which they can move and act into the world.

This chapter explains how to use the animation system of Unity, with a particular focus on 2D animations. We will cover artificial intelligence and what it can do in video games later in the book.

The first part of the chapter will focus on the rich and sophisticated animation system of Unity (sometimes referred to as Mecanim). In explaining each part, we will bring, bit by bit, our evil pandas to life.

However, in the second part of the chapter, we will give the evil pandas the possibility to move around the map, to trigger actions such as dying or eating so much cake that they will explode… *literally*!

In particular, we will see:

- Animation clips and how to create and handle them from Sprite Sheets
- The Animator and how to build a finite state machine for animations
- Scripting objects with an Animator component to trigger animations and make the animation machine working
- Implementing a waypoint system to move the sweet-tooth pandas around

Like all the other chapters of this book, you will find the *Homework* section at the end. It has a range of different exercises for you to do to improve your skills and implement a range of different functionalities in your game. So, let's get ready to learn how to bring our evil pandas to life.

Getting ready

The graphic package that we are using for this book contains an animation Sprite Sheet for our terrible sweet-tooth pandas. Therefore, be sure to have the Sprite Sheet imported as **Sprite** and to set **Sprite Mode** to **Multiple**. In fact, you should have all single frames in a different sprite. Remember to rename them so that you will be less confused later on. The same applies if you are using your own graphics.

An evil panda is looking forward to eat your cake

Animations

Life and all of its creatures are dynamic. We move, and our movements, even the subtlest of ones, express emotions. If we were to remove such things, even the tiniest smile, life would become dull and static. Animation effects can range from the simplest of things such as a flag waving to a dragon flying. Just look around you, inside and outside; something will be moving or will move from time to time. Even stones move, albeit with wind, something knocking them, or someone skipping them across water.

Unity has a complex animation system, also known as **Mecanim**, which requires time to get used to. It includes different components. Some of these are specifically for 3D animations; others can be used for both 2D and 3D. Usually, animating in 3D is harder than in 2D since it requires tweaking of many parameters, and therefore much more practice is needed to master it. If you are interested in learning more about 3D animation in Unity, I suggest that you to read a specific book about it.

In this book, we will focus on animating only in 2D. As such, our workflow becomes simple enough that it can be explained within this chapter. In particular, we will go through the following workflow:

- Creating some files called animation clips, to store our animations. We will do this starting from animation Sprite Sheets.
- Building a finite-state machine to control the flow of the animations.
- Writing a script to control the finite-state machine triggers.

Specifically, in this section, we will see how to animate our terrible sweet-tooth pandas. In our graphic package, we can find the animation Sprite Sheets of the panda under the `Graphic/Enemies` folder. Of course, all the Sprite Sheets should already be sliced, as we have seen back in `Chapter 1`, *A Flat World in Unity* and if you are using your own graphics, it is better if all the single sprites have the same dimensions. But before we go any further in exploring Mecanim, let's go through some background information about animation in the next two sections.

A historical overview

The term *animation* derives from the Latin word *animates*, which is the past participle of the verb *animare*; that means *give breath to*. The verb derives from the word *anima*, which means *life, breath*, originating from the Greek word *anemos*, literally *wind*, which in turn descend from the Sanskrit word *aniti*, meaning *breathes*. It was only during the 1742 that the verb *to animate* was used for the first time with the sense of *give life to*.

Modern animations are based on the concept of motion. Therefore, it's worthwhile to mention that the first studies of motion were conducted by the Greek Philosopher Ζήνων ὁ Ἐλεάτης (known in English as *Zeno of Elea*) during the 4th century B.C. We can read about many of his ideas in works by another Greek philosopher: Ἀριστοτέλης (known in English as *Aristotle*). Zeno is famous for conceiving many paradoxes about motion, exploring the problem to prove the inexistence of motion. One of these paradoxes is the arrow paradox (also known as **Fletcher's paradox**). We can read a little bit about this from Aristotle's book Physics IV, as follows:

> *"If everything when it occupies an equal space is at rest, and if that which is in locomotion is always occupying such a space at any moment, the flying arrow is therefore motionless."*

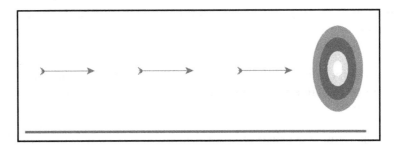

The Zeno's Fletcher's paradox described by Aristotle. You don't see the arrow moving towards the target, but just moments in which the arrow is static, albeit in different positions. Therefore, motion is an illusion.

As we can see from the preceding picture, the paradox claims the motionlessness of the arrow, since in each instant the arrow is in a very particular position in space and it is static in that instant. Besides the many philosophical implications and solutions to the paradox, it's interesting to note that the same concept applies nowadays for animation. Animations in movies and video games (to name a few) are just a series of static frames, which, in a rapid succession, give the illusion of motion.

Animations in video games

Animations help to bring our creations to life. They make the living more vibrant and the dead even creepier! The development of animation has come a long way since the pixel art graphics to what can only be described as an uncanny valley of movement. In some cases, the animations are so life like that for a moment we forget that we're in an alternate reality.

Now, let's go back to the start of game animation. Space Invaders, Donkey Kong, and Tempest. If you have ever experienced one of these games, then you will know what I mean when a lot can be conveyed by very simple animation, whether it is translating side to side with Space Invaders, jumping to dodge barrels in Donkey Kong, or rotating in Tempest. However, as time progressed, so too did the animation techniques that we have become all too familiar with. With the introduction of 3D games and consequently characters, we have seen animations enter another dimension… literally. But despite their polygonal bodies and ridged movements, such as the following image of Lara Croft (though not so much nowadays), animations allow us to simply interact with a game.

Taken from the gameplay of Lara Croft in Tomb Raider I

One good philosophy behind including animation is to think of animations as a way of communicating with your audience. Sometimes, emotions such as love, excitement, and hate are great ways to communicate feelings, just like body movements such as running, jumping, and attacking are good ways to indicate a state that the player is currently experiencing. However, animation doesn't just include the player; objects such as trees, and animals, and those who are not playing, or NPC, also interact and move about the game space, sometimes just as any controlled player would. Some of the most prolific examples of the use of animation with NPCs are in **Role Playing Games (RPGs)**.

Many characters that you interact with develop a feeling about you. For example, if you constantly answer them with an abrupt response, they are likely to display facial expressions of despise, or shock like the next image. Where, on the other hand, if you're warm, friendly, and offer a helping hand, then their facial expressions are likely to be more welcoming.

Shepard, clearly not laughing at a joke (Mass Effect series)

Timing is everything, so when it comes to animations, make sure that they happen when they are supposed to. Pressing X to jump and the jump happening only 3 seconds later is not going to end well, for your game or the player. It is not enough to just animate a character or an object, but you've to add them up to create an immersive environment. The importance of being immersed within a game is vital if you want your player to come back for more. If you have clunky animation that causes frustration, chances are that the player won't be persistent, unless perhaps the story is extremely intriguing. Even the trees in most games animate, even with subtle swaying or leaves flickering with the wind. In this way, it's better than having giant poles of static wood sticking out from the ground.

Another thing to consider when it comes to animation is the frame rate and, in turn, the hardware. You may have a wonderful animation sequence, such as the epic cut scene like the fight in Crisis Core: Final Fantasy VII between Sephiroth, Genesis, and Angeal (as shown in the following image); another example is the gameplay while you're killing enemies in Battlefield 4. But if there were a delay, well, it would have been pretty much nothing! When creating games for Unity, it is very important to consider this, especially when you are targeting mobile devices. While many mobile devices have the ability to play some resource-heavy media, not all do. Therefore, if your ultimate device won't be able to keep up, your intense efforts are likely to go in vain, unless of course you find another device to target. This is mostly the case with 3D games on mobile devices, and you can find out more here in the official Unity documentation:

`https://docs.unity3d.com/Manual/MecanimPeformanceandOptimization.html.`

I recommend that you visit the preceding link once you've finished the chapter so as to have a better understanding of the animation system in Unity.

Gameplay screenshot of Genesis and Sephiroth fighting in Crisis Core: Final Fantasy VII

Check out this site for some great tips for using animation in mobile games:
`www.teksmobile.com.au/blog/15-animation-tips-to-make-your-mobile -games-more-engaging.`

Now that we have an overview of animations in video games, let's head back to Unity to discover what it handles with animations, starting with the general workflow.

Workflow for animations

Now that we have understood why animations are so important for video games, let's give them a closer look. Unity's animation system is based on the concept of animation clips; we will explore this in more detail in the next section. As the name suggests, they are just clips containing data for a single animation (with a few exceptions).

Animation clips are organized into a structure that is similar to a flowchart system, where different nodes are connected to others (like the next screenshot). This system is called an Animator Controller and it acts as a state machine. It keeps track of which clip should currently be played and determines when the animations should change or blend together.

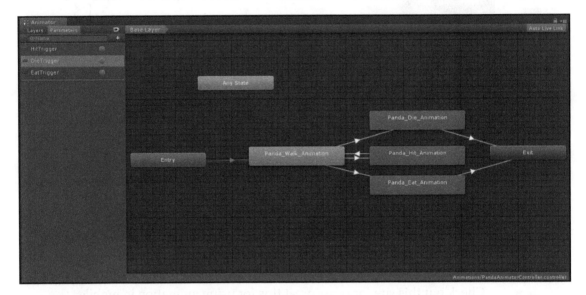

A very simple Animator Controller might only contain a small amount of clips. For example, one clip may be an object breaking, the other a fan rotating. On the other hand, a more advanced Animator Controller is likely to contain a lot more animations, for instance, all actions related to the main character, such as running, walking, idling, dying, and so on. In addition, animations may blend between multiple clips in order to look more fluid-like and less robotic, unless of course that is your intention!

Unity's animation system also has many special features, especially when using humanoid characters. These features allow you to retarget human-like or humanoid animations from any source, such as motion capture, the Unity asset store, or software such as Maya or Blender, and then apply them to your own character model. In addition to applying these animations, you are also able to adjust muscle definitions on characters. These special features are enabled by Unity's Avatar system, where humanoid characters are mapped to a common internal format (we won't see this in detail, but you can learn more in the optional section at the end of the chapter).

Ultimately, the animation clips, the Animator Controller, and the Avatar, are brought together on a gameObject via the Animator Component. This component references an Animator Controller and (if required) the Avatar for the model in question. The Animator Controller in turn contains the references to the animation clips it uses.

Animations clips and the Animator component

At the heart of Unity's animation system, there are Animation Clips. These components contain information that relate to an object's animation, such as whether or not they need to change their translation (position), their rotation, and so on, as the animation takes place. Animation clips can be 2D or 3D and are often made in programs such as 3D Studio Max, Flash, Maya, Blender, and even Photoshop. In addition to using software, animations can be created manually, such as rigging a 3D character (giving it a skeleton to move) or creating movement-by-movement sprites where each movement is drawn out. Remember the old Disney cartoons? Well they used similar processes to bring us some of our most beloved memories. However, if your game requires something that isn't too complex such as opening and closing doors, you are able to do this in Unity. Unity offers a tool known as the the Animation window (more about this later in the chapter).

In the case of 2D, these animation clips can contain an arbitrary sequence of sprites, like single frames in a movie, and change them over time so to give the illusion of motion. Usually, in 2D game development, sprite sheets are used for these purposes (like we anticipated in `Chapter 1`, *A Flat World in Unity*). As such, our graphic package contains these animation sprite sheets as well.

Another useful way to think about Animation clips is to pretend that they are actions, such as pick up an object, walk, or jump.

 In most advanced cases, Animation clips can contain part of an action that can be blended or merged with other animation clips.

For our pandas, we have the following animations:

- **Walk**: When our panda will move along the path
- **Die**: When the player's cupcake towers will take the panda down

- **Hit**: When the player's cupcake towers will hit the panda
- **Eat**: When the panda reaches the end of the level and eats a slice of the player's cake

As such, we need to create four different animation clips, one for each of these.

Creating Animation clips with a controller

The method explained in this section is a rapid way to start to create the first Animation clip, starting from a sprite sheet, and as a side effect, a controller will be created. However, we will deal with it later in the chapter.

First of all, create an empty game object in the scene, and rename it to Panda (or if you prefer, Sweet-Tooth_Panda). Eventually, you'll want to store it, once finished working on it, inside a prefab.

Now in the project panel, if we select animation_panda_sprite_sheet and expand it, we will have something like this:

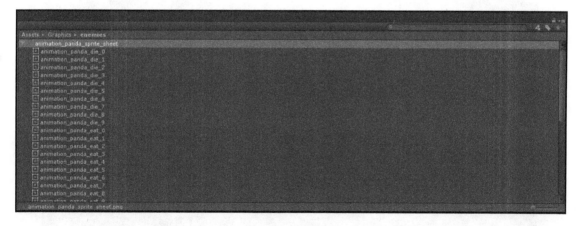

All the single Sprites/frames of the animation should be the same size. By ensuring this in the beginning, it allows you to avoid many headaches later on. Therefore, if the Sprite Sheet is well done, it should be sliced without difficultly with the **Grid By Cell Count** mode in the Sprite Editor, as we did in Chapter 1, *A Flat World in Unity*. In our package, our Sprite Sheet is already good to go with each Sprite distributed evenly, but if you're using your own graphic and the Sprite Sheet doesn't have all the frames of the same size, you might want to modify it within a graphics program (such as Photoshop or Gimp) so that the sprites are distributed accordingly.

This is the final result in the Sprite Editor:

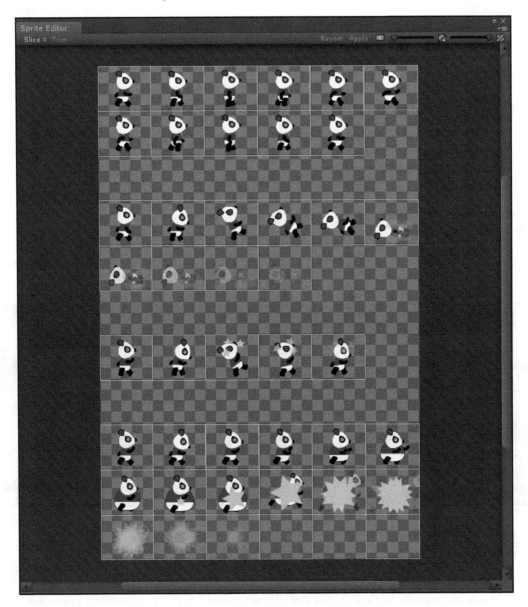

However, if you move the slider at the bottom part of the project panel (as we learned in Chapter 1, *A Flat World in Unity*), you are able to see all the single sprites, as the following image shows:

Select all the Sprites that belong to the animations of the walking Panda, and drag them onto the **Panda** game object we have created before:

In our case, we have 11 sprites for the Walking animation, then 5 sprites for the Hit animation, 10 for the Die animation, and finally 16 for the Eat animation

It may happen that the last Sprite is equal to the first one. Depending on the case, you might not want it because it is likely to cause a disruption in the animation, such as a delay in a walking sequence. In that case, you can just select all the sprites but the last one.

Unity will ask you where to save the animation clip and under which name. We can name it `Panda_Walk_Animation` and save it in our `Animation` folder. If you don't have it, you can create it under the `Asset` folder. In this way, as we discussed in `Chapter 1`, *A Flat World in Unity*, we keep our project clean and tidy.

When we select the `Panda` object, we can notice that in the Inspector two components have been added. One is a **Sprite Renderer**, which we have already discussed in previous chapters. The other is an **Animator** component. Let's see it in detail in the next section.

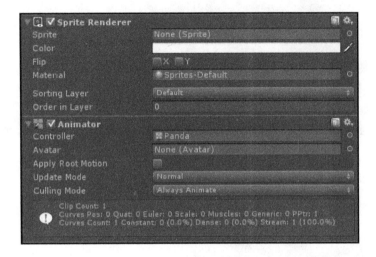

If you navigate in the **Animation** folder, other than the animation file we have just created, you will also find an Animator controller called `Panda` (or `Sweet-Tooth_Panda`, since the name is taken from the Game Object). For our purposes, it's better to rename it as something that describes it better, such as `PandaAnimatorController`. We will learn more about this later in the chapter.

The Animator component

The main function of the Animator component is to hold a reference to an Animator Controller, which defines how our animation clips should be played. Furthermore, it controls when and how to blend and/or transition between them. We will explore the controller in the next sections.

The Animator component has some parameters that can adjusted. Let's see the main ones:

- **Controller**: This is the reference to the Animator Controller, and it's the most important variable. If not set, the Animator component can't work. In the previous picture, the controller is set to `Panda` (or `PandaAnimatorController` if you have renamed it), which is a controller we just created.
- **Avatar**: A parameter only for 3D Humanoid characters, so you can ignore it (however, if you are interested in learning more, check out the *More about Animations* section later in the chapter).
- **Apply Root Motion**: You can ignore this too (however, if you are interested in the learning more, check out the *More about Animations* section).
- **Update Mode**: Specifies when the Animator is updated and which timescale it should use. The **Normal** mode updates the controller in sync with the update calls, and the Animator's speed matches the current timescale. If the timescale is slowed, animations will slow down to match. The **Animate Physics** mode instead updates the Animator in sync with the **FixedUpdate** calls, which are used by the Physic engine. This is useful when the object you are animating has a physical interaction, for instance, if a character needs to push or pull a rigid body (more about Physics in the next chapter). Finally, the **Unscaled Time** mode updates the Animator in sync with the Update calls, like the **Normal** mode, but the current timescale is ignored and it always plays at 100% of its speed. For instance, this mode is useful when you pause the game but you still want to animate part of the UI or the pause menu itself.
- **Culling Mode**: Specifies the culling mode for animations (more on this in the *More about Animations* section later in the chapter).

Furthermore, at the bottom of the Animator component, there is an information box with some useful information about the Animator controller we are using. For now, the only information that is relevant is **Clip Count**, which tells you how many animation clips are used by the controller. You can find out more about this information box in the *More about Animations* section.

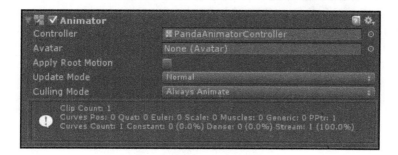

Creating the other animation clips

Now, we need to create the remaining animation clips respectively for when the pandas die, eat or get hit. This time, we want to do it without generating the controller. We have two choices. In the first, we still keep dragging and dropping the other groups of Sprites onto the **Panda** game object as we did previously. As a result, Unity will still ask to give a name and a location for the animation clip, but it won't generate another controller. This is the fastest way. However, there is another one. It involves the **Animation** window, but for the sake of learning we will use this second method to create the remaining Animation clips.

To do so, open the **Animation** windows (click on the top bar menu on **Window** | **Animation** or use the shortcut *Ctrl + 6*). Then, select your **Panda** from the **Hierarchy** panel. You should see something like this:

The **Animation** window allows you to create animations within Unity. It uses interpolation techniques between key frames to compute the position and rotation (along with other parameters) between each frame. It also supports a recording functionality as well as a curve editor. In 2D game development, this is not much used if animation Sprite Sheets are available, like our case (unless you need to fine-tune the animation). Yet, this is an important tool that avoids the need for third-party programs to create your animations. Also, it is useful for prototyping animations. Unfortunately, we don't have enough room in this chapter to talk in detail about the **Animation** window, but you can read more about it in the official documentation here:

`https://docs.unity3d.com/Manual/animeditor-UsingAnimationEditor.html`.

In our case, however, we will use it just to create and save animation clips starting from our Sprites. As we can notice from the preceding picture, there is already the Walk animation created in the last section. To create a new animation clip, click on **Panda_Walk_Animation** and a drop-down menu like the following should appear:

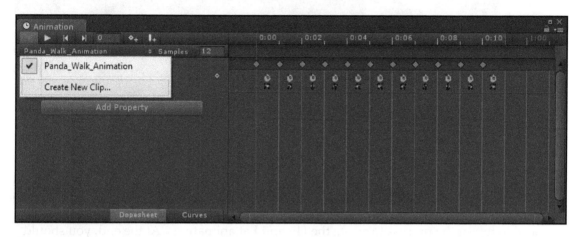

Click on **Create New Clip...** and Unity will ask you where to save this new file and its name. We can name it Panda_Die_Animation and save it within the Animations folder. As a result, the **Animation** window should now be cleared, as shown here:

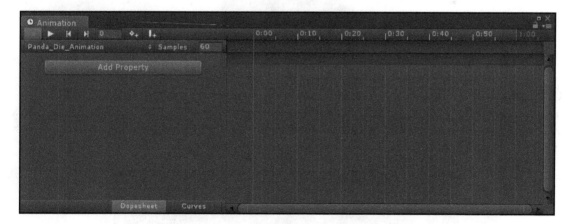

Now, we can select the Sprites of the die animation, and drag and drop them within the window. Thus, the Sprite animation is loaded within the animation file, as we can see from the Animation window:

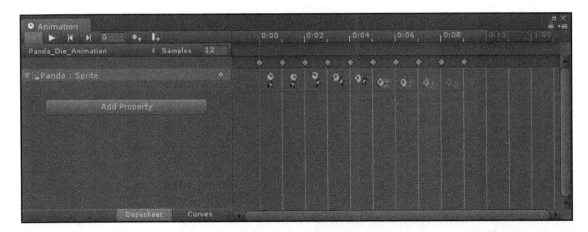

We need to repeat the process to create the Hit and Eat animations. At the end, you should have the following files in the `Animations` folder:

One more thing. If you click on one of them, in the **Inspector**, you can see some options about whether the animation can be played in loop and how, along with an information box with some the amount of certain kind of data for the animation, such as how many muscles (but this is for 3D animation, and we won't use this information).

Not all our animations are supposed to be played in loop. In fact, all but the walk animations are not supposed to loop. Therefore, for them, just uncheck the **Loop Time** variable in the **Inspector**, like this:

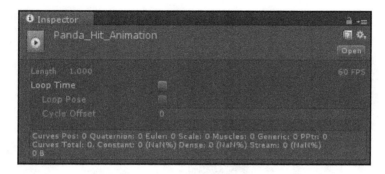

So far so good. Before you proceed, I advise you to create a new prefab in the `Prefab` folder, called `PandaPrefab`, and drag your **Panda** there.

The Animator

Imagine all of the different types of actions that you perform throughout the day-from the moment you wake up, to making coffee, having a shower, and getting ready for work. Each of these would have a different animation. The same goes for characters. In most games, characters or other animated objects (animals, trees, and so on) have a range of animations. Just like our example before, each animation will correspond to a different moment during gameplay. For example, when a character is just standing and being idle, they aren't doing much, but it is likely that they are still breathing. In some games, if characters remain idle for an extended period of time, other animation sequences are then triggered, such as impatient foot tapping or something completely unexpected. In first-person shooters, objects within the game environment may have the ability to be affected by things such as bullets or force (such as running hard into a wall), and as a result, they might break, crack, open, or even close. Mecanim uses a visual layout system similar to a flowchart to represent a state machine and enable you to control and sequence the animation clips that you want to use on your character or object. We will discuss this in more detail later.

The Animator window

The Animator window allows you to create, view, and modify Animator Controller assets within Unity.

Now that we have all our animation files, we need to embed them within the Animator Controller in a meaningful way. If you double-click on `PandaAnimatorController`, the **Animator** window opens, and you should have a screen similar to the following one:

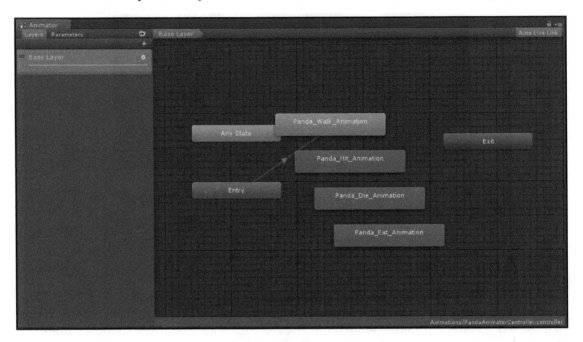

In case you don't see your panda animations within rectangles, like the preceding image, it is probably because you have created the animation clips without having the animation window linked to a controller. That is not a problem; you just need to select the animation clips you want in the controller and drag them into the **Animator** window, and they will be added.

The **Animator** window is divided into two sections. The main section with the dark gray grid is the layout area. You can use this area to create, arrange, and connect states in your Animator Controller.

You can right-click on the grid to create a new state node. Using the middle mouse button or *Alt*/Option, drag to pan the view around. Click to select state nodes, so as to edit them in the **Inspector**, and click and drag state nodes to rearrange the layout of your state machine, like this:

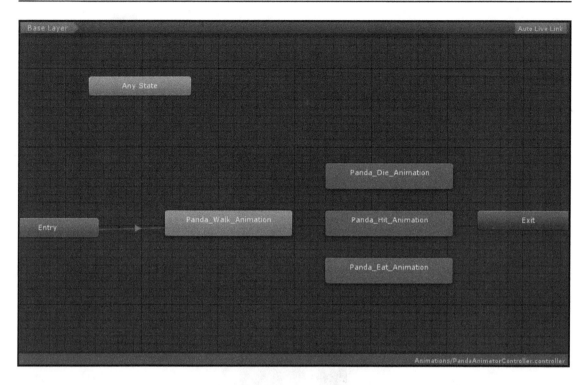

In this way, our state machine will be clearer and tidy for what we are going to do. The second section of the **Animator** window is the left-hand pane, which can be switched between the **Parameters** tab and **Layers** tab (if you want to learn more about layers, you can read the optional section of this chapter, **Layers** in the **Animator**, inside the *More about Animations* section). The **Parameters** tab allows you to create, view, and edit the Animator Controller parameters. These are variables that you define, which will then act as inputs into the state machine. We will see them in detail soon.

Also, toggling the eye icon on or off (highlighted in the next image to easily locate it) will show or hide the **Parameters** and **Layers** side pane, allowing you more room to see and edit your state machine.

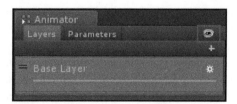

Furthermore, if we enable the lock icon (as in the next image) in the top-right corner, we are able to keep the **Animator** window focused on the current state machine. If the lock icon is disabled, clicking on a new Animator asset or a Game Object with an Animator component will switch the **Animator** window. As a result, we are then able to show that item's state machine. The benefit of locking the window is that it allows us to keep the **Animator** window from showing the same state machine, regardless of what assets or Game Objects are selected.

The last useful toggle (located just below the lock icon) is **Auto Live Link**, which allows us to see the machine in action at runtime. For your convenience, it is highlighted in the following image, but we will talk more about it when we need to test the machine we are building up:

The Animator state machine

As we already have mentioned, the Animator controller is a flowchart system; specifically it is a kind of finite-state machine. But what is a finite-state machine? From Wikipedia, we can read:

> *"A finite-state machine (FSM) or finite-state automaton (FSA, plural: automata), or simply a state machine, is a mathematical model of computation used to design both computer programs and sequential logic circuits. It is conceived as an abstract machine that can be in one of a finite number of states. The machine is in only one state at a time; the state it is in at any given time is called the current state. It can change from one state to another when initiated by a triggering event or condition; this is called a transition. A particular FSM is defined by a list of its states, its initial state, and the triggering condition for each transition."*

In our specific cases, the states will be the animations. So, saying that our Animator is a specific state means that the Game Object with that Animator controller is playing that specific animation. If it is not completely clear right now, it will be a while before we explain the different parts.

 We will explore finite-state machines a bit more in detail later in the book, when we deal with Artificial Intelligence.

Unity generated an Animator controller for us when we created the first Animation clip. But if you need to manually create it, here's how to do it. From the **Project** panel (possibly within a meaningful folder, such as `Animations`), right-click and select **Create** | **Animator Controller**. Once renamed, double-click on it to open it in the **Animator** window. Contrary to the automatically generated controller, which already contains all the states of our Panda animation, here there are no such states. In fact, we need to manually import them. In the case of our Pandas, we just need to select the animations file that we have created before from the **Project** panel and drag them into the grid of the **Animator** window. If you remember, we stored them inside the `Animations` folder. Always remember that you can move any state just by dragging it. This is useful, because you can reorganize states so as to have a visual order and improve the readability of your work.

Now, it's time to dig deeper and see how to actually build an animation machine for our pandas. If you created a new Animator controller, discard it, and let's take the one we had before.

The Animator states

Animations bring characters to life, and therefore Animation states provide the foundations for the Animation State Machine within Unity. Each state contains an individual animation sequence (or blend tree), such as running, walking, climbing, jumping, and so on. All these animation sequences will then be triggered and subsequently played when the character is in that respective state. When an event in the game triggers a state transition, such as the player jumps over a ledge while running, the character will be left in a new state whose animation sequence will then take over.

When you select a state in the Animator Controller, you will see the properties for that state in the inspector, as shown here:

These properties and their functions are listed here:

- **Name**: Is just how the state will be referred in the Animator, and it is also the name showed on top of the state. If it is automatically generated from an animation, as a default, it will have the same name of the animation clip. In fact, our four panda states have the same names as their respectively animation clips.
- **Tag**: Just another way to identify a state or a set of them. It is useful when you need to control animation machines from a script. For our purposes, we can leave it in blank.
- **Motion**: This is the animation clip assigned to this state, for example, one of the animation clips that we have created before, such as `Panda_Walk_Animation` or `Panda_Die_Animation` (actually, it can also be a blending tree; see the optional section *More about animations* later in the chapter).
- **Speed**: The default speed of the animation. For example, the default speed of an animation may be too slow, such as a running animation, and therefore, the speed needs to be increased. By changing the value of **Speed**, the animation is able to player faster.
- **Multiplier**: A number that is multiplied by **Speed** to increase it or decrease it. Next to it, there is the parameter checkbox. This allows us to transform this number into an animator parameter (please also note that the multiplier cannot have an independent value, but just be linked to a float parameter). In this way, we can control the speed of some animations, without touching the **Speed** settings (given that all of them are linked to the same parameter).

- **Mirror**: Should the state be mirrored, which means if the animation clip should be played like in a mirror, exchanging left with right and vice versa. This is only applicable to 3D humanoid animations, and therefore we won't deal with it. Note that can be transformed into a parameter Boolean.
- **Cycle Offset**: Determines if the animation loop should start to a different point, and the value indicates the offset from the beginning of the animation. Also this acts as a **Multiplier** and can be set to be a parameter.
- **Foot IK**: Should **Foot IK** be respected for this state? This is applicable to 3D humanoid animations, so we won't deal with it.
- **Write Defaults**: This decides whether or not AnimatorStates writes back the default values for properties that are not animated by its motion. By default, it is set to true, but unchecking it means that the non-animated properties of a state will keep the value they had previously.
- **Transitions**: The list of transitions originating from this state. It is equivalent to identify under which conditions this state changes into another one. We will see transitions in detail in a couple of sections.
- **Add Behaviour**: For the description of this button see the optional section *More about Animations* later in the chapter.

The default state, displayed in brown, is the state that the machine will be in when it is first activated. If you want, you are able to change the default state of the state machine by right-clicking on another state and selecting **Set As Layer Default State** from the context menu.

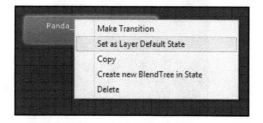

In our case, the default state is the **Panda_Walk_Animation** state, so be sure that it is selected as the default state. In addition, to add a new state, right-click on an empty space in the **Animator Controller** window and navigate to **Create State | Empty** from the context menu. Another way to create a state, as we have already pointed out, is to drag an animation into the **Animator Controller** window, and as a result, you will create a state containing that animation.

As far as our panda's animation states are concerned, we don't have particular needs or settings to tweak. After all, what we are building is a relatively simple finite state machine compared to big, complex 3D animation machines. But, if at any moment you feel that one of the four animations that we have is too fast or too slow, just select it and change its speed. In that case, you can do it at the end, when we finish the state machine, so as to have better and complete vision of the panda animation as a whole, and tweak these values to improve it. For instance, I slowed down the walking, hit, and eat animation to 25%, which means a speed of 0.25, whereas for the die animation, I used 0.2. Usually you find these values by trial and error.

Note that you can only drag Mecanim animations into the controller; non-Mecanim animations will be rejected. Moreover, states do not necessarily contain single animation clips. In fact, they could also contain Blend Trees. You can read more about them in the optional section, *More about Animations*, later in the chapter.

Special states

An animator machine also has some special states, which are presented in this image:

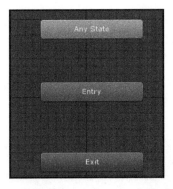

Any State is a special state that is always present. **Any State** implies that it cannot be the end point of a transition. For example, jumping to *any state* cannot be used as a way to pick a random state to enter the next. **Any State** exists for the situation where you want to go to a specific state regardless of which state you are currently in. This is a simpler way of adding the same outward transition to all states in your machine. **Entry** and **Exit** are states that determine the beginning and the end of the Animation State Machine.

There are other special states to handle sub-machines. For more information, check out the *More about Animation* section later on in the chapter.

The animator parameters

As we already introduced before, on the left-hand side of the **Animator** window, there are two tabs: **Layers**, which we won't deal with here (but I remind you that you can read the optional *Layers in the Animator* section), and **Parameters**, which we will learn in this section.

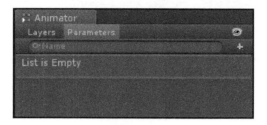

Animation **Parameters** are variables that are defined within an **Animator Controller**. These parameters can be accessed and their values assigned from scripts. As a result, scripts can control or affect the flow of the state machine. For example, a script can set a parameter that indicates how fast an animation should be played, such as running or walking; these can be the same animation, just played at different speed. In a more sophisticated behavior, the same parameter can be a condition to switch between a proper walking animation and a running one, based on the player's input.

To add a parameter, click on the small + button, as highlighted in this picture:

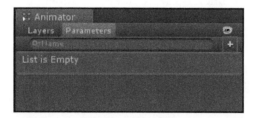

 However, if you want to delete a parameter, select the parameter in the lists and press the *Delete* key.

A drop-down menu appears, asking which kind of parameter we want to add:

They can be of four basic types:

- `Int`: An integer (whole number)
- `Float`: A number with a decimal part
- `Bool`: A true or false value (represented by a checkbox)
- `Trigger`: A Boolean parameter that is reset by the controller when consumed by a transition (represented by a circle button)

Parameters can be assigned values from a script using functions in the `Animator` class, specifically with the following self-explanatory functions: `SetFloat()`, `SetInt()`, `SetBool()`, `SetTrigger()`, and `ResetTrigger()`.

As we have already seen, parameters can be linked to transition conditions or even to state variables (such as the speed multiplier), and then be controlled by scripts. To give an example, imagine the heroine of your game is riding a horse. A script can change a float parameter, which is linked to the speed multiplier of the galloping horse animation, based on how much the player spurs the horse. As a result, the animation of the horse will change in real time, based on the player input (if the player is controlling your heroine), and the horse will move faster.

However, for our Tower Defense game, we just need triggers, in particular, three: one for when the panda is hit, another one when it reaches the end and eats the cake, and the last one when it dies under sprinkles hit. We can respectively name them `HitTrigger`, `EatTrigger`, and `DieTrigger`. At the end, you should see the following:

Of course, this is not the only way to implement this system. Refer to the *State machine behaviours* section later to learn how to use behaviours within a state so that in the *Homework* section you can test yourself with this new technique in order to implement this kind of behaviours in a different way.

The animator transitions

Transitions allow us to change from one state of the Finite State Machine into another one. They can be triggered when certain conditions are met. As the name suggests, they handle how the current state transits into the destination state and how these two should be merged to have a smooth transition.

They are represented as mono-directional arrows between two states. To create a new transition between two state, right-click from the state where the transition should start (in our case, Panda_Walk_Animation) and select **Make Transition**, as shown in this screenshot:

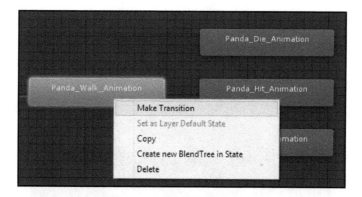

Then click on another state to make the transition between them. In this example, we are doing a transition from `Panda_Walk_Animation` to `Panda_Hit_Animation`, as shown here:

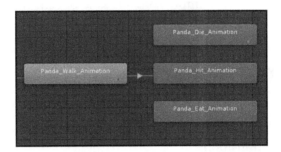

Transition settings

If you click on the arrow, you can see the transition settings/properties in the **Inspector**, like the following screenshot:

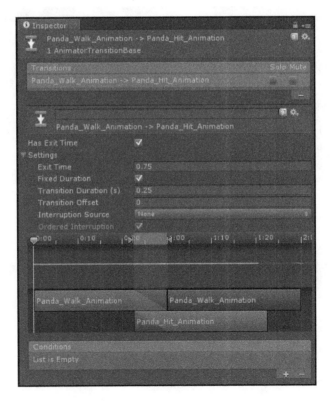

If you wish, you can assign a name to the transition, by typing it in the field shown next (you need to press *Enter* to confirm your choice):

As a result, its name will be shown in the state that contains that transition (for instance, in our example, within the `Panda_Walk_Animation` state):

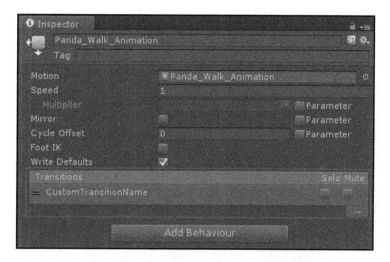

Renaming transition is your choice. Someone prefers to give proper names, someone else references to it as initial and final state, which is the default name. However, if you decide to rename them, remember to give meaningful names; it doesn't matter if they are long.

Let's cover in detail each of these settings so as to have a better understanding of what they mean. Keep in mind that some of them refer to certain conditions, which we will explore soon.

- **Has Exit Time**: If this is set to true, the transition can only happen at the time specified in the **Exit Time** variable.

- **Exit Time**: If **Has Exit Time** is enabled, this value represents the exact time for the transition to take effect. This is represented in normalized time (percentage value); so, for example, an exit time of 0.65 means that on the first frame where 65% of the animation has played, the **Exit Time** condition will be true. On the next frame, the condition will be false. For looped animations, transitions with exit times smaller than 1 will be evaluated on every loop, so you can use this to time your transition with the proper timing in the animation, for every loop. Transitions with exit times greater than 1 will be evaluated only once, so they can be used to exit at a specific time-after a fixed number of loops. For example, a transition with an exit time of 4.5 will be evaluated once, after four and a half loops.

- **Fixed Duration**: If enabled, the transition time is interpreted in seconds; otherwise, it is interpreted in a percentage between 0 and 1 (normalized time), such as 0.5, which would represent 50%.

- **Transition Duration**: This is the duration of the transition. This will also determine the length between the two blue markers in the Transition Graph (see the next section).

- **Transition Offset**: This is the offset of the time where the animation (in the destination state that is transitioned to) begins to play. For example, a value of 0.4 would mean the target state will begin playing at 40% of the way through its own timeline.

- **Interrupt Source**: This allows you to control the circumstances that allow a transition to interrupt the current one. In particular, you can select five different modes:
    - **None** won't allow anything to interrupt the transition.
    - **Current State** allows only transitions, within the current state, to interrupt the transition.
    - **Next State** allows the transition to be interrupted by other transitions, but only if those are within the destination state. Therefore, if the destination state has a transition that is ready to fire, it will interrupt this one and will be triggered.
    - **Current State then Next State** allows the transition to be interrupted by transitions from either the current or the destination state. However, if the conditions of a transition becomes true on both the current state and the destination one, then the former will take the priority. For example, if two transitions are ready to fire but one is on the current state and another one on the destination one, the first transition will be triggered and will interrupt the current playing transition.

- **Next State then Current State** still allows the transition to be interrupted by either transitions of the current or destination state. But in contrast to **Current State then Next State**, if the condition of a transition becomes true on both the current state and the destination one, then the latter will take priority.

- **Ordered Interruption**: This determines whether the current transition can be interrupted by other transitions independently of their order.

> Now that you can make transitions, remember to rearrange often your finite state machine so as to improve readability. You should always place the states in such a way that all the transitions are nicely visible, and ideally they shouldn't cross each other much.

Transition graph

Unity also provides a useful way to tweak these properties (listed just now) in a visual way, through the transition graph, which is located just below the settings of the previous section.

The transition settings can be adjusted either manually by entering numbers into the fields that we saw before, or by using the transition diagram, which will modify the values when the visual elements are manipulated.

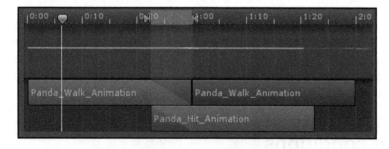

The Transition Graph with a clear timeline; we can tweak how the transition will happen in a visual way

In the preceding diagram, you can do one of the following things:

- Change the duration of the transition by dragging the *out* marker.
- Change the duration of the transition and the exit time by dragging the *in* marker.
- Adjust the transition offset by dragging the animation clips shown in the bottom part of the graph.

- Preview the transition by dragging the playback marker and navigate frame by frame to adjust how the animation clips blend together. The preview window is located at the bottom of the inspector.

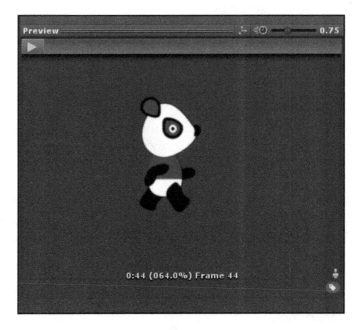

This is the preview window, where you can rotate, scale and play animations, as well as display their pivot point (or center of mass in the case of 3D models) and change the time scale to which you want to play the preview

 If the transition involves a blending tree as one of the two states (or both), the blend tree parameters will also appear in the transition graph. You can find a bit more about blending trees in the *More about Animations* section later in the chapter.

Transition conditions

So far we have seen many settings for our transitions, but when are they actually triggered? That's why, at the bottom of the settings, there are the transition conditions. You can see them here:

To add a condition, press the + button. To remove, select one of them and click on the –
button. Besides, you can reorder them by dragging their left handle. However, the order
doesn't affect the logic behind the transition (just the implementation of it, and maybe the
readability of your project).

These conditions can be checked against the parameters. For `int` and `float` parameters, we
can check them against a fixed number. So if the value in the parameter is **Greater** or **Less**
than the fixed number. For `int` parameters, we can also check whether they are **Equals** or
NotEqual compared to the fixed number. Bools, instead, can be checked to find out whether
they are true or false. Finally, triggers cannot be checked against something, but the
condition checks whether they fire.

Here is an example of conditions using all of the four kinds of parameters:

Please note that the transition is executed/performed only if all the conditions are verified in
that moment. A transition without conditions is triggered at the time specified in **Exit Time**.

 If **Has Exit Time** is not checked and the transition has no condition as
well, then the transition is ignored by Unity. So it is as if the transition
didn't exist.

Now that we have learned how to set a transition, we will explore some useful
functionalities to test them in the next section.

Testing transitions

There are two useful functionalities to know about if you need to test the transitions. The first one is **Solo** and second is **Mute**. If you select a transition, you can see them at the top of the **Inspector**:

However, I suggest you to set **Solo** and **Mute** in another way. In fact, if we select a state, we can find in the **Inspector** all the transitions from that state with the **Solo** and **Mute** functionalities. As a result, we will have a handy view, since we can look at and set all the transitions from that state in one go, shown as follows (all the transitions in this picture will be made in the next section):

When the **Mute** checkbox is selected, that specific transition will be ignored completely. Whereas, when the **Solo** checkbox is selected, all the other transitions will be considered muted. Furthermore, in the **Animator** window, it is possible to see **Mute** transitions in red, whereas **Solo** transitions are in green:

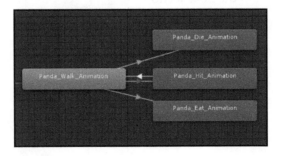

An example of Solo and Mute transitions

If you have the hard copy of this book (so without colors), the transition that goes from `Panda_Walk_Animation` to `Panda_Hit_Animation` is a **Mute** transition, so the arrow is red. Both the transitions from `Panda_Walk_Animation` to `Panda_Die_Animation` and `Panda_Eat_Animation` are **Solo** transitions, and the arrow is green. The remaining one is neither a **Mute** nor **Solo** transition, and therefore it is white. However, this is just an example; feel free to test in the best way that suits you.

Moreover, from the official documentation we can read a rule of thumb about **Solo** and **Mute** functionalities:

> *"The basic rule of thumb is that if one Solo is ticked, the rest of the transitions from that state will be muted. If both Solo and Mute are ticked, then Mute takes precedence."*

Finally, it's worthy to keep in mind that at the time I'm writing this sentence, there is a known issue (always from the official documentation):

> *"The controller graph currently doesn't always reflect the internal mute states of the engine."*

The panda's Animation State Machine

Now that we learnt a bit more about how to use Mecanim system, we will do what we started-have a complete controller for the animations of our pandas. This is how the controller should look once finished:

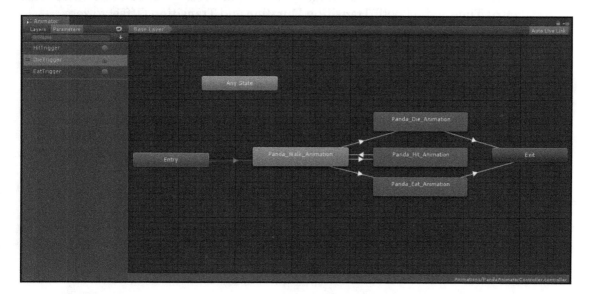

As you can see, there are four transitions, and we've got only one. But we still need to properly set all of them. Therefore, create and complete the transitions in the following way:

- `Panda_Walk_Animation` to `Panda_Hit_Animation`: When the panda is walking and a sprinkle hits it, the panda will play the Hit animation. Therefore, let's add `HitTrigger` as a condition and uncheck **Has Set Time** to trigger the transition at any moment during the walk loop. Furthermore, to make the transition instantaneous, let's set **Transition Duration** to zero to make it start playing the Hit animation from the first frame set **Transition Offset** to zero.

- `Panda_Hit_Animation` to `Panda_Walk_Animation`: After the panda has been hit, he will then keep walking again towards the player's cake. As a result, we need to recover the panda from the `Panda_Hit_Animation` state as soon as the animation finishes. So, let's set **Has Exit Time** to true and **Transition Duration** and **Transition Offset** to zero, since we want the transition to be instantaneous.

- `Panda_Walk_Animation` to `Panda_Eat_Animation`: When the panda finally arrives to the player's cake, the panda will eat so much of it that he will explode! Therefore, the transition needs to be triggered with `EatTrigger`, so add it to the conditions and uncheck **Has Exit Time**. Moreover, as all the transitions of the panda should be immediate, set both **Transition Duration** and **Transition Offset** to zero.

- `Panda_Walk_Animation` to `Panda_Die_Animation`: Being under fire by sprinkles is tough for our panda. If it cannot hold anymore, it will die, leaving the player's cake untouched. This is a transition triggered by `DieTrigger`, which we need to add to the conditions. Again, for the same reasons as before, uncheck **Has Exit Time** and set both **Transition Duration** and **Transition Offset** to zero.

- `Panda_Die_Animation` to `Exit`: Once the panda is dead, we want to get rid of it. Going in the `Exit` state, actually (since we don't have any sub-machines), will make the controller start again from the enter state/node. However, we will see how to destroy the panda before this happens. It doesn't matter if this animation goes in any other state, but choosing exit makes more sense, and so it helps in the readability of your controller. Once more, we want the transition to be instantaneous, so we set both **Transition Duration** and **Transition Offset** to zero; but we want to trigger this transition as soon as the animation finishes, which means having **Has Exit Time** set to true.

- `Panda_Eat_Animation` to `Exit`: The same reasons we said for the previous transition hold for this too. The panda will eat so much cake that it will explode, and again the panda will be removed from the scene. Check **Has Exit Time** and set **Transition Duration** and **Transition Offset** to zero.

Testing the panda's Animation State Machine

Before we move on to the next section, we should check whether what we have done so far works. However, the whole system will be completed only when we finish the game. Therefore, we need to find a smart and fast way to test the controller.

The easiest way is to create a new scene and drag and drop the panda Prefab into it. Then, build an UI interface with three buttons. Change their text so that you will have `Trigger Die Animation`, `Trigger Hit Animation`, and `Trigger Eat Animation`, as shown in this screenshot:

As we learnt in the previous chapter, the buttons have the **On Click ()** event, which allows us to call some functions when the button is pressed. However, we didn't have chance to use this functionality. In fact, we will work more on UI events in the next chapter.

For now, you can select all the three buttons, and click on the small + button in the bottom-right corner of the **On Click ()** event. We can see this in the following image:

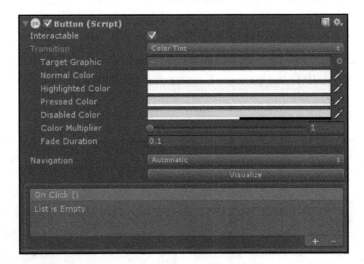

A new event appears, as shown here:

Drag the panda from the **Hierarchy** panel, into the object variable, so that you will have the following:

From the drop-down menu, navigate to **Animator | Set Trigger (string)**. In this way, we can set the triggers of our Animator. So at the end, you should have this:

Now, select each button separately, and assign to each one of them the respective trigger. For instance, in the **Trigger Die Animation** button, you should write `DieTrigger`, as shown in this picture:

Using the `Set Trigger (string)` function is not the best option, since it involves the use of strings. But for testing purposes, it's more than fine. In the next section, when we build a script that controls the Animator, we will see how to use hashes to refer to Animator parameters as numbers, and improve efficiency.

As a result, each one of those buttons now acts as a trigger for our panda. Therefore, we can press **Play**, and finally see our panda walking. Then, by clicking on the buttons, we can trigger the transitions in the Animator and see the panda changing state/animation. As a result, we can test if the transitions work well or not. Feel free to tweak any parameters you want, such as the speed of an animation or the transition graph of one of the transitions to suit your needs.

Do you remember the **Auto live link** toggle when we talked about the **Animator** window? Once you are in **Play** mode, that is the right moment to activate it. As a result, you will be able to have a visual representation on your **Animator** window of the state of your machine.

For instance, in the following screenshot, the walk loop is performed and it also shows a bar with the progress of the animation. This can help you a lot to tweak the Animator controller.

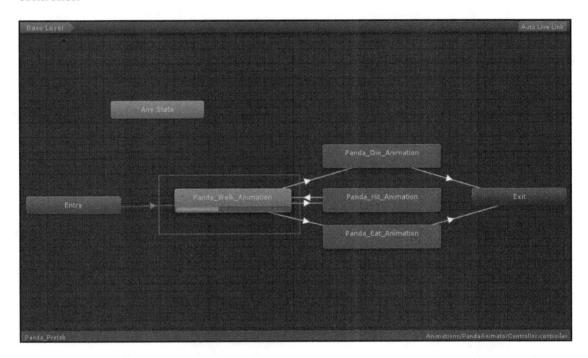

Now, once you are happy with your changes and you have applied them, save the scene if you want, but come back to our main scene. Then, we are ready to create a script, or two, for our pandas.

Scripting Animations

Finally, we've got all the animations for our pandas and a controller that changes them based on some triggers. However, so far nothing will ever set a trigger of the Animator (except our UI test buttons in the other scene). Therefore, we need to create the script for the panda, which will not only include the behaviour of the panda, but it will also trigger the right animations. In the next section, we will learn how to tweak the parameters of an Animator within a script. But before we get there, let me to introduce you a very powerful tool: State Machine Behaviours!

State machine behaviours

Each state of the animation machines can contain one or more behaviours. These are scripts that extend the `StateMachineBehaviour` class, which include the following functions/events, with self-explanatory names regarding when they are called/triggered: `OnStateEnter()`, `OnStateExit()`, `OnStateIK()`, `OnStateMove()`, and `OnStateUpdate()`.

In particular, you need to override these functions from the mother class, and they take as input three parameters. The first is the Animator itself, the second is an `AnimatorStateInfo` that stores information about the current state, and finally we have an integer that represents the layer. In our case, since we won't use any other layer than the base one, it will be always zero. They have the following signature (take `OnStateEnter()` for example):

```
override public void OnStateEnter(Animator Animator, AnimatorStateInfo
stateInfo, int layerIndex)
```

As a result, we can control everything within a state. In fact, State Machine Behaviours are a very powerful tool. Once you have created a script that extends the `StateMachineBehaviour` class, select the state where you want to add it. Then, click on the **Add Behaviour** button at the bottom of the **Inspector**, like this:

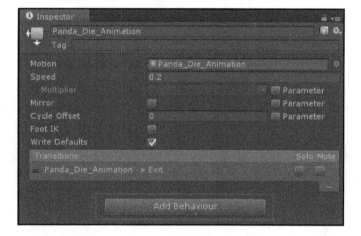

If your class contains variables, they are shown in the **Inspector** as for any other script, and they can be configured for that specific state. Here is a State Machine Behaviour that contains some variables and how they are displayed:

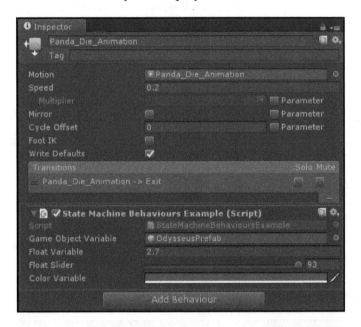

 Be careful when using static variables, because they are shared among all the instances of the State Machine Behaviour among all the controllers! In fact, it's good practice to not use static variables in this context.

Now, imagine that the hero of your game that has the ability to carry and hold different weapons. In this case, with a machine behaviour, you can check which weapon the character is holding, and if it matches with the legendary fire sword, add a fire particle effect when our hero slashes an enemy. Another example could be where some characters share the same animation machine, since they are really similar, but some of them can glide after a jump. As such, you'd want to check this and, in some way, modify some parameters of your animation machines.

To put simply, the only limit is your imagination (and computational power), and you can enhance your animation machine. Of course, all that you can achieve with State Machine Behaviour can be done in other ways, but they offer a simple and quite intuitive way to do it. It doesn't take much to get used and learn how to deal with this tool.

Now that we know what a State Machine Behaviours is, let's make one for our panda!

The destroy behaviour

When our panda is killed either by a terrible rain of sprinkles or by eating too much cake, in some way we need to make the panda disappear from the scene. However, we need to do it, after that the death animation is played, and eventually also after we have updated the gameplay (which we will see later in the book).

That's why we have created two extra transitions from the **Die** and **Eat** animations into the **Exit** state. These transitions will be executed once the respective animation has finished playing. Moreover, these animations are triggered by us in a separate script (see the next section), so before the panda dies, we have a chance to update the gameplay, such as the amount of sugar or health of the player.

A State Machine Behaviour allows us to have this level of control, that is to destroy the panda when it finishes to play that particular animation. Therefore, we can create a new script and call it something meaningful, such as `StateMachineBehaviour_DestroyOnExit`. Now, double-click on the script to open it.

First of all, we need to extend `StateMachineBehaviour` and not `MonoBehaviour`. We can just replace the latter with the former. Since the script doesn't extend `MonoBehaviour` anymore, we can also remove the `Start()` and `Update()` functions. At the end, we should come up with the following:

```
using System.Collections;
using System.Collections.Generic;
using UnityEngine;

public class StateMachineBehaviour_DestroyOnExit : StateMachineBehaviour {

}
```

Next, we need to override one of the aforementioned functions of a State Machine Behaviour. In particular we want to override the `OnExit()` function. So every time the state changes to another (which in the case of the **Die** and **Eat** states means immediately after their animations are played), the panda will be destroyed. We can do this easily, since one of the parameters of the function is the Animator itself, and from it, we can retrieve the gameObject to which the Animator is attached and destroy it. Therefore, we can just add this function:

```
override public void OnStateExit(Animator Animator, AnimatorStateInfo
stateInfo, int layerIndex) {
    //Destroy the gameobject where the Animator is attached to
    Destroy(Animator.gameObject);
}
```

Save the script, and select the **Die** and **Eat** states. From there, click on **Add Behaviour** and select `StateMachineBehaviour_DestroyOnExit`.

Once you have done all of this, we are done! Now, every time the **Die** or **Eat** animations are played, on their completion, the panda will be destroyed. The next step is to see how to actually trigger the states within the controller.

The panda script

We need to create a new script, and this time let it be derived from `MonoBehaviour`. We can call it `PandaScript`. Then, we can start to create some variables inside it. Let's start with a public variable to keep track of the panda's life and another one for its speed:

```
//Public variables that express the characteristic of the Panda
public float speed;      //The movement speed
public float health;     //The amount of health
```

Then, we need a variable to store the reference to the Animator. So, we can use this variable when we need to trigger an animation in the Animator:

```
//Private variable to store the Animator for handling animations
private Animator Animator;
```

As we learned in the *Animator Parameter* section, there are different methods to set parameters within the Animator. However, there are two versions of them: one refers to the parameter with an ID or Hash, the other one as a string. The latter is for sure the most intuitive, but since it relies on string processing, it's a bit slower than the first one. As such, whenever this is possible, it's better to use a hash (see the information box) to refer to a specific parameter within the Animator. Therefore, we can store these hashes inside some variable, so to fast use them.

 In computer science when we need to map data of an arbitrary size onto data of a fixed size, we use a `Hash` function. The result of this function is called *hash values, hash codes, digests,* or simply *hashes*. The main uses of these `Hash` functions are in cryptography and digital security. Whenever you digitally sign a document, behind the scenes there is a `Hash` function somewhere too. However, they are also used in other contexts, such as to optimize, as in the case of Unity.

In our very specific case, we have a set of parameters, which need an integer ID so that they can be referred to quickly in the Animator. A `Hash` function is applied from the name of the parameter, which is a string, and so potentially with infinite combinations, since a string can be long arbitrary, onto a finite set of the Integers which may be expressed with a single `int` variable (so only up to two billion, one hundred and forty-seven million, four hundred and eighty-three thousand, six hundred and forty-seven). So every time in your video game use an `int` variable for storing money or lives, like we did in the last chapter, 2,147,483,647 is the maximum amount. Usually for video games, this limit is more than fine for any integer parameters you may want, although it is possible to overcome it if needed with special data structures. As a result, from the name of the parameter of the Animator, we can have a number with which we can refer to the parameter.

These hashes are Animator independent, since they are based only on the name of the parameter itself. So they can be calculated or retrieved from the static function `Animator.StringToHash()`, which takes as input the name of the parameter and returns as output it's numerical representation to use in an Animator.

In our specific case, we have the three triggers, and we can store their hashes in the following variables:

```
//Hash representations of the Triggers of the Animator controller of the
Panda
private int AnimDieTriggerHash = Animator.StringToHash("DieTrigger");
private int AnimHitTriggerHash = Animator.StringToHash("HitTrigger");
private int AnimEatTriggerHash = Animator.StringToHash("EatTrigger");
```

The next step is to get the reference to the Animator controller in the `Start()` function, so to be used in the other functions. We can achieve this by using the `GetComponent()` function, which returns the component specified as `Type` attached to the same gameObject of this script. Therefore, we can simply add this line in the `Start()` function:

```
void Start () {
    //Get the reference to the Animator
    Animator = GetComponent<Animator>();
}
```

Now, as for a modular workflow, we can create some private functions to implement the logic behind controlling the state machine. However, we will deal with them when we need to call them later on.

So now, we need a function that allows our panda to move towards a point in the map. This function takes a `Vector3` as input parameter, which is the destination point on the map. Based on the speed variable, it creates a step for our panda. Then, using the `MoveTowards()` function, it moves the panda of one step towards the destination point:

```
//Function that based on the speed of the Panda makes it moving towards
the destination point, specified as Vector3
private void MoveTowards(Vector3 destination) {
    //Create a step and then move in towards destination of one step
    float step = speed * Time.deltaTime;
    transform.position = Vector3.MoveTowards(transform.position,
destination, step);
}
```

Another function will be called when the panda is hit by a sprinkle from one of the player's cupcake towers. It has as input a float, which is the amount of damage the panda has taken from the hit. So, the function subtracts this value to the health of the panda, and then checks if the health is less than zero. If so, the function triggers the Die Animation by set the `DieTrigger` parameter. We don't need to then destroy the panda because once death is triggered, the state machine behaviour will take care of it. On the other hand, if the panda is not dead yet, the function, instead, plays the Hit Animation:

```
//Function that takes as input the damage that Panda received when hit
by a sprinkle.
//After have detracted the damage to the amount of health of the Panda
checks if the Panda
//is still alive, and so play the Hit animation, or if the health goes
below zero the Die animation
private void Hit(float damage) {
    //Subtract the damage to the health of the Panda
    health -= damage;
    //Then it triggers the Die or the Hit animations based if the
Panda is still alive
  if(health <= 0) {
        Animator.SetTrigger(AnimDieTriggerHash);
    }
    else {
        Animator.SetTrigger(AnimHitTriggerHash);
    }
}
```

One last function we need to add is for when the panda reaches the end of its path and it's standing in front of the player's cake. Here the function just triggers the `Eat animation`. How to damage the player is something that we will deal in the next chapter:

```
//function that triggers the Eat animation
private void Eat() {
    Animator.SetTrigger(AnimEatTriggerHash);
}
```

We can save the script for now. It should appear like this in the Inspector:

No need to worry now about how to set the speed and the health! We will see this when we will talk about gameplay programming.

Unless you want to read the next optional section, which will guide you through more advanced topics, we can say that we have finished with animation. If you don't want to read the next section, or want to come back to it later, maybe once you've finished the whole book, you can skip directly to the homework and summary sections. Otherwise, take a break and continue with the next section.

More about Animations

We have seen a lot about the Animation workflow in Unity, yet a lot has been left out. This section presents some relatively advanced topics of the Animation workflow in Unity, and they are not needed to develop our Tower Defense Game. In fact, some of these applies only on 3D, but I feel that it's worthwhile to mention them to have a rough, but complete picture of the whole workflow for Animations in Unity. Therefore, feel free to skip this section, or read without focus to understand completely what's written. You can always come back here later, maybe when you've finished the book, for a deeper look to its content.

All the following sections are not intended to explain in detail how to use these tools in Unity, but rather to be aware of their existence and functionalities so as to learn them later on when you are a bit more practical with Unity.

Avatars

In the case of 3D characters, and especially for humanoids, you need to *rig* your character, which means to match all bones of the 3D model into a Unity Avatar. If the model is well done and optimized for Unity, this process can be automatized; otherwise it needs to be done by hand, as shown in this picture:

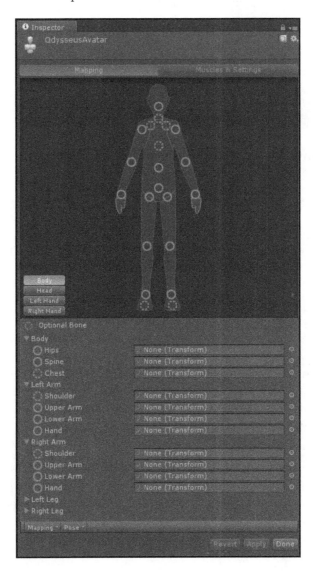

In the scene view, there is your 3D model, from which you can drag and drop the parts of his/her/its body in the avatar.

In this way, Unity stores additional information about the 3D model. It stores not only the matching bones, but also muscles. The main reason is that by doing it in this way it is possible to perform retargeting, which means using the same animations for different character. Suppose you have a beautiful walking animation, and you want to apply it to all your characters. But some of them are tall. Others are fat or full of muscles. The Avatar stores this additional information to overcome the problem and adapt the walking animation to each character.

Furthermore, Unity also allows masking, which means to discard part of the Animation clip data and uses specific parts only. For instance, imagine you have a beautiful walking animation and an animation of someone drinking a glass of water. Suppose you want to make your character to drink a glass of water while he or she keeps walking. By masking the drinking animation, we are able to crop it just onto the upper body part. As a result, we can leave the walking animation playing on the legs, while the drinking one is playing on the upper body of the character.

If you imagine a complex game, where the characters can do many things while walking (such as shoot, reload or talk) this functionality is really helpful. Keep in mind that masking can be done to different levels. For instance, you can merge more than two animations together with respect to different body parts, as well as sub-masking. The possibilities are endless!

That's why Unity offers also a more detailed mapping when required, for instance, for the head or the hands, as the next picture shows, where we can see the mapping for the left hand:

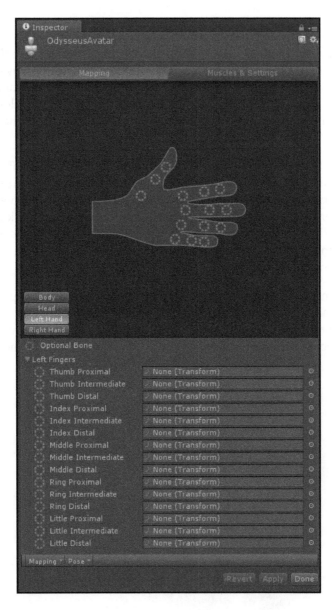

All of this is really powerful when used in combination with sub-state machines, state-behaviors and Layers in the Animator.

Sub-state machines

Previously, we have seen that the Animator is a finite state machine with different states, each one of them as an animation clip. But in actual fact, not all of the states are animation clips. Some of them can be something else, such as sub-state machines. This means, that a state can contain another whole finite state machine!

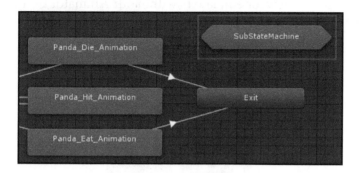

A sub-state machine appears into the upper level like a state, though with a slightly different shape. In fact, transitions can both start or end on a sub-state machine like any other state.

 You can recognize a sub-state machine since the shape around the name is slightly different.

In this scenario, the exit state/node becomes important, because it allows us to finish/exit from the sub-state machine and continue in the next state. Of course, also a sub-machine can be interrupted if set to do so when some conditions are met. Needless to say, being able to nest animation machines is indeed a very powerful tool to build very complex Animators.

The hierarchical location menu

As we have seen, states can contain sub-states and trees and these structures can be nested repeatedly. When drilling down into sub-states, the hierarchy of parent states and the current state can be viewed on the top bar (highlighted in the following picture):

Clicking on the parent states allows you to jump back up to parent states or go straight back to the base layer of the state machine.

Layers in the Animator

Now, if we want to create, view, or edit layers within our Animator Controller, we need to make sure that the left-hand pane is set to Layers view, like this image:

This allows you to have multiple layers of animation within a single animation controller. All these layers are then able to run at the same time, where each layer is controlled by a separate state machine. This process is commonly used when, for instance, you have a separate layer playing upper-body animations over a base layer that controls the general movement animations for a character (to use in combination with Avatar Masks).

To begin, click on the plus icon to add a layer. On the other hand, to delete a layer, select the layer and press the *Delete* key.

Blending trees

Besides Animation clips and sub-state machines, a state in the Animator can be also a blending tree. A common process to apply between different frames of an animation is to blend two or more similar motions, so that it feels like one fluid animation. For example, walking and running animations may require that key frames are blended between one another according to the character's speed. Ideally, you want the player to be slower if they are walking and faster if they are running. In some cases, the speed of how fast a player runs can also be increased again with game elements such as items (speed boosts). Another typical example is to lean the character left or right while they are turning to achieve a more realist behaviors. This can be obtained with blend trees, which are able to *blend* animation clips.

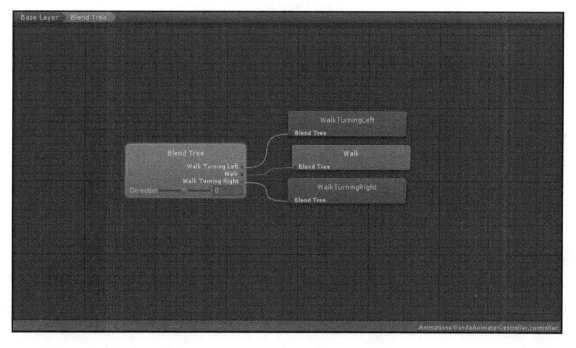

An example of a very common blending tree; Here the walking animation is split in three animation clips, so the character can lean to the left or right as he/she turns during the walk

In fact, they use linear interpolation, which can be controlled by some weights and parameters. Unity supports both 1D and 2D interpolation for blending trees.

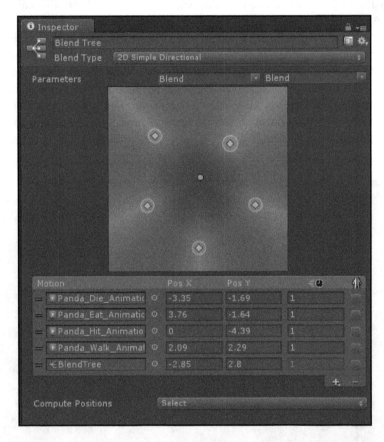

2D interpolation of Blending trees. Numbers and animation clips are placed at random, the aim of the figure it's showing the 2D interpolation in the upper part, where the diamond shapes are the different animation clips and the circle shape is the 2D value that controls the blending among the clips.

We won't go further into blending trees, but keep in mind that they can be used to blend more animations together in real time to achieve incredibly real behaviors and smoother animations.

Animator Override Controller

Imagine that you have just created a beautiful Animation State Machine, full of layers and transitions, since it is super detailed. Your character has states that allows her to cast a spell, to grab a coffee or to swing a sword. However, now, you need to consider that also a Goblin can do that. And even the Ogre of your second level as well as the elf that your protagonist has to fight later on in your game. Should you create again a very similar Animation Machine for each one of them, but just changing the Animation clips? And what if later on you decide to slightly change the controller, do you have to slightly change all of them? Thank God, Unity offers an easier way, called the **Animator Override Controller**.

You can create an **Animator Override Controller** by right-clicking on the project panel and navigate to **Create | Animator Override Controller**. It will be an asset as the others Animator controllers. However, you cannot open it in the **Animator** window. If you select it in the **Inspector**, you will see that you can link a normal Animator controller to it, as shown in this screenshot:

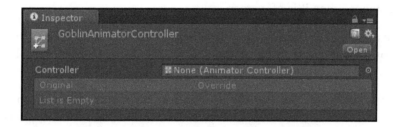

Just for the sake of learning, we drag and drop the only controller that we have in our project, the panda controller. As a result, all the Animator states we used will appear in a list, and we can assign a different animation clip from the original controller.

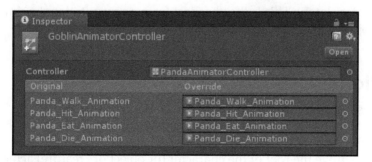

In this way, you don't need to replicate the Animator controller but just assign new animation clips. Once the Animator controller changes, all the **Animator Override Controllers** will change accordingly, updating all the characters in your game that use that controller. Not bad, isn't it?

Culling Mode in the Animator component

For a moment now, picture a beautiful animation of a shiny coin. It is so beautiful that you decide to include many coins in your game. As a result, it might be computationally heavy to make rotate thousands of coins if then the player can see just three on his or her screen.

Consider, instead, this other case. The player just turned a switch that triggers a really heavy and slow door. So, while the door is opening, the player explores a bit the environment. When he or she comes back, the player would expect that the animation of the door is complete and so the door is open. This means that the animation of the door should run also when it is not visible, whereas the coin is not needed to be animated in any moment, for instance when it is off screen.

To optimize this issue, Unity offers an option in the Animator component, the **Culling Mode**. This allows us to specify when the object should animate. The possible values are the following:

- **Always Animate**: The most expensive, although realistic, solution. As the name suggests, the object is always animated, so in the case of the door also, when it is off screen, it will keep opening.
- **Cull Update Transforms**: This is a mid-solution; it disables only some parts, such as Retargeting and IK, to improve performance, but still has a certain degree of realism when needed, without paying too much in computational cost.
- **Cull Completely**: This is the cheapest from a computational point of view, since the object stops being animated completely when it is off screen.

Root motion

Some animations, in theory, should displace the character, such as walking but not drinking a glass of water. So in order to fix this issue in Unity, you can either move the character with a script, as we did in our case, or use root motion. As the name suggests, this allows the animation itself to move the root of the character (or object or creature) achieving a more realistic motion in space.

However, it is not straightforward and has some drawbacks. For instance, it is more expensive from a computational point of view, and as such, many characters with root motions on low-end devices could be prohibitive. Furthermore, it requires different tweaks, especially if the animation is not really well done.

Inverse Kinematic

Inverse Kinematic is something relatively new in video games. It allows you to have a target into the animation, and sometimes compute in real time an animation that suits the target. For instance, imagine a character who just wants to rest his or her hands on the wall. The Inverse Kinematic should allow you to control the animation to place the hand on the wall, regardless of whether the wall is 1 centimeter further or closer.

Usually animations use what is called Direct Kinematic (or Forward Kinematic). Based on the position and rotation of the joints, it is possible to determine the position of each part of the skeleton. So imagine having an arm, and based on the positions and rotations of your shoulder, elbow, and wrist, you can determine the position and rotation of your hand. In fact, these techniques come from robotic research.

The inverse problem, known as Inverse Kinematic, is to determine the positions and rotations of your shoulder, elbow, and wrist starting from the position and rotation of your hand. However, this problem is not uniquely determined, since it might have infinite solutions. Therefore, solving this problem wasn't straightforward. In any case, different techniques (which in the case of robotics may involve inverting the Jacobian matrix) were developed to solve this problem.

The problem with having different solutions is that some of them may lead to very unusual poses. Following again the example of the arm, a solution that, in order to rest the hand to the wall, brings the elbow up to the eye is not really believable (see the next image, on the left). Whereas this might be a relative problem if applied to robotics, in animation this is indeed a big problem, because we want our characters to be believable.

So, other techniques have been developed to solve the problem, and the study of social behaviors (for humanoid characters) have been conducted to understand why some poses are more realistic than others. For instance, the pose in the preceding picture is tiring; nobody will ever rest his hand on the wall in such way. In fact, this also deals with physics, since our brain tries to control our body in such a way to spend as less energy as possible. This results in an unconscious behavior that we recognize in other people, and our videogame characters need it as well.

Unity implements some of these techniques, and Mecanim supports some kind of Inverse Kinematic for humanoid characters, given that they have a correct configured avatar. However, we don't want to dig any deeper in this. I just leave the most curious reader with the link to the Official Documentation here:

`https://docs.unity3d.com/Manual/InverseKinematics.html`.

Another example where Inverse Kinematic is studied and used is for virtual presence in virtual reality. The recent Oculus Touch allows you to have your hands within the Rift Headset, but not your elbow and/or shoulder. While implementing inverse kinematic-even taking into account the believability and the less energy pose-the software is yet not able to precisely map your arm positions in space, because you will feel awkward. However, in multiplayer games, you can see other people in the virtual world but not in reality (or feel their bodies like they do), and therefore Inverse Kinematic can be applied. Although it won't give the exact position of the elbows of the other players in the game, it is close enough to be believable. A game that uses this mechanism is for instance Dead and Buried. As you can see from the next picture, you can see only your hands, but of the other players, you can see their whole bodies.

Animator component information box

As we already mentioned before, the Animator component has an information box at the bottom, which may contain some useful data. Here is a picture of the information box again, for your reference:

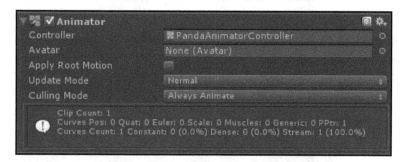

Besides the **Clip Count** that we already have seen, here is a briefly list of the other information:

- **Pos**, **Rot**, and **Scale**: These indicate the total number of curves used respectively for the position, rotation and scale. The animation window, the one we didn't see in detail, allows you to create such curves.
- **Muscles**: The number of muscles used in the Animator in case of Humanoid characters.
- **Generic**: The number of numeric curves used by the Animator to animate other properties.
- **PPtr**: The total count of sprite animation curves; it is useful when we work in 2D.
- **Curves Count**: The total combined number of animation curves.
- **Constant**: The number of animation curves that are optimized as constant values. Unity selects this automatically if your animation files contain curves with unchanging values.
- **Dense**: The number of animation curves that are optimized using the *dense* method of storing data (discrete values, which are interpolated between linearly). This method uses less significantly less memory than the *stream* method.
- **Stream**: The number of animation curves using the *stream* method of storing data (values with time and tangent data for curved interpolation). This data occupies significantly more memory than the *dense* method.

Legacy animation

A simpler animation system was used by Unity prior to the introduction of Mecanim (in year 2012, with Unity 4.0). Given that some time has passed since then, backward compatibility is still available. As a result, it is still possible to continue working on older projects without having to update Mecanim or worrying about other issues arising from the software.

Some people find the Legacy animation system useful for fast prototyping and/or testing animation clips, especially when the object has only one animation clip. This is because it was based on the Animation component (picture given next), and it should not be confused with the Animator component that we have seen before in the chapter.

You can find out more about the Legacy animation system here in the official documentation: `https://docs.unity3d.com/Manual/Animations.html`.

So, unless you have a specific need for it, you can completely ignore the Legacy Animation system, but it was worthwhile to mention it so that you don't get confused in case you found the Animation component and didn't know what it was.

In saying that, and while the legacy animation is still available, it is not recommended that you use it for new projects with Unity.

Get animated!!

One practical example to do that takes you outside of Unity is to think about the movement involved in animation. For example, when you are walking, typing, drinking, eating, any kind of movement, do it in slow motion. What you begin to notice is how subtle movements can make animations distinct and give it character. For each animation, such as drinking a glass of water for instance, do it in a different way. Pick up the cup, perhaps with a different grip such as using your whole hand or a few fingers around the handle. As you begin to become more conscious about movement, you should be able to gain some insight into how you might need to adjust an animation in Unity when something doesn't quite feel right. To get a better idea again, search for videos, even books to explore the uses of animation and › some of their underpinnings. While this book is in no way a how to on animation, understanding the fundamentals not only help you to improve your own understanding about animations, but also help you to better understand the role of an animator and what it entails. This kind of information will be valuable to you later if you ever work or need to work with an animator.

Homework

In this chapter, we faced many aspects of Animation clips and Animator controllers. However, before we go to the next chapter, I invite you to give a look to these exercises to improve your skills:

1. **Becoming an animation designer**: Think of five games that you play, and select a part of each game such as the tutorial level, fighting a boss, walking through a forest, or even the main menu. Now, write down a list of animations that each of them have. Next, remove some animations, or even add some and think how it would alter the experience. Does it improve it, or does it change the atmosphere entirely? Could you make a relatively happy atmosphere really dark by changing some of the animations, and vice versa? By doing this, you will begin to understand the importance that animations play on not only providing life to your game, but also emotion and setting the atmosphere.

2. **Drawing an animation (Part I)**: Imagine that you need to create an animation; you can do this simply in a graphics program. Begin by blocking out the arm; you can use a square for the hand, a rectangle for the forearm, and a longer rectangle for the upper arm. Now, move each one so that it performs a swing animation. It would be ideal to set it up like the Sprite Sheets that we have used so far. Then, import them inside Unity and test it out.

3. **Drawing an animation (Part II)**: Now, add details to your animation, or other body parts such as legs. Moreover, feel free to add some special effects, like the Hit animation of the panda. Once you have you animation ready, try to create a second and a third one. Then, import them all, set them up, and build an Animator controller to see how they are animated. Furthermore, you can polish your animations in order to improve the transitions between them.

4. **A less dauntless Panda (Part I)**: As we have scripted, when the panda is hit, it keeps moving forward. However, the panda should be a little stunned. Only when the animation finishes, the panda should continue its advance towards the player's cake. Fix this problem with any technique you come up, so you can modify the **Panda Script** or create Machine State Behaviours.

5. **A less dauntless Panda (Part II)**: If you have done the previous exercise and found a solution to the fix, it's time to make your code a bit more robust. Add a Boolean value in the **Panda Script** and stop the panda from moving when it is hit, but only if the Boolean is set to true. In this way, we can expose this variable in the **Inspector** and give more possibilities of which kind of panda the player has to face (continued in the next chapter).

6. **State Machine Behaviour as a listener**: We have implemented the **Panda Script** in such a way that triggers are set in the Animator controller to change animations. Now, remove both the Hit and Die triggers from the **Panda Script** and implement other Machine State Behaviours that retrieve the value of panda's health and respectively trigger the Hit animation when health is decreased from the last time or the Die animation if it is below zero.

7. **Explore the Animation window**: Even if we didn't deal with the animation window, you can try to explore it, maybe by following the link to the official documentation provided. Then, try to make some animations for our sprinkles so that they can rotate while they are flying towards an evil Panda. Maybe you can also create a collision animation. Wrap these animations within an Animator controller and modify the Projectile script if needed.

Summary

Thus, we created four different animation clips for our panda, one for each of its possible actions: Walk, Die, Hit, and Eat. Then, we wrapped them within a controller and built a finite state machine to define how these animation clips are linked, through transitions. Finally, we wrote a script to trigger the different states of the machine.

Now that we have seen how to animate our Pandas, it's time to move on to the next chapter, maybe after a coffee break.

5

The Secret Ingredient Is a Dash of Physics

"Sprinkles may seem soft, but they are an excellent sharp weapon against sweet-tooth pandas, who are trying to steal your delicious cake!"

This chapter explains how Unity deals with 2D physics and provides descriptions for each of the components, along with useful examples of usages. Although we will use just a small portion of the Physics engine of Unity for our game, in this chapter you can find some foundations of physics to better face the topics covered, and a full insight of 2D physics in Unity.

In the first part of the chapter, we will acquire some basic notions about physics so as to better face the topics to come. We will learn about mass, forces, and torques, just enough to understand physics in Unity.

Then, most of the chapter will focus on explaining, bit by bit, the 2D Physics engine of Unity along with all its components and functionalities. Many examples will be provided in order to facilitate the learning.

Finally, in the last part of the chapter, we will use some of the notions learnt and apply them into our game. In fact, we will transform simple sprinkles into terrible weapons against the sweet-toothed pandas by enabling and handling collisions between the two.

Therefore, we are going to learn these topics:

- Basic notions of physics
- Understanding the Physics engine of Unity
- Physics settings, which are general properties for the whole project/game
- Rigidbody components with different body types and their usage

- Colliders and how to use them
- Joints to impose constraints on rigidbodies
- Effectors to change physics properties in particular region of the game world
- Physics materials to determine friction and bounciness on colliders
- Using the physics components in our game

Like all other chapters in this book, you will find the *Homework* section at the end. It has a range of different exercises for you to do to improve your skills and implement a range of different functionalities into your game.

Getting ready

This chapter does not need any particular prerequisite to learn about the Physics engine. However, at the end of this chapter we will continue our tower defense game from where we left it in Chapter 4, *No Longer Alone – Sweet-Toothed Pandas Strike*. Therefore, if you want to keep developing the *Tower Defense* game, you need to have done all the other steps in the previous chapters.

For those of you who are newcomers to physics, a great deal of patience is required, but once you master these concepts, a world of new possibilities for your own games will open. So don't give up!

Physics in video games

From bullets flying at different speeds and trajectories to gravity playing a role between keeping you grounded and allowing you to float, physics in video games plays an essential part in making experiences realistic and definitely enjoyable (for the most part). Imagine if every weapon fired a bullet in the same way, regardless of the firepower. Then what would be the point between having a sniper rifle or a revolver? This is only one aspect of the role that physics plays in games. Physics in games does not just revolve around trajectories and force; it can include gravity, time travel, and fluid dynamics.

Some great examples of games that use physics include *World of Goo, Portal 1* and *2, Mario Galaxy,* and *Kerbal Space Program.*

Image by Portal 2 – An orange liquid that reduces friction so much to give you a substantial boost

Of course, at the other end of the spectrum, games don't always replicate physics in the most accurate way but rather exaggerate it or dismiss it altogether to allow for innovative and unique gameplay. An example of this would include taking a *Leap of Faith* from great heights in *Assassin's Creed*, into conveniently placed stacks of hay (and even water). Some people have even studied how much hay that you would actually need in order to survive such jumps, which you can find here:
http://www.kotaku.com.au/2009/06/kotaku-bureau-of-weights-measures-studies-fall out-physics-also-beer/

When it comes to adding physics to your own game, you must ask yourself to what extent you want your gaming experience to be real. If you want your game to be 100% identical to reality, then you must also consider things like death. If a character can be shot by a bullet, do they bleed out or can they heal themselves? In some cases, your game may end up more of a simulation than a game itself if the interaction is too real. An example is **permadeath** (where the player must restart the game from the beginning after they have died), which you may or may not want in your game/simulation. All of these factors need to be considered when adding physics into games because both the cause and effect will all contribute to how believable the game is and ultimately how enjoyable it will be.

Physics – basics

In this section, we will learn some basic notions of physics, to better understand the Physics engine of Unity later on, and overall become better game developers.

First of all, what is physics? Aristotle (the same guy from the previous chapter) wrote a treatise entitled *ta physika*, which literally means the natural things. From this treatise (although many before Aristotle have written about natural phenomena), physics has become a science. Nowadays, physics investigates matter, its motion both in time and space, through mathematical models. Ultimately, the goal of physics is to describe how the whole universe works. Physics is divided into four big branches:

- **Classical mechanics**: This deals with the motion of objects
- **Thermodynamics**: This deals with the temperatures of bodies
- **Electromagnetism**: This deals with electromagnetic waves/particles
- **Quantum mechanics**: This deals with the study of subatomic particles

You don't need to see these as separate entities but just faces of the same coin, which is the model of the world that physics over the centuries has tried to unravel. Therefore, many topics cross them all, and so the division in not univocal. But, it's a good way for newcomers to physics to get an overview.

In this chapter, we will deal only with classical mechanics, and in particular with the motion of rigid bodies. However, other branches and sub-branches of physics are also really useful in game development. For instance, we can use light equations, which are implemented in shader, or fluid dynamics to simulate oceans and waves. Even when the evil wizard casts his most terrible fireball, we need to calculate many different physics equations to have a realistic behaviour and look. Imagine just simulating the fire around the ball.

Most of the time, you don't want to go into that much detail, if you already have a game engine like Unity (or Unreal). In fact, their programmers will take care of this for you. However, sometimes you may have special needs, and you need to write your own shader or code some physics-based behaviours. As such, knowledge of physics is greatly and immensely helpful.

Of course, this is not a course in physics nor a book dedicated to physics programming (for example, algorithms that can simulate more or less approximately and efficiently some physical behaviours). However, in this chapter, we will consolidate the really basic concepts of physics so that we can have a rough idea of how it all works together. As such, this and the upcoming sections will be dedicated to building a foundational understanding of physics so that we can better grasp the Physics engine behind Unity.

I know that some of you might find physics somewhat boring. This may be the case if it awakes some bad memory (or memories) from high school. But my personal opinion is that knowing physics is really important to be a good game developer, especially when you need to program realistic behaviours. With this said, I promise that in this section, I'll try to be as clear as possible and use an informal language instead of the strict mathematical one so that these concepts can be understood by anyone.

Classical mechanics of rigidbodies can be divided into two sub-branches:

- Kinematics: Which deals with the study of the motion.
- Dynamics: Which deals with the causes of the motion.

Of course, once again, they are faces of the same coin. In fact, dynamic equations need kinematic ones, so as to describe and predict the motion of rigidbodies. We will see them in a bit more detail soon, but first let's focus on some basic concepts.

World coordinates and local coordinates

As we have already seen in `Chapter 2`, *Baking Cupcake Towers,* there is a difference in using world coordinates and local coordinates. This is also an important concept in physics: which one is your reference frame (or coordinate system)? The question is key in determining also the values of the different physics quantities. Therefore, every time you have a physical quantity, you need to ask yourself in which reference frame are you working.

In any case, there isn't a frame that is privileged with respect to another (although some physical systems are easier to describe within a frame instead of another). So, by convention, a world frame is defined when we start the description of a physical system. For example, if you are driving your car, what is your velocity? Well, the answer depends on the coordinate system, or reference frame in which I'm describing the car moving. In the car itself, the speed of the car is zero, but rather the world is coming towards the car. Whereas for a pedestrian, the car is moving, and the world is not. An astronaut on the moon will see both the pedestrian moving really fast, along with the whole Earth, and also the car, at two different speeds. All of these descriptions are physically correct. Therefore, all quantities in physics depends on the reference frame.

In game engines such as Unity and/or Unreal, there is always a defined world frame (when you have the position with all zeros at the center of the world frame) as shown in the following diagram:

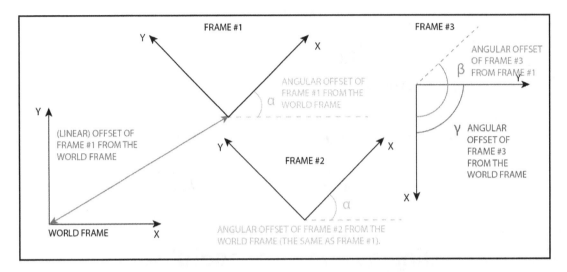

The preceding diagram shows how other frames are described in terms of linear and angular offset from the world frame. Moreover, you can describe a frame in terms of another, which is not the world frame (in the preceding diagram, look at the angular offset of frame #3). In Unity, you can consider the world frame as the global coordinates and the different frames as the local coordinates of game objects in the game. Children of game objects will be expressed in terms of the frame of the parent.

Velocity

Velocity in physics describes a relation between the space and the time of an object; in other words, how the object changes position with respect to a reference frame as a function of time. When the object is not accelerating, velocity is defined as distance covered in space divided by time.

 For those of you who are curious, when an object changes its velocity in each instant, and we need to get the velocity in a specific instant, it is possible to retrieve it by using derivatives (this is a topic of calculus, and I won't adventure deeper in this book).

Velocity is a vector, and therefore it has two coordinates in the 2D world (three in the 3D world), which express a direction and an intensity. The intensity of a velocity is also called **speed**. So it's important to not get confused between the two. In fact, speed is a scalar, just a number, acting independently if we are dealing with 2D or 3D games; velocity, instead, does change (from two numbers to three numbers to express respectively the 2D or 3D vector).

Whenever we use the term velocity, we mean the velocity in the defined world frame (or coordinate). When we use the term relative velocity, we are taking the velocity with respect to another frame. For instance, imagine that there are two cars that are heading against each other, both at 50 Km/h (in the world frame, because when you look at your tachymeter, by convention, that is the velocity with respect to the Earth). For one of the two drivers, the car he is driving is not moving (in fact, when you drive, your steering wheel is not going 50 Km/h away from your hands, but it is always at the same distance from you). However, he will see the other car with the other driver coming at 100 Km/h towards him.

Mass

In classical mechanics, every rigid body has a mass, which you can imagine as the amount of matter that forms that body. Thus, it is considered a property of the physical body. Often in spoken language, mass is confused with weight. In fact, mass is measured in kg (kilograms) in the International System of Units, whereas weight is measured in N (newton) in the International System of Units. Therefore, a scale is not measuring your weight, but rather your mass. Weight is a force and depends on the location where you are. Your weight is different on the moon, but your mass is the same.

Sometimes, mass is also defined as the measure of an object's resistance to acceleration (a change in its state of motion) when a force is applied. In fact, you need much more force to move a truck than your laptop.

However, it is worthwhile paying attention that, for instance, both the laptop and the truck (in absence of other external forces) are attracted by the gravity of the Earth and that both will fall down and touch the ground at the same time. In fact, when the universal gravitation equation of Newton is applied, the forces applied are different but the resulting gravitational acceleration is the same for both objects (since the mass is simplified from the equations).

For the more curious of you, this was discovered by the famous Italian astronomer, physicist, engineer, philosopher, and mathematician Galileo Galilei, much before Newton formalized gravitation. There is an anecdote in which Galileo had dropped balls of the same material but different masses from the Leaning Tower of Pisa to demonstrate that their time of descent was independent of their mass. In this way, he proved that Aristotle's idea that heavy objects fall faster than lighter ones, in direct proportion to weight (at that time intended as mass) was wrong as shown in the following diagram:

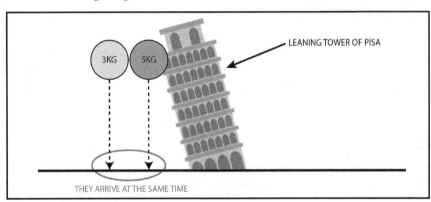

Centre of mass

Imagine you need to calculate or predict the trajectory of an arrow. Taking into consideration the whole shape of the arrow and knowing that different forces come into play at each point ends up in a really tricky calculation (although possible). Therefore, the center of mass is an approximation that works pretty well for rigid bodies. It consists of concentrating the whole mass of an object into a single point (which is an abstraction to imagine all of the mass of that body in that single point). Where this point is depends on the shape of the object (since it is weighted among all the points the object is composed of), and this carries enough information about the shape to do really precise calculations. Especially in real-time applications, this becomes critical, since calculations of motion are greatly simplified. In fact, Unity will only do calculations using the center of mass.

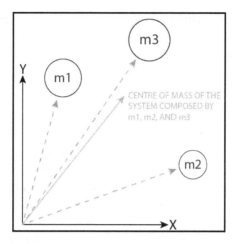

The center of mass is the weight average of all the points in the system, where the weights are the different masses. From the diagram, we can see that center of mass is closer to m1 and m3, since they are bigger (have more mass) than m2.

Kinematics

The term kinematics was used for the first time around 1840, as the translation of the French term *cinématique*, which was used by *André-Marie Ampère* (the famous French physicist and one of the founders of classical electromagnetism — so famous that the electric current unit in the International System of Units, the ampere, was named after him). However, the origin of the term derives from the Greek word *kinesis*, which means movement or motion.

To have a better understanding of what kinematics is in physics, let's refer to Wikipedia:

> *"Kinematics is the branch of classical mechanics which describes the motion of points (alternatively particles), bodies (objects), and systems of bodies without consideration of the masses of those objects nor the forces that may have caused the motion. Kinematics as a field of study is often referred to as the geometry of motion."*

Kinematics takes into consideration just the motion of an object and not the causes of the motion. This gives us some advantages when it comes to game development. First of all, it is cheaper from a computational point of view to take into consideration just the kinematics of an object. Then, we might not want to have a fully realistic object in our scene, and so we can just define its kinematic properties. We will see this in detail later when we will deal with kinematic bodies in Unity.

Of course, in our world, a pure kinematic body doesn't exist; all of them are dynamic. Yet, studying just the kinematics of an object gives us insights into its motion.

Dynamics

The term dynamic was used in the 19th century in the meaning of pertaining to the force producing motion, as opposite to static. Once again, it takes its origin from the French term *dynamique*, although it was introduced by the famous German mathematician and philosopher, Gottfried Wilhelm Leibnitz. However, the origin of this term is again from the Greek word *dynamikos*, which means powerful, and also from *dynamis* (power) and *dynasthai* (to be able to, to have power, and to be strong enough).

If not already explicitly suggested, every time we deal with something dynamic in physics, we are dealing with forces (which have a certain power to move objects). From Wikipedia we can read:

> *"Dynamics is a branch of applied mathematics (specifically classical mechanics) concerned with the study of forces and torques and their effect on motion, as opposed to kinematics, which studies the motion of objects without reference to its causes. Isaac Newton defined the fundamental physical laws which govern dynamics in physics, especially his second law of motion."*

Therefore, dynamics is built on top of kinematics and gives a better description/prediction of how the body will move. In fact, by taking forces into consideration, mass, gravity, drag, and many other things become really important and relevant.

Force and torque

> *"Forces are those things that allow motion; they are responsible for creating a motion."*

Every force applies an acceleration to a body, which is calculated with Newton's second law. It is so simple and elegant that it's easy to understand. We can see this law as follows:

$$\vec{F} = m\vec{a}$$

Where *F* represents the force, which is a vector (so the arrow above the formula), *m* is the mass, and *a* is the acceleration, which is another vector (so the arrow above its symbol in the formula).

This means that if you apply a force to an object with mass *m*, you know that the acceleration is *F/m*. So, just divide the force by the mass of an object and you can calculate how much it will be accelerated. Please note that if we have two objects on which we apply the same force but they have two different masses, the one with the higher mass will have a lower acceleration, because the force is divided by a greater number.

The concept of force is important because it is the cause of motion, and many Physics engines (including the one of Unity) allow you to specify forces.

Another important concept is torque, also called moment of force or just moment, which in some way expresses a force that makes an object rotate along an axis instead of moving it. If you think of force like a pull or push, you can imagine torque as a twist.

 To those of you who know a bit more about the cross-product of vectors, torque is defined as the cross-product between the force vector and the distance vector from the application point of the force. As a result, it tends to produce rotational motion. Therefore, the formula is:

$$\vec{\tau} = \vec{r} \times \vec{F}$$

Where τ (read tau) is the torque, *F* is the force vector, and *r* is the distance vector, also called offset.
In the the International System of Units, torque is measured in $N \cdot m$ (Newton meter).

The formula of torque is a bit more complicated since it involves the cross-product, and one who has just started to deal with physics in video games and uses a graphics engine like Unity doesn't need to know/understand the formula straightaway. However, it is important to understand that this quantity deals with rotations, and applying a torque on a rigid body means that it will rotate along an axis depending on where the torque is applied. Just remember that torque is not a force, although it might seem so due to the way we will deal with it within Unity.

Collisions

In classical mechanics, there are different kinds of collisions between rigid bodies that may happen. They are divided into two categories:

- Elastic collisions, in which all the kinetic energy is conserved.
- Inelastic collisions, in which part of the kinetic energy is transformed into another form of energy.

To go through this chapter, it's not important to understand them well, but it is important to understand that the type of collision may change the behaviour of what happens after the collision. Imagine two balls: one rolling towards the second, which is not moving. At a certain point, the first one will collide with the second. Depending on which kind of collision happens, the result may differ. In one scenario, both the balls will roll in the same direction and they will be as if they were attached. In another scenario, the first one stops and the second one starts to roll. In a third scenario they roll at different velocities and directions after the collision.

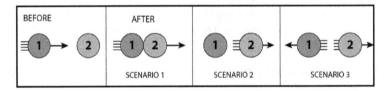

The three possible after-collision scenarios

If you want to learn more, a web page that explains the basic concepts of different collisions in a quite simple way is `http://hyperphysics.phy-astr.gsu.edu/hbase/elacol.html`. However, it is intended for those who already have a clear knowledge of the basic concepts and formulae of physics.

The website itself, `http://hyperphysics.phy-astr.gsu.edu`, is a good source for quick references to the main concepts of physics. However, a minimum of prerequisites are needed to fully understand what's on it. The best way to start is always with a physics book, which may be boring, but mastering those concepts is a great advantage.

Rigid body

A rigid body, as the name suggests, is a body that translates and rotates all together. So for instance, a Christmas ball, a television, or a flying disk are rigid bodies, because all their parts move together. A laptop is not, because its lid can rotate, as well as a door if you consider the frame too as a part of the whole. But, these kinds of objects can be described with two different rigid bodies, such as the door-frame and the door itself, which may constrain each other (in this case with a Hinge). Water, air, toothpaste, or a dress are not considered rigid bodies, because all their parts don't move together.

Most of the objects in your game will be rigidbodies (I'm writing it attached because this is the way Unity will refer to them), or they can be approximated to rigidbodies, so knowing them well is key to learning physics in Unity. In fact, most of the 2D Physics engine of unity is focused on rigid bodies (as we will see soon), and therefore this chapter is about them.

Simulating clothes, liquids, and other physical entities that are not rigidbodies is generally harder, although possible. But often they are used in 3D games, and we won't deal these aspects in this chapter.

For the most curious of you, here is a more precise definition:
A **rigid body** is the idealization of a solid body, where deformation is neglected. Therefore, the distance between any two points within the rigid body remains constant over time, independently of the forces that will apply on the rigid body.
Of course, in our world such objects don't exist. In fact they are idealizations, but they approximate the behaviour of solid objects pretty well (unless the speed of an object is near the speed of light).

Friction – linear and angular drag

If a kid were to ask me, "what is friction?" I would reply, "friction is the thing without which all things wouldn't stop moving". Even if this is not a formal definition, it helps to understand what friction is. It comes into play when you consider the dynamics of an object, because friction generates a force that opposes to the motion of the physical body. There are many types of frictions and they depend on different factors. For instance, air drag depends on the velocity of an object, whereas dry friction depends on the normal force (which depends on the surface, position of an object, its weight, and therefore also its mass).

In games, except for specific needs, you don't need all these kinds of frictions and drags. For instance, in Unity you can control just the linear and the angular drag. The first one opposes the motion of an object along a trajectory (or better, the trajectory of the center of mass of the object; otherwise it would be too complicated to do in real time) and the angular to the rotation of an object. So, in Unity, an object that has both nonzero values for linear and angular drag will eventually stop moving and rotating (in the absence of other forces).

The Unity Physics engine

Unity has a Physics engine integrated into it, which is able to handle both kinematic and dynamic types of rigid bodies as well as other physical entities such as clothes. It is divided into two parts: 2D Physics and 3D Physics. It's important to understand that although they can coexist together in the same scene, they are two separate entities; they cannot communicate between themselves. Physical objects under 2D Physics will not interact with physical objects under 3D Physics.

In this section, we will explore most of the 2D Physics engine of Unity. Although we will not use all the components presented here, it's important to master them all to become a better Unity developer.

Understanding Physics in Unity

In Chapter 2, *Cooking Cupcake Towers*, we learnt about script ordering and how it is executed. The first question we may wonder is when does the Physics engine occur when a frame is rendered? The answer is not straightforward, because the Physics engine runs multiple times during a frame render. In any case, except particular cases (such as the application has paused or particular game objects are enabled/disabled in that frame), the Physics engine runs after the initialization (so all the `Awake()`, `Start()`, and `OnEnable()` functions) and before to gather inputs from the player and update the game logic.

As a result, when we do a physics calculation (we will see these later in the chapter), we need to use the `FixedUpdate()` function, which is called more than once per frame, and all the times just before the Physics engine performs its calculation. As such, if we need to retrieve the time, we cannot use `Time.deltaTime`; instead we need to use `Time.fixedDeltaTime`.

Another question we may wonder is when it is appropriate to use the Physics engine of Unity. In theory, you don't need to use it, because you can program from scratch all the collisions and/or physic behaviours. In practice, it solves many common problems with minimum coding and it is indeed useful. These problems are not necessarily physics problems. In fact, some of them include certain game mechanics that may enhance the quality of your game when using a physics approach (such as the movement of the character). Others include gathering information from the environment for scripting other behaviours (such as a script that needs to know how many targets there are within a zone).

Physics settings in Unity

First of all, the Physics engine of Unity has some general settings, which should be taken into account. They define global physical properties of your game, such as the value of gravity, what will collide with what, and how accurate the Physics simulation should be.

You can have access to the Physics settings in Unity by navigating through **Edit | Project Settings | Physics 2D** as shown in the following screenshot:

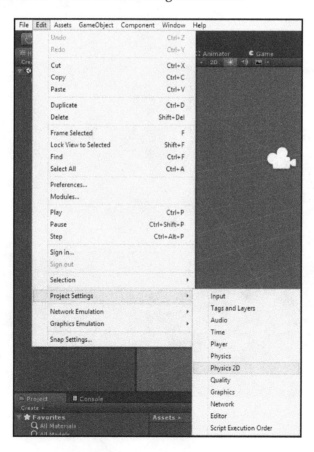

Similarly, you can have access to the 3D Physics setting by navigating through **Edit** | **Project Settings** | **Physics**.

The following screen will appear in the **Inspector** view (the most important parameters are highlighted, which we will see in detail in this section):

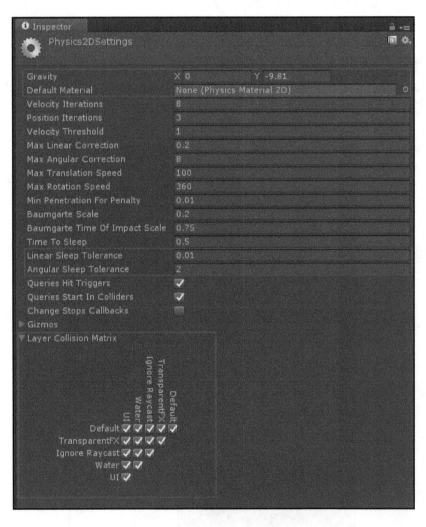

As you can see, there are many options you can tweak. Most of the time, especially for simple games (like the one we are building), the default settings will be more than fine. But Unity offers you the chance to adapt them to your game.

Most of them deal with how accurate the Unity Physics engine is. Therefore, there is a trade-off between accuracy and efficiency, since more accurate means more expensive from a computational point of view.

Let's go through the main ones in detail (if you are interested in learning also about the others, see the optional, *Other things about Physics* section later in the chapter):

- **Gravity**: The vector that defines the gravity acceleration. By default, it is a negative value only along the *y*-axis. In particular, the absolute value of 9.81 corresponds to the one on the Earth, if we let the Unity units be meters.
- **Default Material**: The physical material used by all the colliders and rigidbodies that don't have one set (we will see more about physical materials later on).
- **Time To Sleep**: The time, expressed in seconds, that needs to pass before a Rigidbody 2D goes to sleep, which means that it is not updated anymore by the Physics engine (we will see more about rigidbodies and their sleeping later on).
- **Linear Sleep Tolerance**: This is the linear speed below which the rigidbody after **Time to Sleep** goes to sleep. Imagine you have many objects in your game that drag is slowing down, and now they are so slow that the player can barely perceive their motion. As such, it's a waste of computational resources to keep them updated in the Physics engine. Therefore, this variable puts a limit to the lowest velocity an object can have before it goes to sleep (no more updates from the Physics engine). The lower this value, the more accurate the simulation will be, but it will also be more expensive if many objects are moving at velocities above that one.
- **Angular Sleep Tolerance**: The angular speed below which the rigidbody after **Time to Sleep** goes to sleep. Imagine the same situation as before, but instead the body is rotating really slowly. The same reasoning applies: the lower the value, the more accurate the simulation, but usually it is more expensive.

- **Layer Collision Matrix**: This determines which kinds of objects collide with others. By default, everything is checked, but you may want to make two particular kinds of objects not collide among them. Objects are discriminated based on the physical layer they are in. If you remember, we talked about layers and tags in Chapter 1, *A Flat World in Unity*. So, through the layer menu, you can create new layers, and in the **Inspector**, you can assign a layer to a particular game object. To make things easier, the **Layer Collision Matrix** is presented in this screenshot:

For our game, we can leave all the default values since they are more than fine for what we need.

Physics components

The Physics engine of Unity works by components. Some describe properties of the object itself, others with respect to each other, or some even within a certain region of the game world.

They can be divided as follows:

- Rigidbodies: Which define a rigidbody within the Physics engine
- Colliders: Which define a physical shape for the rigidbodies
- Joints: Which impose one or more constraints on the rigidbodies

- Effectors: Which change the physical property in some region of the game world, influencing all the rigidbodies within that region

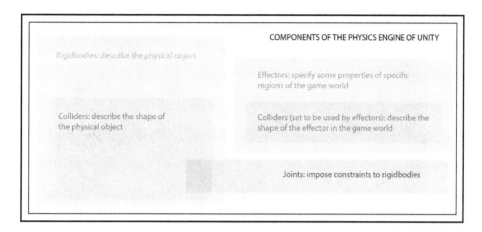

COMPONENTS OF THE PHYSICS ENGINE OF UNITY

Rigidbodies: describe the physical object

Effectors: specify some properties of specific regions of the game world

Colliders: describe the shape of the physical object

Colliders (set to be used by effectors): describe the shape of the effector in the game world

Joints: impose constraints to rigidbodies

A summary diagram of the different components of the 2D Physics engine of Unity

Now, let's see them in more detail.

Rigidbodies

Rigidbodies are, along with Colliders, the core of the Physics engine beneath Unity. When they are attached to a game object, they place it under the control of the Physics engine, which will take care to properly move its Transform. In fact, they should be moved with other functions, and scripts shouldn't touch the Transform. We will see this in detail later.

The exact name of the component is **Rigidbody 2D** (whereas **Rigidbody** is for the 3D Physics engine, but for brevity many times we will use the term rigidbody to specify a **Rigidbody 2D** component).

From Unity 5.4, and then again in Unity 5.5, the **Rigidbody 2D** component has slightly changed. In fact, many improvements have been made to the Physics engine of Unity.

Once the component is added to a game object, it looks like this:

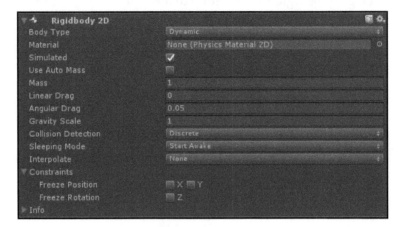

How a Rigidbody 2D works

Every time we wanted to position an object (or its children) or move it, we changed its Transform, which defines where it is in the space as well as how it is rotated or scaled. However, the Physics engine will simulate how the object will interact in a world where physics is simulated. So, if the object has a collision with another one, it will change direction or speed. This means that the Physics engine has to change in some way the Transform of the object (that's why we shouldn't touch it with scripts for physical objects; we will see later how to deal with them by scripting). This way is the Rigidbody component, which is a sort of hub between the Physics engine and the properties of the object, including the Transform.

Therefore, after the Physics engine has made its calculation, it communicates with the rigidbody, which needs to be in its next position, and the Rigidbody component provides to change the Transform to match that new position.

The same applies to colliders (we will see them in detail soon). Each collider attached to the same object of the rigidbody (or to some of its children) will be linked to the rigidbody, and we shouldn't modify the collider or move it but instead move the whole rigidbody. These colliders, which are linked to the rigidbody, allow the rigidbody to actually collide with colliders of another rigidbody and give them a shape in the physics world.

Body types

The most important variable in a **Rigidbody 2D** is the **Body Type**, which is highlighted in the following screenshot:

> If you are using a previous version of Unity (older than 5.5), this variable won't be available. However, you can still get the kinematic mode by checking the **Is Kinematic** parameter, which is available in older versions (from 5.4 and below). You can see this highlighted in the following screenshot (Unity 5.4):
>
>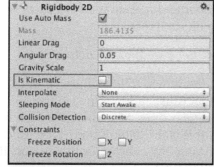
>
> And here in Unity 5.3:
>
>
>
> Older versions, such as 5.2 and below, are similar to the 5.3.

In fact, depending on how the **Body Type** is set, it affects the other settings available on the component. Moreover, it's important to remember that any **Collider 2D** attached to a **Rigidbody 2D** inherits the **Rigidbody 2D** component's **Body Type**.

The **Body Type** determines how the object will move, how the colliders will interact, and therefore also how computationally expensive that rigidbody will be.

Changing the **Body Type** of a **Rigidbody 2D** at runtime can be complicated. There are a few things that you need to consider; for example, when a **Body Type** changes, various mass-related internal properties are recalculated immediately. In addition, all existing contacts for the Collider 2D components attached to the Rigidbody 2D need to be reevaluated during the GameObject's next `FixedUpdate`. As a result, depending on the number of contacts and Collider 2D components that are attached to the body, when you change the **Body Type** of the rigidbody, it can cause variations in performance.

 It's worthwhile to mention that sometimes rigidbodies are described as colliding with each other. Although this is true when we talk about physics (so when we talk of rigid bodies), it is not true in the case of Rigidbody 2D (the component of Unity). In fact, in terms of the Physics engine of Unity, only colliders attached to rigidbodies will collide. However, saying that two rigidbodies have collided is a short way of saying that their colliders have hit each other.

The **Body Type** can be set to be of three types. Let's see them in detail:

- **Dynamic**: This means that the rigidbody will follow all dynamic calculations, which means dealing with forces that cause motion. In fact, the rigidbody will have a mass and both linear and angular drag. Moreover, the body will be affected by gravity as well. In fact, this is the default body type, since it is the most used and collides with everything. But exactly for this reason, it is also the most computationally expensive body type.

- **Kinematic**: This means that the body is still able to move as a physical object, but there are no forces for its motion, and therefore it is not affected by gravity either. In fact, you need to script its motion with any formula (we will see this later), which may or may not be physically realistic (or maybe it is in your game world). However, it is still able to collide, which means the Physics engine will notify your script that the rigidbody has collided, and then it's up to us what happens next. In the case of a collision with a dynamic body type, the kinematic one is considered immovable, which means with an infinite mass. In fact, all dynamic properties, such as mass, are not available. From a computational point of view, the kinematic body type is faster than the dynamic one, since not calculating all the dynamic forces demands less resources from the Physics engine.

- **Static**: This means the rigidbody is not supposed to move at all under the Physics engine (or under simulation). This is intended for an object with infinite mass. Under a simulation, a static Rigidbody 2D is designed to not move. In the instance of something colliding with it, a static Rigidbody 2D behaves like an immovable object (as if it has infinite mass). It is also the least resource-intensive body type to use. A static body only collides with dynamic Rigidbody 2Ds. Having two static Rigidbody 2Ds collide is not supported. This is simply because they are not designed to move. As a result, there are a limited number of properties that are available for this body type.

To better understand the differences between these body types, here is a table with the different features available for each one of them (we will see them in detail in the next section):

Kind of Parameter	Body Type / Feature	Static	Kinematic	Dynamic
Physic Engine	Material	✔	✔	✔
Physic Engine	Simulated	✔	✔	✔
Dynamic	Auto Mass			✔
Dynamic	Mass			✔
Dynamic	Linear Drag			✔
Dynamic	Angular Drag			✔
Dynamic	Gravity Scale			✔
Physic Engine	Use Full Kinematic Contacts	✔	✔	
Kinematic	Collision Detection		✔	✔
Physic Engine	Sleeping Mode		✔	✔
Physic Engine	Interpolate		✔	✔
Kinematic	Constraints		✔	✔
Kinematic	Freeze Position		✔	✔
Kinematic	Freeze Rotation		✔	✔
Physic Engine	Info	✔	✔	✔

Rigidbody properties

In the previous table, we saw many properties; they may or may not be available for some body types. But what do they actually do and what do they determine for the rigidbody? Let's explore these properties in detail:

- **Material**: A physics material that determines properties of collisions, such as friction and bounce (we will see more about physics materials later). This material will be applied to all the colliders under the control of the rigidbody (we will see more about colliders in the next section). This comes in handy when you need to have many colliders with the same physics material.

- **Simulated**: A checkbox that enables the rigidbody to interact with the Physics engine. If it is unchecked, then the rigidbody and so all the colliders referring to it will be disabled and transparent for the Physics engine as if they don't exist. This is useful to enable and disable many colliders at runtime (see the optional *More about physics* section to know more).

- **Use Auto Mass**: A checkbox that, if enabled, allows Unity to calculate the mass of the object by itself. These calculations are based on the dimension and density of each of the colliders that are referring to that specific rigidbody.

- **Mass**: If the previous checkbox is disabled, we can manually specify a mass for our rigidbody.

- **Linear Drag**: The value of the linear drag that affects the rigidbody. If it is different from zero, the object will eventually stop moving.

- **Angular Drag**: The value of the angular drag that affects the rigidbody. If it is different from zero, the object will eventually stop rotating.

- **Gravity Scale**: This is a multiplier to the gravity value for that specific rigidbody. This means that a value of 0.4 will reduce the gravity to 40% of its original value. This is useful when in your game you have objects that react to gravity in a different way. Imagine a fireball cast by your wizard; you may want it to have a rather straight trajectory (even if it is still a parabola, unless the trajectory is completely straight and the **Gravity Scale** is set to 0, which means no gravity affects the rigidbody). Whereas you want the grenade of your soldier to have a clear parabolic trajectory, since it is affected by gravity. Values greater than 1 lead to a stronger gravity than for its original value as shown in the following diagram:

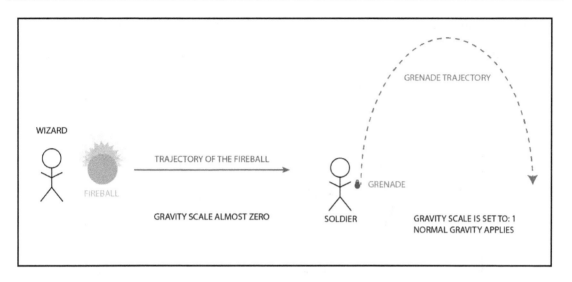

On the left in the preceding diagram is a fireball, which is not affected by gravity when the gravity scale is set to zero, leading to a straight line trajectory. On the right is a grenade, which is affected by gravity (because the gravity scale is greater than zero; in this case, it is exactly 1, which means normal gravity). Without other forces, rigidbodies with a linear velocity and affected by gravity have a parabolic trajectory.

- **Use Full Kinematic Contacts**: A checkbox available only for kinematic body types. If enabled, it allows the kinematic rigidbody to collide with other kinematic rigidbodies. By default, it is set to false, which means that the rigidbody will only collide with dynamic rigidbodies (with the exception of colliders set as triggers).

- **Collision Detection**: The way Unity detects collisions. It can be either **Discrete** or **Continuous**. In the first case, collision detection is calculated only on the position of the physical objects, and if they collide (which means that if the colliders overlap after the update of the positions of the objects, then Unity calculates the collision). On the contrary, continuous collision detection is calculated on the trajectory itself and not only on the positions of the objects. Imagine you have a really fast bullet, which is heading against a really thin wall. Since the game is discrete (the game renders frame by frame), when the bullet is near the wall, in the next update, it can be so fast that its new position is behind the wall. As such, with discrete collision detection, the bullet has crossed the wall without problems, because the Physics engine doesn't detect any collision. With continuous collision detection instead, the Physics engine is aware of the trajectory that the bullet has followed and does calculations on it. So, even if the

the final position of the bullet is behind the wall, the collision is detected and it is properly handled by the Physics engine, which recalculates the new position of the bullet taking the collision into account as shown in the following diagram:

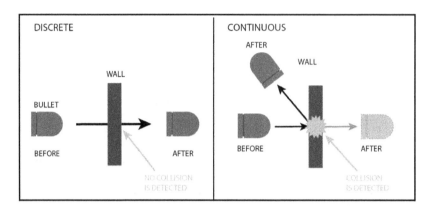

On the left in the preceding diagram is the discrete method, in which only the different positions between frames are taken into consideration. Therefore, if the position of the bullet in the next frame is behind the wall, the discrete method won't detect the collision. On the right is the continuous method, in which the whole trajectory of the bullet is taken into consideration. Therefore, even if in the next frame the bullet is behind the wall, the collision is detected and a new position is calculated based on the collision. This second method is a bit more computationally expensive.

- **Sleeping Mode**: This is the way Unity deals with whether a rigidbody should be awake or sleeping at the beginning, or whether it has the possibility to sleep at all. The possible choices of this variable, with self-explanatory names, are: **Never Sleep**, **Start Awake**, and **Start Asleep**. A rigidbody is sleeping when it is not taken completely into consideration by the Physics engine (it differs from not being simulated, and now we see why). Imagine how many objects in your game could be potently moving but they don't at the moment. For example, imagine a ball pit with thousands of balls, but at the moment none of them are moving. In this scenario, it's useless to call each one of them in the Physics engine for void calculations. Another example: imagine a pendulum that is stopping, and its oscillation arc is too small to be perceived by the player. Calculating the exact position of the pendulum on this arc is a waste of computational resources. It's better to stop the pendulum or the balls (set them into sleeping mode) until an event, such as the player diving in the ball pit or pushing the pendulum. So, for performance reasons, not all rigidbodies are awake at any moment. However, they can be awoken by an event, which is usually automatic in the Physics engine. But it can also be controlled by you within a script (we will see more details about this in the next section).

- **Interpolate**: When a rigidbody is moving, maybe under a force, the Physics engine performs some calculations on which will be its next position. However, the Physics engine is not perfect and cannot replicate our physics. In fact, algorithms are subjected to numerical instability, which may result in a jerky motion in our case. Therefore, Unity offers you two ways to smooth the motion and make it less jerky, plus the option **None**, in which no smoothing is performed. The first way, called **Interpolate**, takes into consideration the previous position of the rigidbody. On the contrary, the second way, called **Extrapolate**, takes into consideration the prevision of the next position of the object. Both methods work well, and you can perceive the difference between them and **None**. However, the difference between the two could be tricky to understand, especially since their behaviour is really similar, and understanding which one is better for your game can sometimes be determined just by trial and error (unless you have really specific needs).

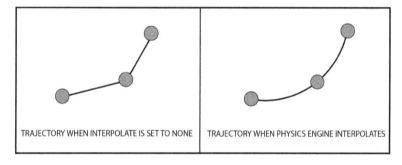

On the left, the trajectory is not interpolated; it leads to a fragmented trajectory. On the right, the trajectory is interpolated and its curve is smoothed.

- **Constraints**: These prevent the rigid body from moving or rotating in a certain way, if not at all. In the case of 2D, you can freeze the motion along x or y or both axes and rotation along the z-axis. All of them are independent checkboxes, which can be selected in any combination. Of course, having all of them selected means that the rigidbody won't be able to move. Imagine you are developing a puzzle game and your main character game needs to move a box, maybe by pushing it. However, we don't want the box to start to rotate on itself if the player doesn't push the middle point of the box. As such, we can freeze the rotation of the box, still allowing the box to move and be pushed by the main character.

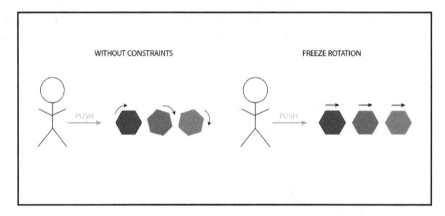

On the left, there are no constraints, and therefore when the player pushes, the object might rotate. On the right, the rotation is frozen, and when the player pushes, the object won't rotate. Which behaviour to choose depends on the design of your game.

 Info: A foldout showing all the other variables of the rigidbody, which is very useful in debugging.

Dealing with rigidbodies

Now that we have explored the Rigidbody 2D component in detail, let's see how we can deal with it within scripts. As previously explained, scripts are not supposed to change the Transform of a rigidbody. So how we can move them? The answer is that some special functions exist.

These functions need to be called on the rigidbody; therefore probably you may want to have a reference to the Rigidbody 2D, like this fragment of script:

```
//Reference to the RigidBody2D component
public Rigidbody2D rb2D;

void Start() {
  //Get the reference to the Rigidbody2D component
  rb2D = GetComponent<Rigidbody2D>();
}
```

As a result, you can call the functions in this way:

```
Rb2D.NameOfTheFunction()
```

Where of course, instead of `NameOfTheFunction` there will be one of the functions listed next. However, if you remember, the Physics engine might be called more than once per frame, and therefore all of these functions should be called within `FixedUpdate()`.

So how can we actually move a rigidbody? For dynamic body types, we can either just leave them at the mercy of the external forces such as gravity, collisions, and so on, or we can apply a specific force.

In order to apply a force to the rigidbody, there are the following useful functions:

- `AddForce(Vector2 force, ForceMode2D mode = ForceMode2D.Force)`: Applies a force specified in the `force` parameter. Moreover, enum `ForceMode2D` is an optional parameter that specifies whether the force should act as an impulse or not. By default, it is not an impulse.
- `AddForceAtPosition(Vector2 force, Vector2 position, ForceMode2D mode = ForceMode2D.Force)`: Behaves like the previous function, but you can also specify an application point for the force.
- `AddRelativeForce(Vector2 relativeForce, ForceMode2D mode = ForceMode2D.Force)`: Behaves like the first function, but the force is specified in local coordinates.
- `AddTorque(float torque, ForceMode2D mode = ForceMode2D.Force)`: This applies a torque to the rigidbody; likewise, the first function applies instead a force.

For kinematic body types instead, we have two functions to explicitly move these kinds of body types and still allow the Physics engine to perform collision detection correctly. Inside these functions, we directly pass a position and a rotation, which can be calculated with any formula. Therefore they can follow any physics law you want (or one that is meaningful in your game):

- `public void MovePosition(Vector2 position)`: Moves the rigidbody to the specified position
- `public void MoveRotation(float angle)`: Rotates the rigidbody to the specified angle

The easiest example is to apply the classical kinematic law for velocity to make the kinematic body move in a straight line indefinitely. For the most curious of you, the formula is the following:

$$\Delta Space = Velocity * \Delta Time$$

The Δ (read delta) in physics means the final minus the initial which can be rewritten (by explicitly separating the delta of the space) as:

$$NextPosition = CurrentPosition + Velocity * \Delta Time$$

We can translate this into Unity with the following fragment of code (instead of `Time.deltaTime`, we need to use `Time.deltaFixedTime`):

```
public Vector2 velocity;
void FixedUpdate () {
   rb2D.MovePosition(rb2D.position + velocity *
Time.fixedDeltaTime);
}
```

Moreover, we have some or the other function for all kinds of body types:

- `IsAwake()`: Returns true if the rigidbody is awake.
- `IsSleeping()`: Returns true if the rigidbody is sleeping.
- `IsTouching(Collider2D collider)`: Returns true if the collider is touching the rigidbody (which means any of the colliders attached to the rigidbody)
- `OverlapPoint(Vector2 point)`: Returns true if the point is overlapping the rigidbody (which means any of the colliders attached to the rigidbody)
- `Sleep()`: Makes the rigidbody sleep
- `WakeUp()`: Disables the sleeping mode of the rigidbody

For the full list of functions and variables of a Rigidbody 2D component, you can consult the official documentation here: `https://docs.unity3d.com/ScriptReference/Rigidbody2D.html`.

Colliders

Imagine that you have the heroine of your game moving in a complex environment; by complex, I mean detailed, for instance, the kitchen of the king's castle. If the Physics engine is super realistic, it should take in consideration that the hand of the heroine can go over the table, as far as the body stays on its side. However, this is impossible (or at least out of reach for the current hardware of your players) to run in real time. So colliders provide an approximate shape for objects and characters that need to have some kind of physical interaction, such as a collision. For instance, characters are often approximated as a capsule-shaped collider and objects with a sphere-shaped or box-shaped collider. Of course, if a deeper level of detail is required, different colliders can act as a more complex one. And ultimately, all the polygons of the 3D model (or perimeter of the 2D Sprite) can be part of the collider, having a much better realism but at the cost of performance. Therefore, you'll want to be careful to always have the right level of detail for each situation.

In Unity, colliders can be of five types, which are:

Name	Appearance in the Inspector	Description
Circle Collider 2D	▼ ○ ✓ **Circle Collider 2D** 🔲 ⚙ ⚓ Edit Collider Material None (Physics Material 2D) ⊙ Is Trigger ☐ Used By Effector ☐ Offset X 0 Y 0 Radius 0.5 ▶ Info	The collider's shape is a circle, which is defined by a position and a radius expressed in the local coordinate.

Box Collider 2D	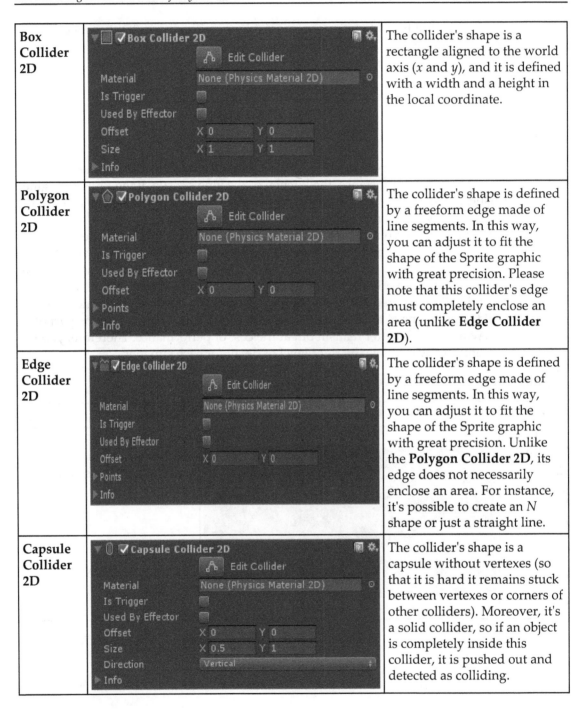	The collider's shape is a rectangle aligned to the world axis (x and y), and it is defined with a width and a height in the local coordinate.
Polygon Collider 2D		The collider's shape is defined by a freeform edge made of line segments. In this way, you can adjust it to fit the shape of the Sprite graphic with great precision. Please note that this collider's edge must completely enclose an area (unlike **Edge Collider 2D**).
Edge Collider 2D		The collider's shape is defined by a freeform edge made of line segments. In this way, you can adjust it to fit the shape of the Sprite graphic with great precision. Unlike the **Polygon Collider 2D**, its edge does not necessarily enclose an area. For instance, it's possible to create an N shape or just a straight line.
Capsule Collider 2D		The collider's shape is a capsule without vertexes (so that it is hard it remains stuck between vertexes or corners of other colliders). Moreover, it's a solid collider, so if an object is completely inside this collider, it is pushed out and detected as colliding.

All of them share the same core settings, and some additional ones to customize the shape of the collider. For instance, for **Circle Collider 2D**, we can decide the center and the radius. However, Unity automatically tries to enclose/envelop the Sprite or 3D model within the collider, though manual tweaking may be required (see further for editing the collider in a visual way).

Since this book focuses on the 2D world, for brevity we will refer to the colliders without the ending 2D, assuming we are always referring to the 2D component and not to the 3D one with the same name. For example, **Box Collider 2D** becomes **Box Collider**.

Let's explore the core options of each collider:

- **Density**: This affects the mass of the rigidbody that it is referring to. A value of zero means that the collider will be completely ignored in the calculation of the mass of the rigidbody. The higher the value, the more the collider will contribute to the mass of the rigidbody.

If you don't see the **Density** option, it's normal. In fact, it will be visible only if the option **Auto Mass** is enabled on the rigidbody associated (so attached on the same game object of the collider or on some of its parents up in the hierarchy). In fact, when the rigidbody component automatically calculates the mass, it takes into consideration all the colliders linked to that rigidbody and their densities.

- **Material**: A physics material that determines properties of collisions, such as friction and bounce (we will see more about physics materials later).
- **Is Trigger**: Check this if you want the collider to behave as a trigger. This means that the collider won't be used to do collisions but rather to trigger something when another collider enters within this one (see the next section for more details).
- **Used By Effector**: Check this if you want the collider to be used by an attached effector (we will see more about effectors later).
- **Offset**: This is the offset of the collider geometry expressed in local coordinates; in other words, how far in terms of x and y the collider should be from the position of the game object on which it is attached.
- **Info**: A foldout showing all the other variables of the collider. It is very useful in debugging.

Then, there are the specific ones for each collider:

- **Radius**: Used only for the circle collider, and it determines the radius of the circle.
- **Size**: This is used only for the box and the capsule collider. In the first case, it determines the size of the box, and in the second the size of the box that the capsule fills up (and therefore indirectly the size of the capsule) as shown in the following diagram:

- **Points**: This is non-editable information for the polygon or edge colliders about their complexity. It describes all the points of the collider and how they are connected in paths.
- **Direction**: This is used only for capsule colliders and it can be set to be either **Vertical** or **Horizontal**. This controls which way round the capsule sets; specifically, it defines the positioning of the semi-circular end-caps.

Furthermore, it is possible to visually edit the colliders by clicking on the following icon, available in all the colliders:

As a result, you will able to modify the collider directly into the **Scene** view. It is quite intuitive, so I'll let you explore this feature by yourself.

You can create a vertex for the edge or polygon colliders by clicking on one of their edges.

Dealing with colliders

Often, in video games, when colliders collide, we want to trigger some actions and run specific code. For instance, imagine a bullet that hits the surface of the wall, we may want to instantiate a particle effect in the point, and remove the bullet. The same applies for a fireball, but with a fire effect. Or imagine the player walks through a door and a cut-scene is triggered. In this case, there is a volume trigger (a collider with **is Trigger** set to true) so that when the player enters, the volume triggers the cut-scene. Another example, is an area full of toxic gasses, and the longer the player stays in that area, his health is gradually reducing.

All of this can be achieved by using some special functions. If you remember, in `Chapter 2,` *Baking Cupcake Tower*, we have seen that every script that derives from monobehaviour could have some functions, such as `Start()` and `Update()` that are automatically called by Unity. Among these functions there are some that are called by the Physics engine of Unity.

For trigger volumes, there are the following functions:

- `OnTriggerEnter2D(Collider2D other)`: This is called on both the rigidbody and the volume trigger when the former enters in the latter. Information about the other collider is passed as a parameter in the `other` variable.

- `OnTriggerStay2D(Collider2D other)`: This is called on every frame on both the rigidbody and the volume trigger as long as the former is within the second one. Information about the other collider is passed as a parameter in the `other` variable.

- `OnTriggerExit2D(Collider2D other)`: This is called on both the rigidbody and the trigger volume when the former leaves/exits the second one. Information about the other collider is passed as a parameter in the `other` variable.

For colliders not set to be triggers, there are similar functions. However, instead of having just information about the other collider, information about the whole collision is available through the class `Collision2D`, which stores — other than the colliders — the contact points, relative velocities, and so on. More information about this can be found here in the official documentation at: `https://docs.unity3d.com/ScriptReference/Collision2D.html`

So, the functions for colliders are:

- `OnCollisionEnter2D(Collision2D coll)`: This is called on both the rigidbodies/colliders that have just made contact (had a collision). Information about the collision can be found inside the `coll` variable.

- `OnCollisionStay2D(Collision2D coll)`: This is called on both rigidbodies/colliders every frame as long as they are touching each other. Information about the collision can be found inside the `coll` variable.

- `OnCollisionExit2D(Collision2D coll)`: This is called on both two rigidbodies/colliders when they stop making contact. Information about their collision can be found inside the `coll` variable.

In our specific case, we will need these functions (the trigger ones) to detect when the sprinkles hit the enemies, to reduce their health, and eventually trigger the right animation. We will see this at the end of the chapter.

Joints

So far, we have talked about rigid bodies and colliders, but they were just single physical bodies. What about more complex mechanical systems? Imagine a rope that is holding a cage with a skeleton and a key inside. So, our protagonist decides to cut the rope to make the cage fall. Once the rope is broken, then the cage falls down. However, even before the rope is cut, the cage was under the effect of gravity. In fact, if our protagonist would have pushed the cage instead of cutting the rope, that would have started to oscillate. The reason is that the rope is giving a constraint to the cage — it is allowed to move only within a circle (or sphere if we are in 3D) that has per radius the length of the rope. Of course, when it oscillates, gravity makes the cage move on the border of this circle (or sphere). What if the rope were a rigid metal bar? Well, the cage would even have a harder constraint, because now it is forced to be only on the border of the circle (or sphere). And if the rope was a spring? Again, this is another kind of constraint as shown in the following diagram:

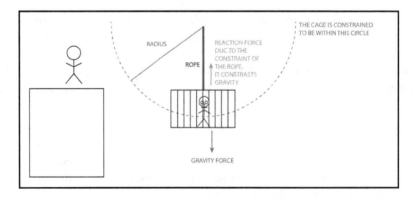

Although the cage is under the force of the gravity, the rope imposes a reaction force. As a result, the cage doesn't fall. Therefore, the rope imposes a constraint on the cage. In particular, it limits the cage motion to be within a circle with a radius equal to the rope length.

Now, imagine placing many of these constraints together. For instance, you tie up the cage to a pending spring, and from the bottom of the cage a rope is holding a metal sphere. The system would start to increase in complexity. But how does Unity handle all of this? The answer is, using Joints components.

 Note that all the joints that finish with 2D belong to the 2D Physics engine; otherwise they belong to the 3D one. So be careful to not get confused or attach the wrong joint. However, from now on, we will always refer to it as Joint 2D, even without 2D, unless otherwise specified. This decision was made to make the chapter clear and more fluid to read.

Main properties of Joints

By using a joint component, you can attach a rigidbody to another one, in order to give them a specific constraint, and still leave some freedom for the motion. In particular, Unity provides nine Joint 2D components. But before we go through each one of them, let's explore some general properties of the joints in Unity.

The other rigidbody

As we've already said, a joint involves two rigidbodies (with the exception of the **Target Joint 2D**). The first is attached to the same object of the joint. The other one can be chosen arbitrarily. Therefore, these two options are available inside the joint components:

- **Enable Collision**: Both rigidbodies will have colliders. If this toggle is true, it means that the two rigidbodies will collide between them according to the Physics engine and what we have seen so far in the previous two sections. Most of the times, rigidbodies with a joint belong to the same big system, and you don't want it to collide with itself. As such, the default value is false.
- **Connected Rigid body**: This is the reference to the second rigidbody of the joint, as the name suggests.

Then, most of the joints (with the exception for the **Relative Joint 2D** and the **Target Joint 2D**) needs the two points of the application of the joint. Imagine again the example of the cage pending from the rope. Where the rope is attached to the cage is an important factor, because if the rope is attached to one of the corners of the cage, this will be rotated, as shown in this diagram:

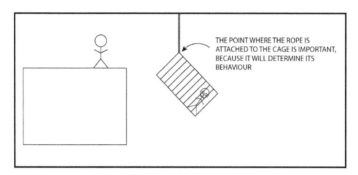

We attached the rope on the cage which is important, because it will affect how it will react to forces. However, it is interesting to note that wherever you append a rigidbody, the line along the rope will pass always through the barycenter (centroid) of the rigidbody.

Plus, you need to consider the possibility that there are other forces that may move the cage, and again where the rope is attached is an important piece of information. The same applies to the other rigidbody; in the case of the cage, the other rigid body is the ceiling.

Therefore, there are some options available to determine these two points of application, which are called **anchors** in Unity:

- **Auto Configure Connected Anchor**: If this is checked, Unity will take care to determine where the two anchors are. Of course, turn it off if you have a specific point of application of the joint in mind and you want to place an anchor there.
- **Anchor**: The position in x and y (with respect to the rigidbody) of the anchor of the joint on the rigidbody where it is attached.
- **Connected Anchor** : This is the position in x and y (with respect to the rigidbody of the other object) of the anchor of the joint on the rigidbody specified in the **Connected Rigidbody** variable.

Breaking joints

Coming back to the example of the suspended cage, imagine that the hero decides that it is a good idea try to jump on top of the cage and then jump on another platform. However, he didn't consider that the rope was really old (in fact, there is a skeleton in the cage!), and once he landed on the cage, the rope breaks making both the cage and our hero fall. Therefore, it's true that joints impose a constraint, but they have limits too. For the same reason, if you pull both sides of a rubber with too much force, the rubber will eventually break.

Also in Unity, Joints can be broken. In particular, in their components there are two variables:

- **Break Force**: This is present in all the joints, and it holds the numerical value of the force after which the joint will break. Breaking a joint in Unity means to erase the Joint component from the object. By default, it is set to be infinity, which means that the joint is indestructible. Otherwise, the lower the value, the easier it is to break the joint. In the example of the cage, if we choose to give a very low value for the joint that simulates the rope, it will be likely that the rope is really old and when our hero jumps on top of the cage, they both will fall in the dungeon of the castle.

- **Break Torque**: This is present in all the joints other than **Distance Joint 2D**, **Spring Joint 2D**, and **Target Joint 2D**. It holds the numerical value of the torque after which the joint will break. As we already have seen, rigidbodies can not only move but also rotate. By default, it is set to be infinity, which means the joint is indestructible. Otherwise, it can be brought to a finite value, allowing the joint to break with torques greater than the value specified.

     For an example of a joint that breaks under torque, you can just imagine something that is rotating but it's motion is blocked by something, such as when you use the screwdriver and keep going until the wood (which was the constraint) is broken. However, here is another example that is less intuitive but more common (even in video games). Imagine you append yourself on the boarder/edge of a shelf. Since there is an offset from the center of mass of the shelf and the point where you have appended yourself (they are likely to be perpendicular if the shelf is flat), a torque is applied on the shelf. Under the effect of the torque, the shelf should rotate around its center of mass, but it doesn't since the wall prevents it. If you are heavy enough, which means the force you apply on the shelf is greater (or also if in some way you are able to increase the offset), the torque increases, until it reaches a breaking point. Then the constraint will break, which may result either in a broken shelf or a broken wall depending which one has more resistance (most probably the shelf will break and the wall will still stand). The following diagram should help you to figure the example out:

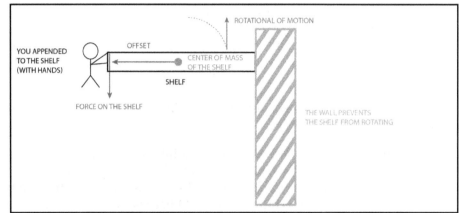

Specific joints

So far, we have seen only general properties of the joints in Unity, but now we will take a closer look at all the nine joint 2D components available.

It's worthy to mention that joints are divided into two classes: spring joints and motor joints. The former uses a spring to impose a constraint, which may be completely stiff so as to simulate a rigid bar. Motor joints, instead, can actively apply forces onto the rigidbodies. Some joints are both, like a spring with a motor.

All the joints in Unity have an icon (visible when, for instance, you place the component in the **Inspector**). In this book, you can see the icon in the top-left corner of the images of the joints (in the next sections). This icon is really useful for remembering what the joint does and also how it works. So, when reading the next section, or programming your game, pay attention to this icon, which might help you to understand the joint better.

Distance Joint 2D

This joint keeps the two rigidbodies at a certain distance apart. The aim of this joint is to keep at a certain distance two rigidbodies, or a rigidbody and a fixed point in the game world. In fact, if you set the **Connected Rigidbody** variable to None, you can then specify the position of the fixed point in **Connected Anchor**.

It should appear like the following in the **Inspector**:

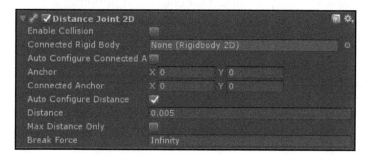

This joint applies a linear force to both the rigidbodies (or just to the rigidbody on which it is attached if using a fixed point) with a very stiff simulated spring (which is not configurable) to keep the distance. The joint doesn't apply any torque.

In addition to the parameters that we have seen in the last section, **Distance Joint 2D** also has the following options:

- **Auto Configure Distance**: If set to true, Unity will calculate the current distance between the two rigidbodies (or the rigidbody and the fixed point) and place its value in the **Distance** variable.
- Distance: Specifies the distance beyond which the two rigidbodies (or the rigidbody and the fixed point) cannot go further.
- **Max Distance Only**: If enabled, the distance between the two rigidbodies (or the rigidbody and the fixed point) can be lower than the value specified in the Distance. If this option is disabled instead, the distance is fixed and the two points cannot be any further or closer than the Distance.

 Remember that if the **Break Force** of the joint is a finite value, it will eventually break, even if the **Max Distance Only** option is set to false.

When **Max Distance Only** is false, the constraint among the two points is rigid, so you can imagine them connected by a metal string/bar along with a hinge (since they can still rotate with respect to each other). An example of how this is used is when you need to connect two couches of a train together, because they cannot get any farther or closer than a specific distance. If **Max Distance Only** is true, instead, they can be closer than the **Distance**, but not further. This is the behaviour of our rope, which holds the cage. that potentially can get closer to where the rope is tied but not further. Another example is a dog with a leash.

However, it is important to keep in mind that both the rigidbodies are free to rotate with respect to each other. In fact, this joint imposes the constraint only on the relative position of the two rigid bodies.

Fixed Joint 2D

The aim of this joint is to keep a certain relative offset (both linear and angular) between two rigidbodies or a rigidbody and a fixed point in the game world (you can specify it by setting **Connected Rigidbody** to None).

It should appear like the following in the **Inspector**:

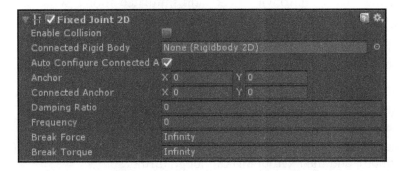

This joints applies both a linear force to compensate the linear offset, and a torque to compensate the angular one. Like **Distance Joint 2D**, it uses a very stiff simulated spring, but you can tweak the spring values, such as the frequency.

Therefore, in addition to the parameters we have seen in the last section, **Fixed Joint 2D** has also the following options:

- **Damping Ratio**: This defines the degree to which the oscillation of the spring is suppressed. Its value ranges from 0 to 1; the higher the value, the less motion. As you would expect from a spring, this joint will overshoot the desired distance and then rebound back, leading the spring to oscillate. The **Damping Ratio** determines how quickly the oscillation is damped (reduced) and thus how fast the spring comes back to its rest position

- **Frequency**: This defines the frequency at which the spring oscillates when the rigidbodies are reaching the separation distance. It is measured in cycles per second, and its value ranges from 1 to 1 million. The higher the value, the stiffer the spring, which means less motion. It's worthwhile to notice that a value of zero means that the spring is completely stiff.

Another way to think of this joint is like parenting GameObjects within the **Hierarchy** so that the children are fixed with respect to their parents. However, the joint offers you more options than a simple parenting, including the possibility to break it.

An example of usage of this joint is when you have a chain of rigidbodies (such as a real chain that hangs from the ceiling, or you can imagine also a bridge made of sections), and you want to hold them rigidly together. The advantage is that you can allow a certain flexibility in the joint, so in the case of the bridge, it can still bend a little within the limits you impose.

Friction Joint 2D

The aim of this joint is to keep to zero both the linear and angular offset, by slowing down the movement between the two rigidbodies or a rigidbody and a fixed point in the game world (you can specify it by setting **Connected Rigidbody** to None).

Friction Joint 2D should appear like this in the **Inspector**:

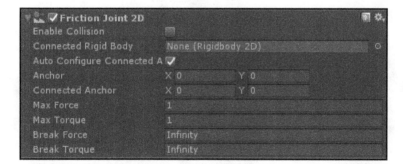

In addition to the parameters we have seen in the last section, **Friction Joint 2D** has the following options:

- **Max Force**: This determines the linear resistance along the line that connects the two rigidbodies. A high value (the maximum is 1,000,000) creates a strong linear resistance; thus the two rigidbodies will not move along the line that connects them much. On the contrary, a low value allows more motion.
- **Max Torque**: This determines the angular resistance between the two rididbodies. A high value (the maximum is 1 million) creates a strong angular resistance; thus the two rigidbodies will not rotate much relatively. On the contrary, a low value allows more motion.

An example of the use of this joint is when there are physical objects in the game that need friction to be believable. So, imagine a platform that is anchored to a big wheel in the background. Since the game is 2D, the wheel is only an aesthetic element; it doesn't actually affect the platform. As such, we need to simulate the friction between the platform and the wheel, and we can achieve that with a **Friction Joint 2D**. In this way, we can have an angular resistance on the platform; thus it can still be rotated, but not so easily. Maybe, the player may drop a heavy box on the border of the platform to make it rotate enough so that the player can pass.

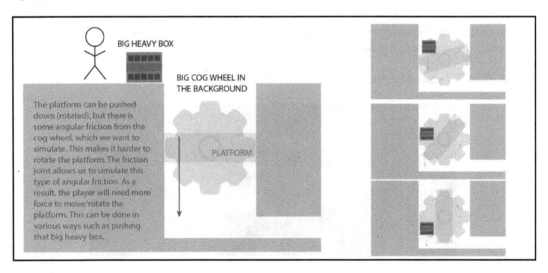

On the left is the representation of the system. On the right is what will happen when the box is dropped onto the platform, which will rotate slowly due its angular friction.

Hinge Joint 2D

The aim of this joint is to constrain the rigidbody to rotate around another rigidbody or a fixed point in space (always specified by **Connected Anchor** if **Connected Rigid Body** is set to None). The rotation can either be left to happen passively (for example, in response to a collision, or under the effect of gravity) or be actively powered by a motor, which provides torque to the rigidbody. Furthermore, limits can be set to constrain the hinge just to rotate at certain angles, or to allow more than a one full rotation around its axis.

It appears like the following screenshot in the **Inspector**:

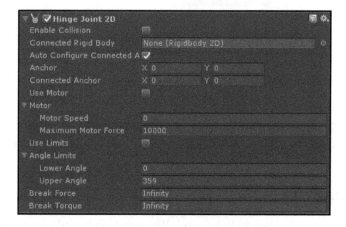

In addition to the parameters that we have seen in the last section, **Hinge Joint 2D** has the following options:

- **Use Motor:** If enabled, it allows the joint to actively apply a torque on the rigidbody, simulating a motor.
- **Motor Speed:** This specifies at which speed the simulated motor should rotate in degrees per second. So a value of 30 means that the motor will do a complete rotation in 12 seconds (*360/30=12*).
- **Maximum Motor Force:** This specifies the maximum force that the motor can apply to reach the **Motor Speed**. Imagine a very heavy object requires a stronger force to rotate and thus reach the **Motor Speed**. If the motor is not powerful enough, it won't make the rigidbody reach the **Motor Speed**. Moreover, if a **Break Torque** is specified, it may break the joint.
- **Use Limits:** If true, the joint limits the angles to which the rigidbody can rotate.
- **Lower Angle:** This sets the lower end of the rotation arc allowed by the limit.
- **Upper Angle:** This sets the upper end of the rotation arc allowed by the limit.

A clear example of the usage of this joint is with doors. They can rotate around their hinges, which connect the door with its frame. We can limit how the door can rotate, so for instance, you may want it to rotate only of 90 degrees. Moreover, if the door is automatic, we can simulate a motor, which actively makes the door rotate. In fact, the motor may be triggered by a script. Finally, if the player wants to push the door beyond its limit (90 degrees in the example), and a **Break Torque** is specified, the player may break the hinge with enough force.

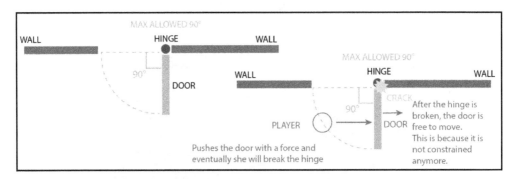

Top view (birds-eye view). On the left is the representation of the system. On the right is what will happen when the player pushes the door beyond its limits.

Relative Joint 2D

This joint makes two rigidbodies to keep a relative position based on each other's position. In fact, the aim of this joint is the same as that of the **Fixed Joint 2D**; the difference lies in how they do it. The **Fixed Joint 2D**, as we already have seen, is a spring kind of joint that will stop to oscillate only when the two rigidbodies are at the specified offset and rotation, and so the spring is in a rest position. Instead, the **Relative Joint 2D** is a motor kind of joint that applies a direct force and torque to rigidbodies so that they are at the same offset and rotation.

Like the **Fixed Joint 2D**, the **Relative Joint 2D** can also work with both of these:

- Two rigidbodies
- A rigidbody and a fixed point

To use the second case, set **Connected Rigidbody** to None and then specify the coordinate of the fixed point in the **Linear Offset** variable.

It appears like this in the **Inspector**:

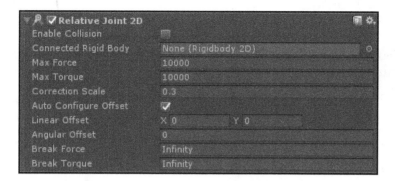

In addition to the parameters we saw in the last section, the **Relative Joint 2D** has the following options:

- **Max Force**: This specifies the maximum force that the joint/motor can use to correct the offset between the two rigidbodies. The higher the value, the better the simulated motor will be able to correct the offset. By default, **Max Force** is set to `10000`, which means a really powerful motor.

- **Max Torque**: This specifies the maximum torque that the joint/motor can use to correct the angular offset between the two rigidbodies. The higher the value, the better the simulated motor will be able to correct the angular offset. By default, **Max Torque** is set to `10000`, which means a really powerful motor.

- **Correction Scale**: Tweaks the joint to make sure that it behaves as it is supposed to. This can be done by either increasing **Max Force** or **Max Torque**, which may affect behaviour (and as a result the joint may not reach its target). Therefore, you can use this setting to correct it. The default setting of `0.3` is usually appropriate (because on an average the joint behaves as you would expect; it's a value that has likely been found by trial and error). But it may need tweaking between the range of 0 and 1.

- **Auto Configure Offset**: When checked, this takes the current linear and angular offsets of the two rigidbodies, stores them in the **Linear Offset** and **Angular Offset** variables, and maintains them.

- **Linear Offset**: This specifies the linear offset that the two rigidbodies should have, expressed in local coordinates.

- **Angular Offset**: This specifies the angular offset that the two rigidbodies should have, expressed in local coordinates.

An example of use of this joint is between the camera and the Avatar in the game. In this way, the camera can follow the Avatar with a slight delay (because if the camera is parented, it will move instantaneously with the Avatar). But it won't oscillate much as with the **Fixed Joint 2D**, since it is a spring kind, which may cause frustration to the player (of course, this also depends on how the **Fixed Joint 2D** is configured, maybe with a real stiff spring; but usually the **Relative Joint 2D** is used for this kind of situations).

Another typical example of the use of this joint is when something should follow the player, such as a life counter above her head or a friendly spirit behind her shoulders.

Slider Joint 2D

Imagine you want to constrain the motion of a rigidbody just along a line, so that it can only slide onto that line. This is what the **Slider Joint 2D** allows you to do. As for the other joints, the line can be between two rigidbodies or a rigidbody and a fixed point in the game world.

It appears like this in the **Inspector**:

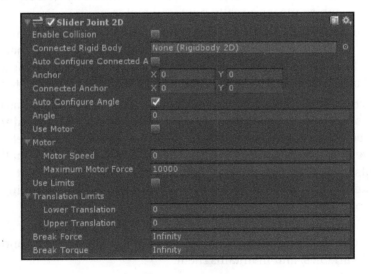

In addition to the parameters we have seen in the last section, the **Slider Joint 2D** also has the following options:

- **Angle**: This specifies the angle at which the rigidbody is constrained to remain. In the 2D world, an angle fully specifies a direction, and this angle specifies in which direction the motion is constrained.

  In order to fully determine the line where motion is allowed by the joint, the current position the rigidbody is taken into consideration as well. Thus, a point (the current position of the rigidbody) and a direction (specified from the **Angle** variable) univocally determine a line where the motion is constrained, as shown in the following diagram:

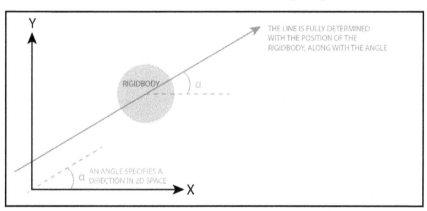

- **Use Motor**: If true, the joint uses a simulated motor as well.
- **Motor Speed**: This specifies the speed of the rigidbody that the motor should achieve.
- **Max Motor Force**: This specifies the maximum force that the motor can use/apply in order to achieve a Motor Speed for the rigidbody.
- **Use Limits**: If true, this allows further constraints on the rigidbody along a segment of the line.
- **Lower Limit**: This specifies the minimum distance the rigidbody should be at from the **Connected Anchor** point.
- **Upper Translation**: This specifies the maximum distance the rigidbody should be at from the **Connected Anchor** point.

Typical scenarios where you may want to use this joint are a sliding door, which goes up and down, and also a platform, which can go left and right, up, down, or even diagonally.

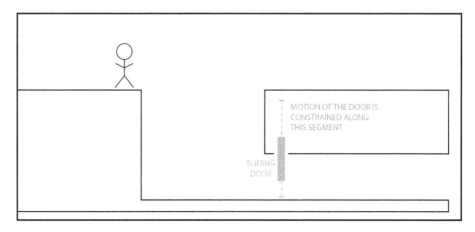

The sliding door in the diagram is constrained along a segment

Spring Joint 2D

As the name suggests, this is a pure spring joint 2D. It actually simulates a spring connected between the two rigidbodies, or a rigidbody and a fixed point. In fact, this joint gives you all the functionalities for a spring joint, and therefore you can simulate all the other pure (without a motor) spring-joints.

In fact, the **Distance Joint 2D** is simulated by using the **Spring Joint 2D** with **Frequency** set to 0 and **Damping Ratio** to 1.

It appears like the following in the **Inspector**:

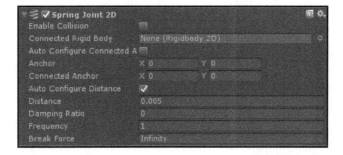

In addition to the parameters we have seen in the last section, the **Spring Joint 2D** has the following options:

- **Distance**: This specifies the distance that the two rigidbodies (or the rigidbody and the fixed point) should keep. You can imagine it also like the length of the spring in its rest position, which means the length of the spring when no forces are applied on it.
- **Damping Ratio**: This specifies how much you want to suppress the motion of the spring. Its value ranges from 0 to 1. Lower values mean a movable spring, higher values mean a stiff spring. If it is set to 1, the spring is not movable.
- **Frequency**: This specifies the frequency at which the spring oscillates while the objects are approaching the separation distance (which is the length of the spring in the rest position) specified in the **Distance** variable (measured in cycles per second). It ranges from 0 to 1,000,000. The higher the value, the stiffer the spring will be.

Whenever you need to place a spring in your game, this is the right joint. So, an example could be a physically realistic Launchpad, which you need to compress the spring, so as to let it have a boost in your jump. However, you don't need necessarily to think of this joint as a normal spring. In fact, you can bring this joint to the limits (such as a very stiff spring). As such, you are able to create other behaviours that in reality don't have a spring, but in the game they look nice when connected by a spring. Have you ever played *Rayman*? The character has its body parts separated, but they still move together in a coherent way in the game. If you are planning to create a similar character, the spring joint can be a valid solution to link the body parts in a realistic way. Here is an image of *Rayman*:

Image of *Rayman*. As you can see, the character doesn't have legs or arms, but has hands and feet. In your game, you can attach them to the chest through a Spring Joint.

Target Joint 2D

The **Target Joint 2D** is a particular spring-type joint that, instead of having a second rigidbody, has a target. The aim is to keep the rigidbody where the component is attached at a certain distance from the target. It only applies a linear force; thus no torque is given to the rigidbody.

It appears like this in the **Inspector**:

Since this component doesn't have a second rigidbody, there are some variables that allow you to specify the target:

- **Anchor**: Defined in local coordinates, with respect to the rigidbody, where the joint is attached on the rigidbody.
- **Target**: Defined in local coordinates, with respect to the rigidbody, where the other end of the joint tries to move.
- **Auto Configure Target**: When checked, it sets the **Target** to the current position of the rigidbody, which is useful when our rigidbody is moved around, maybe driven by other forces. Furthermore, when this option is selected, the **Target** changes as you move the rigidbody; on the contrary, it won't if the option is not selected.

Moreover, it is possible to control the characteristic of the spring with the usual parameters:

- **Max Force**: This specifies the maximum force that the joint can use on the rigidbody
- **Damping Ratio**: This specifies how much the motion of the spring is suppressed (refer to either the *Spring 2D Joint* or *Fixed 2D Joint* section for more details)
- **Frequency**: This specifies the frequency of the spring (refer to either the *Spring 2D Joint* or *Fixed 2D Joint* section for more details)

An example of the use of this joint is when the player needs to drag objects with the mouse. In this scenario, you can set the target of the object dragged to the cursor, so it will follow the cursor, without having a rigid movement (as if we would set frame after frame the position of the object to the mouse coordinates). Moreover, you can use the **Anchor** to specify where the object should be attached. For instance, if the player started to drag from a corner of the object, you can set the **Anchor** to be there, and as a result, the object will hang from that point.

You can find this joint in one of the exercises of the last chapter to improve the look of your game.

Wheel Joint 2D

The Wheel Joint 2D is a combination of a spring and motor kind of joint, and it has a very specific usage. As the name suggests, it simulates the constraint that a wheel can impose on a body. In particular, it can rotate the wheel with a motor (the wheel moves) and simulate suspensions with a spring.

More specifically, the joint applies a linear force to both connected rigid bodies to keep them on the line, an angular motor to rotate them on the line, and a spring to simulate the wheel suspension.

It is interesting to note that you can reconstruct a **Wheel Joint 2D** with the combination of a **Slider Joint 2D** (with both **Use Motor** and **Use Limits** off) and a **Hinge Joint 2D** (with **Use Limits** off).

It appears like the following in the **Inspector**:

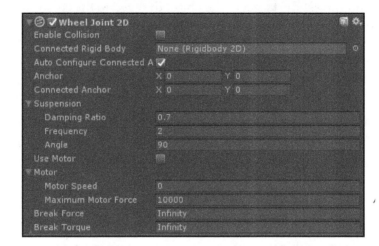

As you can see from the preceding screenshot, the parameters are divided into **Suspension**, which defines a spring, and a motor. Both use the same parameters we have already seen respectively for springs (with the exception of **Angle**) and motors.

The suspension is defined by the following:

- **Angle**: This specifies the angle (in degrees in world coordinates) where the suspension happens. By default, it is set to 90 degrees, which means the suspension will happen upwards, as usually happens for a car (the body of the car is on top of the wheels, so the direction of the suspension is along the positive *y*-axis, which means 90 degrees) as shown in the following diagram:

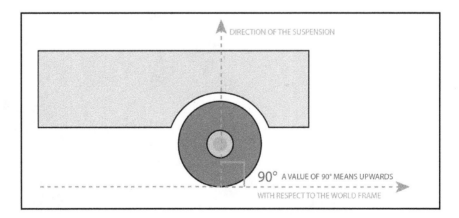

In this diagram, we can see the the angle of the suspension for the wheel of the car is at 90 degrees, which means upwards in the game world. This is the default value. Imagine you want to have a car that is able to run on the ceiling thanks to magnetic wheels; you may consider changing the angle of the suspension. In the case of the ceiling, it is the opposite of the normal situation, so the angle will be 270 degrees.

- **Damping Ratio**: This specifies how much the motion of the spring is suppressed (refer to either the *Spring 2D Joint* or *Fixed 2D Joint* section for more details).
- **Frequency**: This specifies the frequency of the spring (refer to either the *Spring 2D Joint* or *Fixed 2D Joint* section for more details).

The motor is defined by:

- **Motor Speed**: This specifies the speed that the motor should achieve on the wheel
- **Max Motor Force**: This specifies the maximum force that the motor can apply on the wheel in order to achieve **Motor Speed** on the wheel

Needless to tell you which is the most common usage of this joint. Every time in your game you have a wheel and it needs to move in a realistic manner, this joint is the deal for you.

If you want to create a car controlled by the player, you can attach this joint to the wheels and set **Motor Speed** to 0 to control this variable through your script based on the player's input. Moreover, you can use **Max Motor Force** to simulate the different gears.

Effectors

Imagine our hero is crossing an enchanted room, so he starts to float due a powerful spell. In this case, while the hero is within this room, gravity should be contrasted by a (magical) force. As a result, we need to specify that in that room, there is a force that makes our hero levitate.

Similarly, imagine the hero drops a box in a lake. The box doesn't sink at the same velocity as it falls; moreover, it might float. Therefore, in our game, we need to specify that the region delimited by the lake has special physical properties.

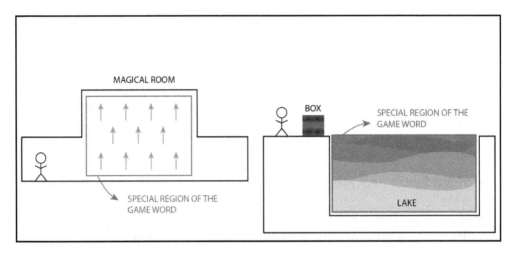

There are some special regions of the game world where the physical laws could be different from the rest of the game world; in Unity, these regions can be specified with effectors

In Unity, this can be achieved by using effectors. Effectors are some components that affect the behaviour of rigidbodies in certain region of the game world. They are really different from each other, because they do different things, although the core concept is the same: they affect one or more rigidbodies that come into the region that they control.

Effectors use collision detection to know which are the rigidbodies within their region, and therefore, as we already mentioned before, the rigidbodies need to have a collider. Otherwise, they won't be affected by the effector.

Moreover, the effectors themselves need their own collider to work. This, in order to be used by the effector they should have the **Used By Effector** property set to true. Otherwise, the effector will not affect any rigidbody. If the collider of the effector should be set to be the trigger or not depends both on the kind of effector and on what are you trying to achieve, although there is a default way to set it (in fact, Unity gives you a warning in case you are using the effector in an unusual way).

We will see this case by case, and here is a summary table with the effectors, saying whether the collider should use **is Trigger** or not:

Effector	Linked collider should be a trigger?
Constant Force 2D	This component is attached to rigidbodies, not colliders
Area Effector 2D	True
Buoyancy Effector 2D	True
Point Effector 2D	True
Platform Effector 2D	False
Surface Effector 2D	False

All of them (with the exception of Constant Force 2D) have a couple of variables to determine which rigidbodies are affected by the effector, and these variables are:

- **Use Collider Mask**: If enabled, this allows you to discriminate the colliders that enter in the area through layers specified in the next variable.
- **Collider Mask**: This determines which layers are affected by the effector. Once again, remember that you can learn how to add layers in Chapter 2, *Baking Cupcake Towers*. So, in this variable, you can specify one of them through the use of a drop-down menu.

Let's see each one of them in detail to better understand how they work.

Constant Force 2D

This is not a proper effector, because instead of acting in an area or region, it is directly applied onto a rigidbody. So it needs to be attached to the same game object that has the rigidbody component.

Here is how it appears in the **Inspector**:

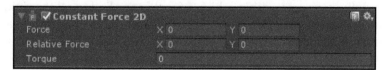

Out of curiosity, for this component, there is a 3D counterpart: **Constant Force**.

As the name suggests, it applies a constant force to the rigidbody. Usually this is used in testing to easily apply a force from the **Inspector**, but it can also be used in the normal gameplay if we need an object that is always under the control of a constant force (so that it will keep pushing). Of course, it's value can be changed through script to make it a non-constant force, but in that case it is preferable to apply the force directly with a function in the script. The component should be used only for constant forces or forces that don't change over time (the force can change, but for long periods of time it remains constant).

Moreover, this component also can be used to apply a torque on the rigidbody.

Here are the three variables:

- **Force**: The constant force to apply to the rigidbody.
- **Relative Force**: The constant force to apply to the rigidbody expressed with respect to the rigidbody coordinates
- **Torque**: The constant torque to apply to the rigidbody

Here is an example of usage that is not testing. Suppose you are doing a game where different objects are affected by different gravitational forces. So for instance, brown boxes will follow on the ground as usual, but green boxes will follow on the right because as per your game design they are supposed to do so. The reason could be an experimental serum invented to change gravity for things that are green. In this scenario, the green boxes cannot be affected by normal gravity, so you can place on them a rigidbody and set **Gravity Scale** to 0. In this way, it won't be affected by normal gravity. Then, place on it the **Constant 2D** force component and set your gravity. Moreover, if all the objects have different **Constant 2D** forces, you can change their gravity force in real time, maybe after the invention of another serum, which changes the gravity on the left instead of the right.

Area Effector 2D

This component defines an area within which a force is applied to all the rigidbodies inside the area. You can configure the force at any angle with a specific magnitude and random variation on that magnitude. You can also apply both linear and angular drag forces to slow down rigidbody 2Ds.

This effector, in order to work, requires a collider with both **Used By Effector** and **is Trigger** set to true. In fact, rigidbodies should be able to enter in it.

The component has two foldouts (expandable menu options) for the relative options to set, **Force** and **Damping**, as we can see from this diagram, which shows the component in the **Inspector**:

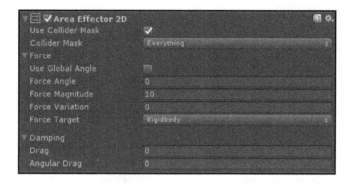

 The two foldouts appear only in recent versions of Unity. So if you are using an old version and you don't see them, don't worry; the options have just been reordered, but they still work as described here.

All the variables have intuitive names, but let's go through them quickly:

- **Use Global Angle**: If checked, the next variable will be interpreted in the world coordinates, and local coordinates otherwise.
- **Force Angle**: This is the angle of the force to apply, and so it defines the direction.
- **Force Magnitude**: This is the magnitude, which means the intensity of the force.
- **Force Variation**: This is the variation of the magnitude of the force so as to not have always a constant force and improve realism. Be careful not to give too high value, which may quickly result in undesired behaviour.
- **Force Target**: This can be either the **Rigidbody** or **Collider**. In the first case, the force will always be applied to the center of the mass. In the second case, if the collider is not on the center of the mass, the force will also generate torque for the rigidbody.
- **Drag**: This is the linear drag to apply within the region.
- **Angular Drag**: This is the angular drag to apply within the region.

Here is an example of the use of this component. Suppose that there is a special device which is able to push the magnetic shoes of the main character to contrast gravity. So, in the area just above this device, you can place an area effector, specifying a force that goes upwards. Please note that if the intensity of the force is less than the gravity, then your character will have a big jump, but eventually she will fall down. Whereas with a greater value, even without a jump she starts to levitate upwards until either an obstacle or the end of the area effector is met.

Buoyancy Effector 2D

This component is used to simulate a fluid, and so it can potentially make rigidbodies floating. It requires a collider with both **Used By Effector** and **is Trigger** set to true. In fact, rigidbodies should be able to enter it.

It appears like the following in the **Inspector**:

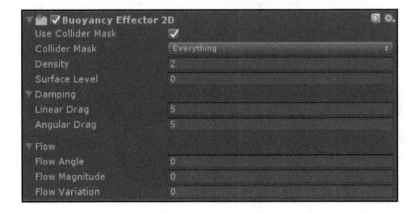

 As we can see from this screenshot, there are two foldouts to help the logical order of the component. Don't worry if they aren't there. You may be using an older version of Unity.

The main variables are the following:

- **Density**: This indicates the density of the fluid, and it affects how the different rigidbodies are affected by the effector depending on the rigidbody density as well. In fact, rigidbodies with a higher density will sink, those with a lower density will float, and those with the same density of the fluid will be suspended in the fluid.
- **Surface Level**: This indicates where the surface of the fluid is with respect to the Transform (the position) of the game object where the effector is attached. A value of zero means that the surface will lie on the center of the object, and it is placed in the middle of the collider (only if the collider doesn't have any offset). You can recognize it from the blue line in the **Scene** view.
- **Drag**: This is the linear drag to apply within the region below the surface.
- **Angular Drag**: This is the angular drag to apply within the region below the surface.
- **Flow Angle**: This specifies the angle, in world coordinates, where the flow force of the effector is applied. Therefore, it defines the direction of the force.
- **Flow Magnitude**: This specifies the intensity of the flow force, and therefore the level of buoyancy of the effector. It can assume negative values, and in this case, it's as if **Flow Angle** has been rotated by 180 degrees.
- **Flow Variation**: This indicates how much **Flow Magnitude** can vary, so as to not have it constant and therefore achieving a higher level of realism.

The component appears like this in the **Scene** view, to actually show where the surface level is:

Furthermore, here is an example of its usage. Suppose that in your 2D game there is the sea, and the main character has to jump on some platforms in the harbor. Placing this effector at the level of the sea will make its behaviour more realistic. For instance, the main character can push a wooden box down in the sea, which will float, and so she can jump on top of the floating box to cross.

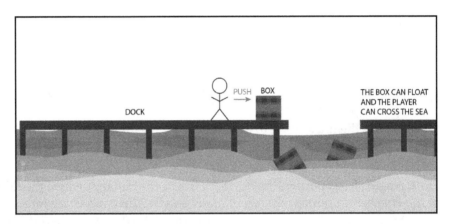

An example of use of the Buoyancy Effector 2D, which is able to simulate the sea and make the wooden boxes float; as a result, the player can jump on top of the wooden box and cross the sea

Point Effector 2D

You can imagine this component to be a magnet of rigidbodies, so it can push/repulse or attract them, which is concentrated at a single point, as the name of the effector suggests. The point can be determined by either the collider (most used) or the rigidbody attached to the same game object of the effector.

The component requires a collider with both **Used By Effector** and **is Trigger** set to true. In fact, rigidbodies should be able to enter in it.

It appears like this in the **Inspector**:

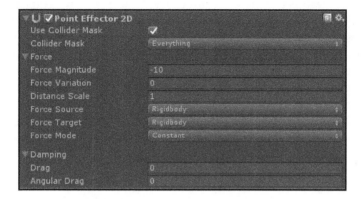

 Once again, the foldouts are only in recent versions of Unity.

The main variables are the following:

- **Force Magnitude**: The magnitude, which means the intensity of the force.
- **Force Variation**: The variation of the magnitude of the force in order not to always have a constant force and improve realism. Be careful not to give too high value, which may quickly result in undesired behaviours.
- **Distance Scale**: When the distance between the rigidbody and the attractive or repulsive point is calculated, it is scaled by (multiplied by) **Distance Scale**. As such, you are able to modify the behaviour of the effector (see **Force Mode** in this list).
- **Force Source**: This can be either a **Rigidbody** or **Collider**. In the first case, the point that attracts or repulses will be placed on the center of the rigidbody (which means at its center of the mass). In the second case, it will be placed in the middle of the collider.
- **Force Target**: This can be either a **Rigidbody** or **Collider**. In the first case, the force will always be applied to the center of the mass of the rigidbody entering in the effector. In the second case, if the collider is not centered on the center of the mass, the force will also generate torque for the rigidbody.

- **Force Mode**: This specifies how the force is calculated, and it can be of three types. **Constant** is the most intuitive. The force is always constant regardless of the distance between the rigidbody affected by the effector and the point that repulses or attracts. This means that only the relative positions between the rigidbody and the point are taken into consideration to determine the direction of the force, which lies on both. Instead, in **Inverse Linear**, the force changes its intensity based on the distance between the rigidbody and the point. For double the distance, half intensity of the force. Finally, **Inverse Squared**, which in most cases is the most physically realistic, takes the square of the distance into consideration. This means, for double the distance, a quarter the intensity of the force.

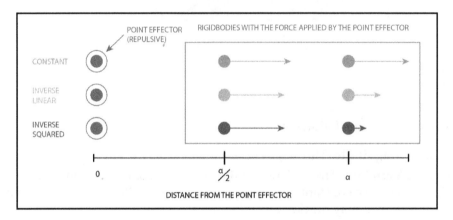

Differences between the different force modes

In this diagram, on the left is a repulsive point effector. Below is a distance scale, all included within the range of the point effector. Suppose that at a distance of half alpha, three different rigidbodies have the same applied force from the point of effect. At a distance of alpha, the constant mode will keep its whole force applied on the rigidbody. The **Inverse Linear** mode will halve the force by doubling the distance. Finally, the **Inversed Squared** mode (which is the most physically realistic, since both the gravitation and the electromagnetic forces have this behaviour) will have a quarter of the force it would have half way closer to the point effector.

- **Drag**: This is the linear drag to apply within the region of the effector.
- **Angular Drag**: This is the angular drag to apply within the region of the effector.

Here is an example of its usage. Suppose the main character has a special ring that, when active, attracts metal (when the ring is not, it will attract the main character's wife). Therefore, every time that the player activates the ring, the game activates a point effector on the main character, and through the **Collision Mask** variable, only metals can be selected.

Platform Effector 2D

This component gives the effect of a platform for 2D games. For instance, it implements the one-way collision. So if the character jumps from below the platform, he will cross it, but when he lands on top, the platform will give a collision, maintaining the character on top of the platform. Moreover, it can be used to remove side-friction/bounce.

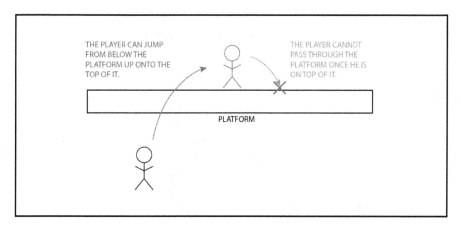

With this effector, the player is able to cross a collider in one direction but not the other way round. In some platform games, the player is able to jump on top of the platform by jumping underneath it, but he or she cannot fall back.

In fact, this is the most used component to build platform games. Think about games like *Braid*, where the player is able to jump on top of a platform from a platform that is underneath.

The component requires a collider with **Used By Effector** set to true but not **is Trigger**. In fact, rigidbodies should be able to collide with it.

This is how it appears in the **Inspector**:

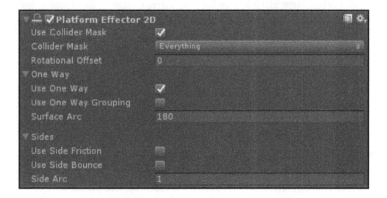

 Once again, the foldouts are present only in recent versions of Unity. Moreover, the rotational offset is a parameter that has been added recently.

And here you can see one possible instance in the **Scene** view of this component.

This is how the effector appears in the Scene view when its gizmos are active

The big arc on top defines from which direction the platform/collider is not traversable, whereas the two small side arcs define which direction is considered the side of the platform.

The main variables are the following:

- **Rotational Offset**: This indicates the angular offset in degrees of the whole platform effector. This has been added recently in Unity, and thanks to it, it is possible to rotate the platform effector so as to have platforms that are inclined, or walls that can be crossed one way. For instance, you can use it also for magical portals that can be crossed one way.
- **Use One Way**: If checked, the platform will collide only in one direction.

- **Use One Way Grouping**: This ensures that all contacts disabled by the one-way behaviour act on all colliders. This is useful when multiple colliders are used on the object passing through the platform and they all need to act together as a group.
- **Surface Arc**: This specifies in degrees how wide the arc on top of which the collision will be performed is. In all the other directions, if **Use One Way** is enabled, it won't allow any collision, allowing any rigidbody to pass through, such as your character.
- **Use Side Friction**: If true, friction is applied to the side of the platform effector.
- **Use Side Bounce**: If true, bounce is applied to the side of the platform effector.
- **Side Arc**: This specifies the degree for both the right and left side (if the **Rotational Offset** is set to 0; otherwise it may indicate up and down) that are considered the sides of the platform effector. So, if **Use Side Frictionor** and **Use Side Bounce** is enabled, this will be applied along the arc specified here.

Besides the classical use of this component to create platform games, let's see another example in which we may want to use it. Imagine a puzzle game where some portals can be crossed only in one direction. As such, we can place a platform effector and set its **Rotational Offset** so as to have the colliding part only on one side of the portal. As a result, the character will be able to cross the magical portal only in one direction, and not in the other way round as shown in the following diagram:

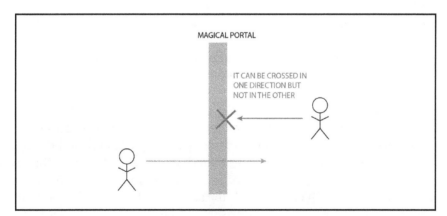

This is an example of how it is possible to use this effector in another way that is not the classical platform. By rotating the component through the **Rotational Offset**, it is possible to make a magical portal which is crossable in one way, but not in another. This could be an interesting game mechanic for a puzzle game.

Surface Effector 2D

This component applies a tangential force to the surface specified by the collider associated with this effector. In other words, you can imagine this as a conveyor belt, which transports rigidbodies along the direction of the force, as far as they are touching the surface.

This is how it appears in the **Inspector**:

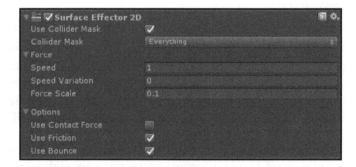

It is possible to have access to the options of the **Surface Effector 2D** through two foldouts, and you can find the parameter that you can set here:

- **Speed**: The speed that the tangential force should maintain. In other words, it's the speed of the conveyor belt.
- **Speed Variation**: The maximum variation of the speed, so as to not have always a constant speed, especially if you have many of these effectors. The random variation ranges from zero to the value in **Speed Variation**. Therefore, a positive value brings a random increment, whereas a negative value brings a random decrement.
- **Speed Scale**: This allows you to scale the tangential force that is applied when the effector tries to accelerate the contacting rigidbodies to the specified speed along the surface. If it is set to 0, then no force is actually applied, and it is like that the component is disabled. On the other hand, if it is set to 1, means that the full force is applied. A useful way to think of this parameter is to think about how fast the rigidbody, which is in contact with the surface, is then accelerated to meet the specified speed; lower values means it will require more time, whereas higher values means it will reach the speed much quicker. However, you should be careful to use the full force, since a rigidbody might face other forces, leading the rigidbody to an undesired motion.

- **Use Contact Force**: If true, a contact force will be used. Although it is more physically realistic, it may impress a torque to the rigidbody contacting the surface. As such, in video games where realism depends on the design, you can choose to enable it, since the default is disabled. An easy way to imagine this is that you are jumping on a real conveyor belt. The contact force along with the tangential force of the conveyor belt will make your legs move forward, but your chest will stay behind due to inertia, which may result in you falling. That means your body has started to rotate due a torque as shown in the following diagram:

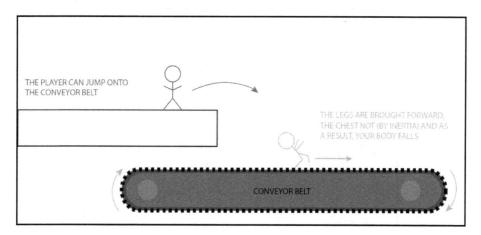

In this example, when you jump on the conveyor belt, your legs are brought forward by the tangential force of the belt. Your chest, instead, stays behind due to inertia, leading to an applied torque on your body, and therefore you will fall. In Unity, it is possible to disable the contact force, so as to ensure that a torque is not applied to rigidbodies that enter in contact with the conveyor belt.

- **Use Friction**: If true, there will be friction on the surface
- **Use Bounce**: If true, there will be bounce on the surface

Of course, the natural example of usage is when in your game a conveyor belt is used. But let's try to find out another example. Suppose that the protagonist of your game has a special glove that when it touches a metal wall, it is able to contrast gravity by creating a magnetic field. You can place a surface effector vertically, and apply a force upwards as far as the player is touching that wall.

Physics Material 2D

Unity also offers the possibility to create physics materials so as to adjust the friction and bounciness of a physical object when it collides with another one. In the case of 2D, this is enabled by the **Physics Material 2D**.

You can create a **Physics Material 2D** by selecting **Assets | Create | Physics Material 2D** from the top-bar menu as shown in the following screenshot:

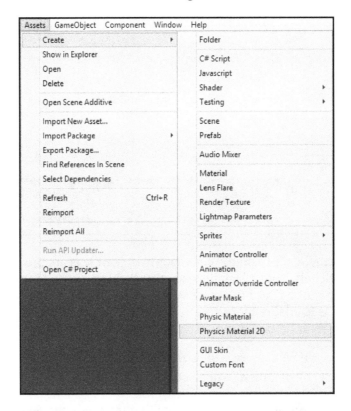

Once selected in the project panel, we can tweak its two values in the **Inspector**, as shown here:

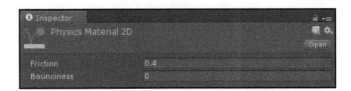

It's worthwhile mentioning that we have seen many variables during this chapter to assign a **Physics Material 2D**, and they are structured in a simple hierarchy:

1. If a **Collider** has a **Physics Material 2D**, this takes the priority and will be set to **Collider**.
2. If a **Collider** doesn't have a **Physics Material 2D**, then it will be assigned the one in the **Rigidbody2D**.
3. If even the **Rigidbody2D** doesn't have a **Physics Material 2D**, then the default **Physics Material 2D** will be assigned. The default **Physics Material 2D** can be set in **Physics Settings**.

Dealing with physics in Unity

So far, everything went smooth and we learned about all the single components of the Physics engine of Unity. However, when it comes to building your own game, dealing with physics might be a little bit tricky. In fact, just some wrong values on some forces and the whole scene can quickly mess up. The best way to solve this is by trial and error. The more you experiment, the more you will become practical with the Physics engine, and you will develop an intuition on how to balance all the values in your game. As a result, you will be able to make your scene act as described in the game design document (or almost).

Dealing with physics isn't just about placing the different components, but also about how to program them. We have already seen some useful functions to apply on a rigidbody as well as some events when two colliders hit each other. But there is more. First of all, it's important to understand that all the variables we have seen of all the components (such as rigidbodies, colliders, joints, and effectors) can be assigned dynamically at runtime with a script. You just need to get a reference to that component, and then you will be able to change its internal parameters.

One more thing that can come in handy is the possibility to query the Physics engine through some functions in order to gather some information about the surroundings. These are static functions of the `Physics2D` class, and so they can be called with the following fragment of code:

```
Physics2D.NameOfTheFunction();
```

Of course, you need to substitute NameOfTheFunction with the function. The Physics2D class exposes many of these, but let's explore just the main ones:

- OverlapCircleAll(Vector2 point, float radius, *[optional parameters]*): This returns the arrays of Collider2D which are all within the circle specified by the radius and point (the center of the circle) variables. In other words, it detects all the colliders that are within the specified circle. From the collider, it is possible to retrieve the game object itself as well. Our cupcake towers will use this function to detect how many enemies there are around. Furthermore, other optional parameters of the function are available to specify a mask of layers and the min and max values for the depth (z-axis) in which the function should search.

- OverlapCircle(Vector2 point, float radius, *[optional parameters]*): The same function as before, but instead of returning the full array, it returns the first occurrence. It is useful when you just need to detect whether something is present within the circle.

- RaycastAll(Vector2 origin, Vector2 direction, *[optional parameters]*): This shoots a ray from an origin towards a direction, and returns all the different colliders that the ray hits within an array of RayCastHit2D (see later), which is a class that specifies all the details of the hit, including the collider. This function is useful when you need to verify if something is present somewhere in the space. Furthermore, other optional parameter can specify the maximum distance that the ray can reach, a mask of layers, and the min and max values for the depth (z-axis).

- Raycast(Vector2 origin, Vector2 direction, *[optional parameters]*): The same function as the previous one, but instead of returning the full array, it returns only the first hit.

You can find all the functions of the Physics2D class in the official documentation here:
https://docs.unity3d.com/ScriptReference/Physics2D.html.

About the RayCastHit2D class, here is the list of information that we can retrieve:

- centroid: The centroid of the primitive used to perform the cast
- collider: The collider hit by the ray
- distance: The distance from the origin of the ray to the impact point
- fraction: The fraction of the distance along the ray that the hit occurred
- normal: The normal vector of the surface hit by the ray

- `point`: The point in the world space where the ray hit the collider's surface
- `rigidbody`: The `Rigidbody2D` attached to the object that was hit
- `transform`: The Transform of the object that was hit

In conclusion, querying the Physics engine is a common practice to gather information, and we will do it with our *Tower* Defense game.

Other things about Physics

As with other chapters, this is an optional section with some deeper insights into the topic covered in the chapter. So, feel free to skip this section if you are not interested, and jump directly onto the next section. Otherwise, just grab some more coffee and keep reading.

The Simulate setting on rigidbodies

This aim of this section is to explain the difference between enabling and disabling physical components on a rigidbody and enabling and disabling the **Simulate** settings on top of the rigidbody component.

Every time that a physical component is either added, enabled, removed, or disabled, the internal memory of the Physics engine is updated (respectively to add or remove the component from the memory). When the **Simulate** setting is disabled, the Physics engine just stops to perform calculations on it – it doesn't erase the object from the memory. As a result, when **Simulate** is checked back, the Physics engine has already all the objects/components in the memory and it doesn't' need to create them from scratch, thus leading to a performance improvement.

Of course, if you need to remove a rigidbody permanently from the scene, then just erase the component, because if you just uncheck **Simulate**, the component will still be in memory, leading to a poor memory management.

Physics Raycaster 2D component

Back in Chapter 3, *Communicating with the Player – the User Interface*, we have seen the Unity UI system, and in the optional section there were the different components of a canvas. One of them was the **Graphical Raycaster**, which is able to detect the input of the user on the screen. This component checks if the player actually went over a slider or clicked a button, and then triggers events by exchanging messages with the event system.

If we have physics objects and we want to exchange events about them in a similar way the **Graphical Raycaster** does for the UI, we can use a Physics Raycaster 2D component on a camera to handle such events.

Once this component is added, you can implement different interfaces in the scripts of your physics objects. As a result, the functions that they will implement will be automatically called when the corresponding event is triggered.

For instance, an event could be that a joint breaks, and you may want to run some code when this happens. Moreover, some information will be provided to the functions; in the case of the joint, the amount of force that broke the joint is passed as a parameter.

The other Physics settings

Here you can find the other Physics settings:

- **Velocity Iterations**: The number of iterations that are made to determine the velocity of a physical body during an update. The higher is the number, the more accurate the simulation will be. The drawback is computational cost. The default value is 8.
- **Position Iterations**: The number of iteration made to determine the position of a physical body during an update. The higher is the number, the more accurate the simulation will be. The drawback is computational cost. The default value is 3.
- **Velocity Threshold**: Collisions with a relative velocity lower than this value are treated as inelastic collisions, which means that the colliding bodies will not bounce off each other.
- **Max Linear Correction**: The maximum linear position correction used when solving constraints. It can have any value between 0.0001 to 1000000. It helps to prevent overshooting.

- **Max Angular Correction**: The maximum angular correction used when solving constraints. It can have any value between `0.0001` to `1000000`. It helps to prevent overshooting.
- **Max Translation Speed**: This is the maximum (translation) speed that a body in your game could have. This value is the upper limit, which means that every object that tries to reach faster velocities, will be cap to this value.
- **Max Rotation Speed**: This is the maximum (rotation) speed that a body in your game could have. The same reasoning as before applies, just with rotations instead of translations.
- **Min Penetration For Penalty**: The minimum contact penetration radius allowed before any separation impulse force is applied.
- **Baumgarte Scale**: This is a scale factor that determines how fast collision overlaps are resolved (see the information box).
- **Baumgarte Time Of Impact Scale**: A scale factor that determines how fast time-of-impact overlaps are resolved (see the information box).

Baumgarte's constraint stabilization method (sometimes just abbreviated to Baumgarte's method) is an algorithm for resolving certain collision constraints, such as with joints, invented by J. Baumgarte in 1972. It is fast enough so that it can be used in real-time applications such as video games or robotics. The trick consists of taking advantage of some derived analytic forms of differential equations that are solved numerically. This allows you to run the algorithm not only faster than its predecessors but also with a higher degree of accuracy.

The **Baumgarte Scale** is the important parameter for the algorithm, which represents the correction ratio to apply. A common value, which is often given as default, is `0.2` and it is also the default value that Unity uses. The higher the value, the more your joints will go wild. On the other hand, the lower the value, the less your joints will do, and it can cause sponginess.

- **Queries Hit Trigger**: This is a toggle that if true allows raycasts to hit also trigger volumes. By default, it is true, but can be unchecked in case you don't want raycasting to hit trigger volumes, but just colliders. When to uncheck this box really depends on the design of your game, and what you have in mind to program it.

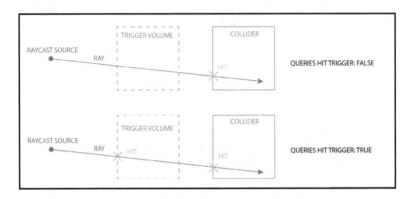

When Queries Hit Trigger is set to false (upper part of diagram), trigger volumes won't be detected by raycasting. On the contrary, when Queries Hit Trigger is set to true (lower part of diagram), also trigger volumes will be detected by raycasting and returned as a hit.

- **Queries Start In Collider**: This is a toggle that, if true, allows raycasts that start within a collider to what hit that collider. By default, it is true, but can be unchecked if many of your raycasts start within a collider and you don't want them to be returned as hits. Again, when to uncheck this box really depends on the design of your game, and also you have in mind to program it.

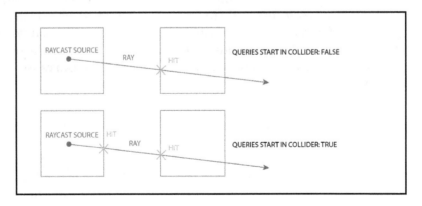

When Queries Start In Collider is set to false (upper part of diagram) and the the source of the raycast is within a collider, this one won't be returned as a hit. On the contrary, when Queries Start In Collider is set to true (lower part of diagram), also the collider in which there is the source of the raycast is returned as a hit.

- **Change Stops Playback**: This is a toggle that, if true, stops reporting collision callbacks immediately if any of the GameObjects involved in the collision are deleted or moved. By default, it is false.
- **Gizmos**: (The description of this foldout is in the next section.)

Gizmos for colliders

This section describes the previous menu item, **Gizmos**, in the **Physics 2D** settings.

Gizmos is a foldout that shows you extra options about the visualizations of colliders within the editor. These options are really useful in debugging. This is how it appears in the **Inspector**:

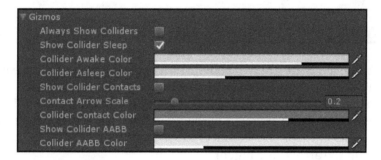

Here is an explanation of the options displayed and their usage:

- **Always Show Colliders**: By default, you are able to see a collider only when a game object (or one of its children) contains such a collider. If you enable this option, you will always be able to see colliders (whenever **Gizmos** are visible).
- **Show Collider Sleep**: When enabled, it allows you to see a collider even when it is in sleep mode within the Physics engine
- **Collider Awake Color**: This specifies the color that awake (no-sleeping) colliders should have when shown. By default, it is a light green with the alpha channel (opacity) set to 192.
- **Collider Sleep Color**: This specifies the color that sleeping colliders should have when shown. By default, it is the same light green as when the collider is awake, but with the alpha channel (opacity) set to 92.
- **Show Collider Contacts**: When enabled, this allows you to see the contacts point of the colliders when they collide. They are shown as arrows (as shown in the next diagram).

- **Contact Arrow Scale**: This value allows you to scale down the arrow showed by the contact points of the collider. By default, its value is 0.2 (as shown in the next diagram).
- **Collider Contact Color**: This specifies the color of such arrows representing the contact points of the collider. By default, it is set to light purple (as shown in the next diagram):

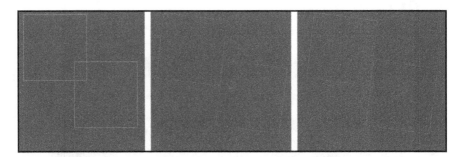

On the left there are two colliders that are overlapping with each other. In the middle, the colliders are updated by the Physics engine to simulate the collisions (since they cannot overlap). Also shown are the points of contact between the two arrows. On the right, there is the same diagram that is in the middle, but with the **Contact Arrow Scale** set to 0.6 instead of 0.2, and as a result the arrows are bigger.

- **Show Collider AABB**: When enabled, this allows you to see the **Axis-Aligned Bounding Box** (**AABB**) of the collider. As the name suggests, it is a box that fully contains the collider, and it is aligned with the axis of the world frame. For example, the bounding box of a polygonal collider is the following (on the left):

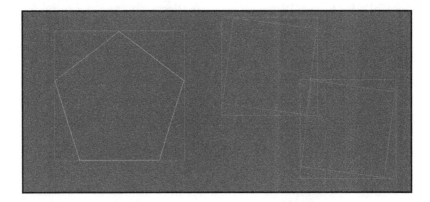

On the left is the polygonal collider with its AABB; on the right is the same diagram as the previous one, but showing its AABB.

- **Collider AABB Color**: This specifies the color of the AABB of the collider, when shown

Physics for our game

In this section we will apply some concepts of this chapter into our game. In particular, we will see how to detect when a sprinkle hits a panda and applies damage to it using the Physics engine.

Set up Pandas as a rigidbodies

Since we will take advantage of the Physics engine, we need to proper set up the Panda as that to be a physical object in the scene. This means giving it a rigidbody component.

Therefore, we can start by adding a **Rigidbody2D** component to the Panda prefab, and set its **Body Type** as **Kinematic**, as shown in the following screenshot:

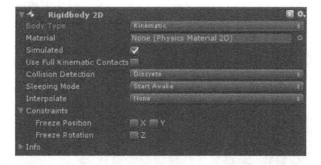

In theory, we should have done, since the Panda is considered a physical object now. However, in the previous chapter, we have written a function that allows the Panda to move by assigning its new position directly on its Transform. Since now the Panda has a **Rigidbody2D** component, we cannot do in this way anymore (as we already explained previously in the *Rigidbodies* section). Therefore, we need to slightly modify the PandaScript. In particular, we need to get a reference to the rigidbody of the Panda, then use the MovePosition() function for Kinematic rigidbodies. Basically, we are applying what we have learnt in the *Dealing with rigidbodies* section.

Hence, open the script, and add the following private variable:

```
//Private variable to store the rigidbody2D
private Rigidbody2D rb2D;
```

Then, in the `Start()` function add this line at the end of the function:

```
//Get the reference to the Rigidbody2d
rb2D = GetComponent<Rigidbody2D>();
```

In the `MoveTowards()` function, we need to use the `MovePosition()` function on the Panda's rigidbody to change its position. In addition, we shouldn't use `deltaTime` anymore, and substitute it with `fixedDeltaTime`. As such, here is highlighted what is changed from the previous chapter:

```
//Function that based on the speed of the Panda makes it moving towards the
destination point, specified as Vector3
private void MoveTowards(Vector3 destination) {
  //Create a step and then move in towards destination of one step
  float step = speed * Time.fixedDeltaTime;
  rb2D.MovePosition(Vector3.MoveTowards(transform.position,
    destination, step));
}
```

We need to remember that the `MoveTowards()` function, now, should be called within a `FixedUpdate()` and not in the `Update()`. We will see this in Chapter 7, *Trading Cupcakes and the Ultimate Battle for the Cake – Gameplay Programming*. But you can have an example in the next section.

Finally, we can save the script, and we have done with the Panda.

Set up projectiles as rigidbodies

Similar to what we did for the Pandas, we need to add a **Rigidbody2D** component to all the projectiles, and again set the **Body Type** to **Kinematic**.

If you remember, also projectiles used to move by changing directly their Transforms, and we need to fix this, since they have a **Rigidbody2D** component as well.

Open the script, and as we did for the Pandas, add the following private variable:

```
//Private variable to store the rigidbody2D
private Rigidbody2D rb2D;
```

Then, in the `Start()` function, let's get the reference to it:

```
//Get the reference to the Rigidbody2d
rb2D = GetComponent<Rigidbody2D>();
```

Now, we need to replace the `Update()` function with the `FixedUpdate()` one, since we are dealing with the Physics engine. Moreover, we need to slightly change the code (note also the use of the `fixedDeltaTime`):

```
// Update the position of the projectile according to time and speed
void FixedUpdate() {
  rb2D.MovePosition(transform.position + direction *
    Time.fixedDeltaTime * speed);
}
```

A careful reader would notice that we are applying the equation of motion explained in the information box within the *Dealing with rigidbodies* section. In particular, here we have split the velocity into a direction and a speed (which multiplied them together give back the velocity).

Save the script, and let's see how we can detect when a sprinkle hits a panda in the next section.

Detect sprinkles

In order to detect a collision between a sprinkle and a Panda, we need to add them both a **Collider2D**. You can choose the one that better suits your needs, I'll go for the **Box2D** collider. Then, you need to make one of them act as a Trigger, in our example we can take the Panda.

The next step is to implement the `OnTriggerEnter2D()` function, which is called from the Physics engine of Unity, on the `PandaScript`. As a result, we are able to detect when something hits the panda, and check if it is an actual sprinkle, so to apply damage to the panda with the `Hit()` function written in the previous chapter.

```
//Function that detects projectiles
void OnTriggerEnter2D(Collider2D other) {
  //Check if the other object is a projectile
  if(other.tag == "Projectile") {
    //Apply damage to this panda with the Hit function
    Hit(other.GetComponent<ProjectileScript>().damage);
  }
}
```

Of course, we need to be sure that every object with the Projectile tag have a **ProjectileScript** component attached. This check is left as an exercise.

Finally, save the script, and we have done with Physics for our game, at least in this chapter. In fact, in the next chapter, we will use again the Physics engine, but for other reasons.

Homework

As in every chapter, here are some exercises that you can use to practice your skills:

1. **The forgotten rigidbody**: Sometimes components in the **Inspector** could be forgotten. However, we can facilitate the process by creating warnings in the code. For both our Panda and the sprinkles, create within their scripts a check, when the game object is initialized, to add a **Rigidbody2D** component, if missing, and set it to be **Kinematic**. Additionally, you can print a warning message (See Chapter 8, *What Is beyond the Cake?*, for more about debugging messages).

2. **Passion for acceleration**: In the chapter, we saw how we could implement motion equations for our **Kinematic** rigidbodies. In particular, the chapter shown an implementation of the velocity equation. Now, try to implement the acceleration equation for a **Kinematic** rigidbody.

3. **Joint Master**: For each one of the joints that Unity offers, think about a possible usage and example (possibly different from the ones already presented in the chapter). Then, sketch the physical system on paper, and determine which are the rigidbodies and where the anchor points are. Finally, reproduce what you have imagined within Unity, and tweak all the settings until it works as you have decided.

4. **Effector Master**: For each one of the effectors that Unity offers, think about a possible usage and example (possibly different from the ones already presented in the chapter). Then, sketch how the effector should work on paper, and determine how the different rigidbodies would interact with it. Finally, reproduce what you have imagined within Unity, and tweak all the settings until it works as you have decided.

5. **A less dauntless Panda (Part III)**: If you also completed the second part of this exercise back in Chapter 4, *No Longer Alone – Sweet-Toothed Pandas Strike*, some pandas will be stunned, others not, depending on the Boolean value. Instead of exposing this Boolean within the **Inspector**, add this property to the Projectile

class, so that if the Panda is stunned or not depends on which kind of projectile the Panda was hit with (we will see this later in `Chapter 6`, *Through a Sea of Sprinkles – Navigation in Artificial Intelligence*).

6. **A less dauntless Panda (Part IV)**: After you have done part three of this exercise, if the poor panda is under attack with too many sprinkles, it might not move anymore because it is always in a stunned state. As a result, it won't able to avoid the sprinkles either. So as to avoid this, we need to modify the Panda script such that if another sprinkle hits the Panda while it is stunned, it detracts the health from the Panda; but doesn't trigger from the beginning the hit animation and/or the stun period.

7. **A less dauntless Panda (Part V)**: Now that you have also completed the third part of this exercise, let's improve the whole system of stunning a Panda. Add to each projectile, a variable that indicates the chance of this projectile to stunning a Panda. Finally, trigger the stunning phase of the Panda probabilistically based on the previous variable.

Finally, if you are into challenges, here is one for you:

8. **The frozen conveyor belt (Part I)**: Imagine a conveyor belt that is made of a big piece of ice and scrolls quite fast. Think and describe what would happen when a box is dropped onto it. Keep in mind that the friction on the ice is really low, and that there is inertia to consider. What if, instead of a box, there was a sphere? The solution is available at the end of the book.

9. **The frozen conveyor belt (Part II)**: Once you have done Part I, reproduce the frozen conveyor belt within the Physics engine of Unity, and try it out with boxes and spheres.

Summary

In this chapter, we started by learning some basic notions of physics so as to better develop our games. Then, we went through the Physics engine of Unity, which is divided into some components. Rigidbodies and colliders describe the properties of physical objects in the game, whereas joints and effectors affect how they react with each other in the environment.

Finally, we saw how to deal with physics and took what we needed for our *Tower Defense* game, so as to implement the collision between a sprinkle and a Panda (and call the right functions to update the Panda's health and animations).

6

Through a Sea of Sprinkles – Navigation in Artificial Intelligence

After having given a rendering (Chapter 4, *No Longer Alone – Sweet-Toothed Pandas Strike*) and a physical shape (Chapter 5, *The Secret Ingredient Is a Dash of Physics*) to our Pandas, it's now time to give them intelligence. In particular, the ability to walk/navigate through the map towards the player's cake to eat it. In fact, as we have already pointed out, **artificial intelligence (AI)** is at the core of giving life to NPCs, so that they can move around and act within the world. However, this chapter will focus on navigation.

In particular, we will implement a waypoint system for our Pandas. We will do it twice, so that we can have two different perspectives on the same thing, and we will highlight the advantages and disadvantages of each method.

Here is an outline of the topics that we will cover:

- The importance of AI in video games
- Navigation in video games and an overview of the main techniques
- Implementing a waypoint system as a static list
- Implementing a waypoint system as a dynamic pool of game objects (and display them as icons on the map)
- Getting an idea of what's beyond navigation

As in all the other chapters of this book, you can practice your skill at the end with the Homework section. So, let's get ready to start!

Getting ready

The only requirement for this chapter, is that you have already done all the parts of the book that dealt with the `PandaScript` so far.

Introduction to artificial intelligence

Artificial intelligence (**AI**) is an extensive topic, even if we limit ourselves just to video games. In fact, due to its complexity, it's one of the hardest parts to program for a video game. A good AI programmer should have knowledge of math (such as graph theory, Bayesian networks, operational research, and so on), physics (such as the motion equations) and psychology (to understand how the player reacts to AI in the game). Whereas the first two are well known, the last one is sometimes neglected, but is just as equally important. In fact, sometimes the most believable behavior of an NPC character is not the most enjoyable for the player. If you are interested in learning more, I wrote an article that you can find on my website at `francescosapio.com`

However, I hope I haven't scared you by quoting such concepts of mathematics. In fact, in these sections, we won't cover such complicated things, but it is useful to have an idea about the foundations of what we will do, even if we will only create a simple ground to make our tower defense game work. In any case, I invite you to learn more about artificial intelligence in video games, since what you can achieve is really awesome!

The importance of artificial intelligence in video games

Imagine a tower defense game without enemies to compete against, it's just you and a bunch of towers. Games like *SimCity* (`www.simcity.com`) would cease to exist. Games would become predictable experiences, their replay value would be greatly diminished, and MMOs would become ordinary. It would be the apocalypse of dynamic gameplay, without being too dramatic. Therefore, for any game to provide a dynamic and growing experience, AI is essential.

Artificial intelligence, or simply AI, allows systems to think and then behave just like humans, *or* animals. Over time, these systems can learn from the behavior of its user; for example, if they are progressing too easily, or if they are struggling, then the system is able to make adjustments to the game (in real time) so that the game adapts to the player. This concept refers to **machine learning**.

AI in computer games refers to the behaviour and decision-making process of game components such as non-player characters, or NPCs for short. In modern games, there is real-time, very dynamic AI that in some cases feels like you're playing against other real players. In this way, well done AI allows you to make fast and intelligent decisions in order to progress through the game and achieve greatness. Some examples of AI in games can range from early arcade games such as *Pac-Man*, to enemies in first person shooters, such as *Battlefield*, *Call of Duty*, and *Alpha Protocol*; or *hordes of orcs* and beasts in strategy games, such as *World of Warcraft* and *Guild Wars 2*.

In a book about AI (*Artificial Intelligence for Games* by Ian Millington and John Funge), which I recommend you to have a look at, we can think of AI as having the following states:

- **Movement**: This refers to AI that involves NPCs making decisions that then produce a type of motion, such as attacking or fleeing the player.
- **Decision making**: As the name suggests, this requires that a decision is made by the NPC about what to do next. For instance, if the enemy sees you, will it attack, run, or call for help?
- **Strategy**: Imagine trying to coordinate a whole team, like in *S.W.A.T* or Tom Clancy's *Rainbow Six*. In these situations, AI does not affect just one or two characters, but the entire team who, in turn, may have his or her own decision making tree, such as what to do when they sight an enemy; do they take them out on their own or do they notify you?
- **Infrastructure**: This refers to how the AI is structured, which will ultimately determine how well it works in a game. This isn't just about creating the write algorithms to make NPCs perform certain actions, it is also about utilizing the computer's resources in an efficient way.
- **Agent-based AI**: This refers to the concept of creating autonomous NPCs that take in information from the game data, determine what actions to take, and then carry out those actions.

A great site to check out is Intel's: `http://tinyurl.com/IntelAI`, which provides a nice explanation and introduction to the use of AI in games.

Navigation

Now, we should have a better understanding of why AI is so important and vital for video games, but it's such an extensive topic that it cannot be dealt with in a small chapter like this. Therefore, we will focus on just one particular aspect, which is navigation. Since this is an introductory chapter to the topic, we will hope to understand the basic concepts of navigation, but implement just one of the simple techniques that we will use in our game.

Aspects of navigation

Game characters move within the game and its levels. The movement can be quite simple, such as that of arcade games or NPCs following or targeting you, and others can be quite complex like in fast paced action and adventure games. Fixed routes are simple to implement within a game, but keep in mind that it is possible to break their illusion when objects and other characters get in the way. For example, in games that are highly populated by NPCs (such as *Assassin's Creed*), characters that roam the environment can get stuck on environmental objects and appear to be moon walking, or in other words moving but not going anywhere. In a more dynamic situation, characters that will follow you or come towards you (friend or foe) will not know your future movements and therefore must act accordingly, as you do. This can range from waves of enemies in real-time strategy games, to guards who you need to avoid in order to infiltrate high-level security buildings.

For each of these characters (and situations), the AI must be able to calculate a suitable route within the game level, ensuring that it can respond to objects that come into its path, in order to reach its goal. Ideally, you want the character to act as natural as possible.

In larger contexts, navigation can be used in a space, which can represent the environment, but also more abstract things, such as the space of moves of a problem. For example, in the famous *Eight queens* game (placing eight queens on a chess board such that each one of them doesn't attack another; you should try it), finding a path in the space of moves might be equivalent to finding a solution.

In video games, navigation can exist in various forms, such as:

- **Steering behaviours**: These find an immediate path in front of the agent to avoid collisions. It can be used for basic obstacle avoidance, also in multi-agent system contexts. Since these behaviours are at a low-level, in video games they always have been implemented in a Kinematic way (in the same way we saw in `Chapter 5`, *The Secret Ingredient Is a Dash of Physics*). However recently, some dynamic steering behaviours have arisen in the game development world, bringing more realistic games.
- **Pathfinding**: These finds a path from a starting location to a destination. This level is the most used, and many techniques have been discovered/invented and implemented. It is this type of navigation that will be the focus of this chapter.
- **Driven pathfinding**: These finds one or multiple paths according to some driven behaviours. This is still a level that has never been implemented in the game industry, but it's a field of research for game development in academia, and therefore it's worth mentioning. This level is placed between decision making and pathfinding. In fact, some decisions are taken at pathfinding time, bringing a more intelligent pathfinding and efficiency in decision processes.

 More information about the different types of navigation can be found in more detail on my website. Moreover, my research involves directly driven pathfinding, such as the BDP (we will see later in the chapter). Here is the link: `francescosapio.com`.

Pathfinding and its techniques

Over the last few decades, many pathfinding algorithms and techniques have been explored. One of the very first pathfinding algorithms that was invented was the **dijkstra algorithm**, which gave the foundation for modern pathfinding algorithms. Of course, since Dijkstra, much progress has been made and algorithms have become much more efficient (especially when we deal with specific information or we have a priori knowledge about the problem that we can use). The most used of these in video games is the **A* algorithm** (along with all its derivations), which uses some additional information about the map. The main concept of Dijkstra was to explore in all directions until a route was found; the main concept of A* is to explore towards the direction of the destination (which may sound simple, but it is not always easy to determine a function that in some way tells you which is the direction towards the destination). Of course, this is a simplification, but good enough to gain a better overview.

The preceding mentioned algorithms work in many situations, but if the route which we want to find is easy enough to be found in a small map, it wouldn't be worthwhile developing such algorithms, since there are easier techniques. One of these techniques is the use of waypoints, which is the technique we will use for our game. The main concept is that the map is split into a graph which, potentially, is very small (enough to be drawn by hand) and finding a path can happen in a distributed way. Of course, there is another entire world beyond distributed pathfinding (a practical application would be IP packets that need to travel the world on the Internet, and the path between the different routers is determined in a distributed way since the map of the network changes continuously).

Another important fact that influences pathfinding (but also other techniques of AI) is whether the algorithm needs to work online or offline. Online means that the algorithm needs to find a solution in real time, whereas offline means that the solution can be found a priori. In video games, there are situations in which we need to use online solutions (such as finding the path for your NPCs) and others where we need an offline solution (for instance, when you have more time to compute, such as with turn-based games, or when some AI calculations are performed at loading time).

Unfortunately, we would need another book just to describe navigation in video games, but this chapter is giving you a nice and gentle introduction to the world that's behind all of this, and you can use the references (suggested books and links) to continue your journey in learning AI in games.

Waypoints for enemies

A waypoint is a special point on the map where NPCs change their direction to move towards another waypoint. They can contain logic to actually lead the character to specific places that change over time, such as next to the player. For instance, in a shooting game, enemies want to get closer to the player to shoot him/her. Waypoints can also perform part of the decision-making process. For example, imagine a tower defense level where the path of the enemies splits in two. In this case, the waypoints can be used to decide which direction a particular enemy should take (we will see this in the last chapter of this book). The advantages of waypoints are that, in some cases, they can be more efficient than implementing a complete pathfinding algorithm.

In more complex implementations, waypoints can be connected in different ways and these connections can also be created automatically by letting the waypoints find each other. Furthermore, they can also contain other information, such as which is the closest waypoint to the player. Here, the enemy can ask or query the waypoints where to head towards in order to find the player without running a complete pathfinding algorithm on the map itself.

At the moment, we don't need to implement a particular logic behind the waypoints. However, they are a useful tool since they allow us to move enemies around the map easily, and they are modular enough so to be able to create other levels of our game without many problems.

In this section, we will learn how to create waypoints. In particular, we will see two ways to implement them.

Getting the waypoint coordinates

Before we start creating waypoints, we first need to decide where to place them on the map. Therefore, we need to find all the places where our Pandas change their direction. In this simple map, they are located at all corners of their path. In the following image, they are indicated by the red dots:

As we can see, there are 11 and we need one waypoint that is on the cake in the map. This final waypoint is the finishing spot, where the Panda has succeeded in his mission to steal a big bite of the player's cake.

Now that we have spotted them, we need to take note of their coordinates on the map. A fast way to do it is to drag the Panda Prefab around the map in the **Scene** view and then take note of the position of our waypoints. In this case, we could obtain the following data:

Waypoint number	X coordinate	Y coordinate
1	-28	8
2	-28	-16
3	-16	-16
4	-16	7
5	-2	7
6	-2	-6
7	12	-6
8	12	9
9	25	9
10	25	-17
11	32	-17

Implementing waypoints – the first/static way

Now that we have all the waypoint coordinates, we can implement them. In this section, we will explore the first way to implement them. The main advantage of this method is the simplicity of the implementation and the possibility to learn more about static variables and iterating over waypoints.

Implementing waypoints in the Game Manager

In this first implementation of waypoints, they won't be separate entities in the game, but rather a collection of positions in a specific order. All the enemies will consult this list, and based on which waypoint they are currently at, take the next one in the list.

Of course, this method has some limitations such as we won't be able to implement custom features in the waypoints, as we will see in Chapter 8, *What Is beyond the Cake?*. However, it is simpler to implement, and it gives us the opportunity to explore how to use static variables.

First of all, we need to create another script, and call it GameManagerScript. We will implement more functionality in this script in the next chapter. But at the moment, it is needed to store the waypoints. In fact, for now, we just need to add an array of positions, so you can write the following in the script:

```
//public waypoint list as an array of positions
public Vector3[] waypoints;
```

It is a Vector3 array, which basically just stores a set of positions in a specific order. Save the code, and create an empty GameObject in the **Scene**, which you can rename Game Manager. Attach the script on it, and in the **Inspector** you should see something like the following:

We need to set the number of elements of our array with the number of waypoints we have found, in this case 11. Therefore, our **Inspector** looks like the following:

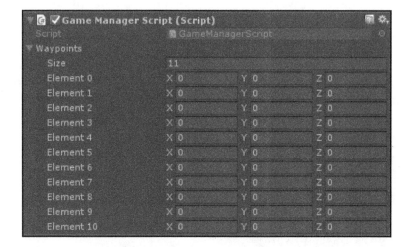

Finally, we can fill all those values with our waypoint positions. But what about the z-axis? Since we don't want the Pandas to change their z-axis, we can just set its value to the same z-axis value of our PandaPrefab, which is –1. At the end, we should have something like this:

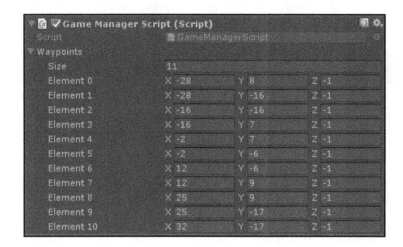

The reader may wonder if it was worthwhile using `Vector2` instead of `Vector3`. The answer is: it's your choice. Nothing prevents you from using `Vector2` and forgetting about `Vector3`. But, since we have made the choice to handle the depth of our game with z-buffering, I personally prefer to have direct control over the z-axis as well, so be sure to achieve the intended behavior.

Moving along the designed path – static

Next, we need to give an opportunity for the enemies to have access to the waypoints stored in the `GameManagerScript`. Therefore, we need to get a reference it. There are many ways to do so, but for learning's sake, we will use a static variable (so as to unravel the use of such variables). In fact, all the Pandas share the same game manager, and it's a waste of computational resources if every time a Panda is created, it needs to search for the `Game Manager`. A static variable is a value which is shared among all the instances of the `PandaScript`. Of course, we need to be careful not to assign this variable many times.

Remember that static variables are persistent over different scenes/levels. Therefore, if you are planning to release a game with more than one level, most likely you will need to reset this variable when the level is changed. We will explore this better in `Chapter 8`, *What Is beyond the Cake?*.

Open the `PandaScript`, and let's add the static variable to store the reference to the `Game Manager`:

```
//Private static variable to store the Game Manager
private static GameManagerScript gameManager;
```

At the beginning of the `Start()` function we need to check if another instance (another Panda) has already been assigned this variable. If not, we will assign it by finding its reference in the scene, even though there will only be one game manager in the scene at the time. As a result, this Panda will actually initialize the variable. As such, all the other instances of Pandas that will be created will have a reference to the `Game Manager` ready, and thanks to this check, we are sure that we are assigning it only once:

```
//If the reference to the Game Manager is missing, the script gets it
if(gameManager == null) {
  gameManager = FindObjectOfType<GameManagerScript>();
}
```

Now, we have to make the Panda move. But first, we need a variable to store the current waypoint that the Panda is heading towards:

```
//Private counter for the waypoints
private int currentWaypointNumber;
```

Then, we need a constant to establish a threshold after which the waypoint is considered as having been reached. In fact, there are numerical instabilities, and we cannot check directly if the distance from the waypoint is actually zero, only a value very close to it. As you can see, the value assigned to this constant is very low:

```
//Private constant under which a waypoint is considered reached
private const float changeDist = 0.001f;
```

Finally, we need to implement the mechanism under which the Panda heads towards the right waypoint, and changes direction to the next one when the previous is reached. Since the MoveTowards() function we will use to move the Panda deals with physics, we need to implement this whole mechanism of the waypoints within the FixedUpdate() function, as we learnt from Chapter 5, *The Secret Ingredient Is a Dash of Physics*. So, we can start writing the following:

```
void FixedUpdate() {
    //Add here the rest of the code of this section
}
```

In particular, we need to do three things within the FixedUpdate() function. The first one is to check if the Panda has reached the end of the waypoint list, which means it is in front of the delicious player's cake. If so, we need to trigger the eat animation in the same fashion we triggered the others in Chapter 4, *No Longer Alone – Sweet-Toothed Pandas Strike*. Then, we need to remove this script from the Panda. In fact, the State Machine Behaviour script we wrote in Chapter 4, *No Longer Alone – Sweet-Toothed Pandas Strike*, will take care of removing the Panda from the scene. Finally, we return so that the rest of the function is not executed:

```
//if the Panda has reached the cake, then it will eat it, by triggering
    the right animation,
//and remove this script, since the State Machine Behaviour will take
    care of removing the Panda
if (currentWaypointNumber == gameManager.waypoints.Length) {
    animator.SetTrigger(AnimEatTriggerHash);
    Destroy(this);
    return;
}
```

The second thing, in case the Panda is not at the last waypoint yet, is to calculate the distance between the current Panda's position, through its Transform, and the waypoint it is heading towards. This value is stored within a local variable `dist`:

```
//Calculate the distance between the Panda and the waypoint that the
   Panda is moving towards
float dist = Vector2.Distance(transform.position,
   gameManager.waypoints[currentWaypointNumber]);
```

The last thing is to check if the Panda is close enough to the waypoint. Enough means below the constant threshold stored in the `changeDist`. If so, we just increase the counter of the waypoints so that at the next iteration, the Panda will head to the next waypoint. Otherwise, we just use the `MoveTowards()` function implemented in the previous chapter to move the Panda towards the waypoint:

```
//If the waypoint is considered reached because below the threshold of
   the constant changeDist
//the counter of waypoints is increased, otherwise the Panda moves
   towards the waypoint
if(dist <= changeDist) {
   currentWaypointNumber++;
}else {
   MoveTowards(gameManager.waypoints[currentWaypointNumber]);
}
```

We can save our script and test it out. By placing a Panda in the scene somewhere near the first waypoint and pressing play, we will see it moving along the path.

Implementing waypoints – the second/dynamic way

In this section, we will explore a second way to implement the waypoint system of our game. Of course, the outcome will be the same, but this approach offers many other advantages. First of all, it's easier for designers to collocate, change, move, and replace waypoints within the map itself. Second, it allows a great flexibility in behaviors, which can be implemented in such a way to make it easier for designers to use the script created. We will exploit some of the potentiality of this system later in the last chapter of the book.

Nonetheless, this approach does suffer from some drawbacks, as with every choice in life. In particular, the complexity of the system increases. Moreover, it uses a different game object for each one of the waypoints, and this is critical if the number of waypoints is really high.

To overcome this last problem of having different game objects for each of the waypoints, we have many possibilities, but making each one of them work is a challenge and at the same time, easy for designers to use. In fact, waypoints can still be stored as a list, not as positions this time, but rather of the `waypoint` class, and at the same time expose functionalities to allow designers to edit and place them within the **Scene** view. This is left as a challenge in the *Homework* section.

Implementing waypoints as separate entities

So far, we have seen a simple implementation of the waypoints. Now, we will implement them again, but this time as separate entities. As such, in `Chapter 8`, *What Is beyond the Cake?*, we will explore how to unlock the potential of waypoints in a game. In fact, at the end of this section, the effect on our game will be the same; however, we will change the script in `Chapter 8`, *What Is beyond the Cake?*, by implementing more features.

First of all, we need to erase the `waypoints` variable from the `GameManagerScript` (but don't erase the script, even if it is empty, because we will use it; for the same reasons, don't erase the `gameManager` variable from the `PandaScript`).

Now, we need to create a new script, which will be the actual waypoint. As such, we can rename it as `Waypoint`.

We need a variable of the same class to store the next waypoint. In this way, each waypoint will be able to point/reference towards another waypoint. The goal is to build a chain which the Pandas will follow. Since the variable is private but we still need to have access to it in the **Inspector**, we need to add the serializable property. So, we can add the following to our script:

```
//Private variable to store the next waypoint in the chain
//It is serializable, so it can be set in the Inspector
[SerializeField]
private Waypoint nextWaypoint;
```

Now, from the waypoint, a Panda would like to retrieve its position and the next waypoint to follow, once the current one is reached. To achieve this, we can expose two functions from our `Waypoint` script.

The `GetPosition()` function will return a `Vector3` with the position of the waypoint, which (in this specific implementation) is stored in the Transform of the waypoint. The code is the following:

```
//Function to retrieve the position of the waypoint
public Vector3 GetPosition() {
    return transform.position;
}
```

The `GetNextWaypoint()` function, instead, will return just the next waypoint (at least for the moment), stored in the `nextWaypoint` variable. In fact, the `nextWaypoint` variable is private, and so Pandas need a function to retrieve it. Therefore, we can just write the following:

```
//Function to retrieve the next waypoint in the chain
public Waypoint GetNextWaypoint() {
    return nextWaypoint;
}
```

We have finished with this script for now, so we can save it.

The next step is to create a Prefab for our waypoints. Create an empty GameObject and attach the `Waypoint` script. Then, in the **Project** panel, create a Prefab called `WaypointPrefab` and drag and drop the empty GameObject you have created. Finally, erase the empty GameObject from the scene, since now we have our Prefab.

Drag and drop as many Prefabs as the number of waypoints you have identified; in our example, there are 11. For your convenience, I suggest you rename them in a progressive order, as shown in the following screenshot:

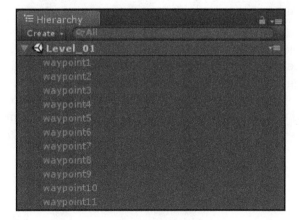

Now, we need to link them to each other. In particular, `waypoint1` will be linked to `waypoint2`, which will be linked to `waypoint3`, and so on. For instance, `waypoint4` should look linked in the **Inspector** as follows:

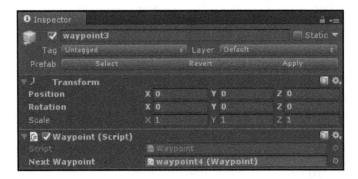

The only exception is in the last waypoint, which has nothing in the `nextWaypoint` variable, as shown in the following screenshot:

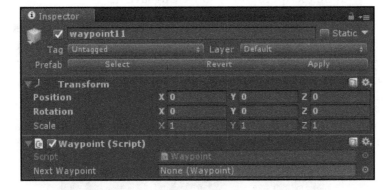

Finally, we need to place them at the coordinates we have identified in the *Getting the waypoint coordinates* section. To quickly recognize them, I recommend that you add a Gizmo icon. As the name suggests, a Gizmo is an icon that will be shown in the **Scene** view to quickly and easily recognize specific objects, but won't be visible once the game is built. Recently, Unity added also the possibility to see them within the **Game** view.

The easiest way to insert a Gizmo is by clicking the cube-shaped icon next to the name of the GameObject, highlighted in the following screenshot:

 The same holds for Prefabs, but their icon is a blue cube.

Once you have clicked on this icon, a menu appears as shown in the following screenshot:

By selecting one of the ellipse-shaped icons, you will place a label to the object with its name in it. We will choose one of these for our waypoints. If you click on the circle-shaped or crystal-shaped icons, the Gizmo will look like a circle or a crystal, without any text. If you click the **Other...** button, you can use your own graphics.

 A more complex way to insert Gizmos is through scripting. In fact, there is a special function called OnDrawGizmos() which is called by Unity when rendering Gizmos is enabled. Within this function, you are able to use any of the functions listed at https://docs.unity3d.com/ScriptReference /Gizmos.html, which allow you to draw shapes on the screen. This is a very powerful tool, because it can enhance tremendously the usability of your scripts. For instance, in our specific case of waypoints, we could draw the path that Pandas will follow. This is left as an exercise in the *Homework* section.

In our case, we can select one of the ellipse-shaped icon for all the waypoints. As a result, we are able to see them in the **Scene** view (even if they don't have any explicit rendering component and thus they won't be visible in any way in the final game) and quickly place them.

At the end, your **Scene** view should look like the following:

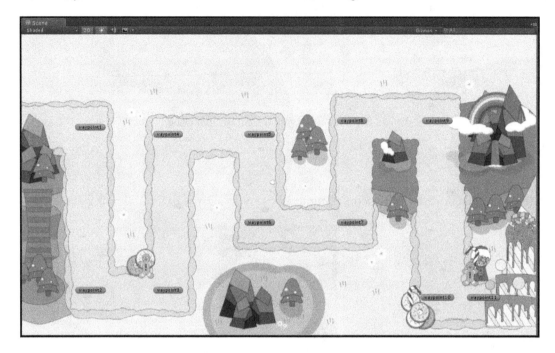

Now, we need to specify to the game, which one of these waypoints is the first of the chain. As such, we can store this information within the Game Manager. So, let's add the following variable to the GameManagerScript:

```
//The first waypoint of the chain
public Waypoint firstWaypoint;
```

Finally, after having saved the script, set the variable in the **Inspector**, as shown in the following screenshot:

In conclusion, we have created a chain of waypoints, which is exactly what we need for our game. However, we still need to define how the Pandas get to them.

Moving along the designed path – dynamic

The next step is to slightly modify the PandaScript to take care of this new waypoint system. So, let's open the script again.

First, we need to substitute the integer variable, currentWaypointNumber, with a proper waypoint variable, as shown here:

```
//Private reference to the current waypoint
private Waypoint currentWaypoint;
```

Then, we need to initialize this new variable; we can do it in the Start() function, by retrieving the first waypoint from the Game Manager, as shown here:

```
//Get the first waypoint from the Game Manager
currentWaypoint = gameManager.firstWaypoint;
```

Then, in the first check of the FixedUpdate() function, we need to check if the variable itself is null (which means that the Panda has reached the cake, because the last waypoint will return a null pointer). Here is the code, with the modified parts highlighted:

```
if (currentWaypoint == null) {
  animator.SetTrigger(AnimEatTriggerHash);
  Destroy(this);
  return;
}
```

Going on in the FixedUpdate() function, we need to change how the distance is calculated, by using the GetPosition() function of our waypoint in the following way:

```
float dist = Vector2.Distance(transform.position,
  currentWaypoint.GetPosition());
```

Finally, we need to change the last if statement of the FixedUpdate() function to get the next waypoint when the previous one is reached. We also need to decide which parameter we should give to our MoveTowards() function. Again, the modified parts are highlighted:

```
if(dist <= changeDist) {
  currentWaypoint = currentWaypoint.GetNextWaypoint();
}else {
  MoveTowards(currentWaypoint.GetPosition());
}
```

Save the script. We have finished this second way of implementing waypoints. Chapter 8, *What Is beyond the Cake?*, will suggest some ways to take advantage of this structure to implement more complex behaviors.

More about artificial intelligence in games

In the previous sections, we have seen a couple of implementations of a waypoint system to move characters within the game environment. However, as we already said in the introduction, this is not even scratching the surface of AI in games. This section presents some techniques, without entering into detail, as they are not needed to develop our tower defense game. In fact, to master AI in games, you need a specific book about it. Therefore, feel free to skip this section, or read it. You can always come back here later, maybe when you finish the book, for a deeper look at its content. The main goal of this section is just to give you a basic understanding of AI in games.

Other techniques for navigation at the pathfinding level

The *Pathfinding and its techniques* section at the beginning of this chapter was in no way exhaustive, and of course thousands of other techniques exist at the pathfinding level which are used in video games.

However, it's worth quoting one in particular: Navigation Mesh. This is important, because it's built into the Unity engine for 3D games. The main concept behind this technique is a pre-analysis of the geometry of the level to extract a graph (this is for instance, an offline algorithm) where other pathfinding algorithms can extract paths when needed (these, instead, work online).

You can generate such a graph by setting some parameters by clicking in the top menu bar on **Window | Navigation**. Specifically, you can set the general options in the **Bake** tab, as shown in the following screenshot:

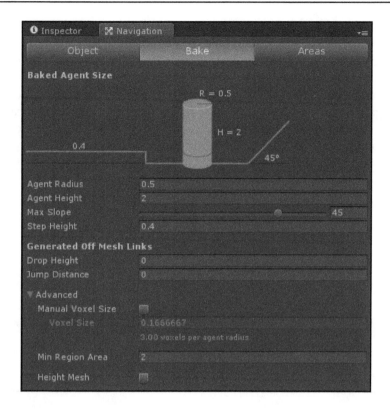

Once this graph is built, agents can have access to it through specific classes in scripts.

In any case, this belongs to the 3D part of Unity, and we won't go into it any further. But if you are interested in learning more, you can start from the official documentation at: `https://docs.unity3d.com/Manual/Navigation.html` (as you may notice from the table of contents, it's quite a large and extensive tool in Unity, but powerful).

Navigation at the level of steering behaviours

Remember how we could implement physics equations in Unity from `Chapter 5`, *The Secret Ingredient Is a Dash of Physics*? We can implement all the equations of the motion and we will obtain any kind of movement. If then, we mix this with a goal, a destination, or even just a direction, along with some obstacle avoidance techniques, we have made a steering behaviour.

For instance, if you implement obstacle avoidance as magnets that repulse the NPC, and the goal as an attractive magnet, you obtain a pretty nice steering behaviour. Characters could reach destinations without any pathfinding algorithms. Note that I said *could*. In fact, they can get stuck, and there are many other issues related to steering behaviours as an end-solution. But integrating steering behaviours in a pathfinding algorithm (the first deals with high-level navigation, such as going from one room to another, the second can navigate within the room to reach the door to the next room) is a great addition, which can lead to highly-realistic behaviours with very low performance overhead.

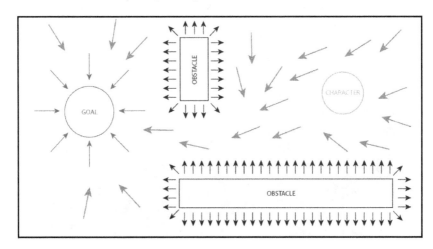

Example of steering behaviour with magnets

Usually, the attraction range of the goal is extended to the whole map, whereas the repulsion force of the obstacles is just local. Moreover, these forces can follow different potential laws, and have different shapes. To help you to visualize magnetic fields, you can give a look at the picture by Dayna Mason at: https://www.flickr.com/photos/daynoir /2180507211. Each compass represents which kind of force the character is subject to when he/she is in that position. The same happens in our example, where the character is pushed away from obstacles and attracted by goals. It is also interesting to note that our goals and obstacles are single pole magnets, but in our physical world they don't exist (only magnetic dipoles exist).

Navigation at the level of pathfinding/decision making – belief-driven pathfinding

As I have already mentioned, research in academia has recently started to merge portions of decision-making within pathfinding. An example of this is one of my own publications about **Belief-Driven Pathfinding** (BDP).

The key concept is that NPCs do not necessarily know the entire map. Imagine there was a bridge to cross a river, but the player had destroyed the bridge; therefore, when the character navigates through the environment, the character should consider the map as if the bridge was still there, because he is not aware that the bridge is down. Only when he approaches the river, he realizes that the bridge is down, and therefore, takes action on it (such as find another path, build another bridge, create a raft with the wood, or swim). That is why it is belief-driven, because the character navigates through the environment as he/she believes the environment is and, as such, makes assumptions.

If you are interested in learning more about BDP, you can check out my website at: `francescosapio.com`.

Beyond navigation

AI in games is not limited to only navigation, but as we said in the introduction, there are many levels that AI can be applied to in video games. Imagine turn-based games, in which NPCs needs to take strategic decisions.

But AI does not only apply to non-player characters. Some games implement algorithms to adapt the difficulty to the game (adaptive and learning algorithms), others handle how the camera should move in order to raise a specific emotional state in the player (such as in the work of Georgios N. Yannakakis in particular, in the paper, *Space Maze: Experience-Driven Game Camera Control*). Other games have algorithms of **Procedural Content Generation** (**PCG**), like the famous *Temple Run* (Imangi studios, 2011) which procedurally generates the level, or even *Minecraft* (Mojang, 2011) in which a whole world is procedurally generated.

AI is also applied for analysis of games and players, such as to study the inner structures of games or to gather psychological player profiles. Regarding the latter, you need to imagine the application in serious games, where games can be used to evaluate the performance of people within specific contexts. You can find an interesting introductory paper titled; *Towards personalized, gamified systems: an investigation into game design, personality and player typologies* by Lauren S. Ferro (available at: `http://dl.acm.org/citation.cfm?id=2513024`).

Lastly, it's worth mentioning that the relationship between games and AI is not mono-directional. In fact, not only do games use AI, but also the opposite applies. Some studies and research on AI are helped by video games, which can provide a perfect simulation environment (for instance, for robots), and also create algorithms that take the place of the player and play the game (without cheating, because the AI within the game always uses additional extra data to gather the specific state of the game).

In any case, keep in mind that when AI is used in games, the most important aim is not to be realistic, but to create an immersive and entertaining experience for the player (which may also result in learning experiences, if the design of the game includes that).

Homework

In this chapter, we gained an overview of AI in games. However, we focused only on navigation, and in particular, implementing the waypoint system for our game. But you can still improve it, and this section proposes some exercises to achieve that. Therefore, before the next chapter, I invite you to do the following exercises to develop your skills even more:

1. **Becoming an AI designer and programmer**: Think of five games that you play, and select a part of that game that contains NPCs such as the enemies or even the boss. Now, write down a list of behaviors that each of them have. Now, remove some behaviors, or even add some and think about how it would alter the experience. Does it improve it, or does it change the atmosphere entirely? Could you make a relatively realistic behavior into intelligent, yet not realistic, by changing some of the behaviors, and vice versa? By doing this, you will begin to understand the importance that some behaviors play in not only providing life to your characters, but in also giving emotions to the player.

2. **Waypoints as colliders**: From the previous chapter, we learnt how to use colliders and detect collisions. In particular, we saw how the sprinkles collided with Pandas to trigger actions (in this case, to shoot down the Panda). However, the same principle can be applied here as well. Instead, to use the `changeDist` constant and check the distance from the Panda to the waypoint, we can use the `OnTriggerEnter2D()` function again to check when a Panda has reached a waypoint. Implement the changing of waypoints in this way, regardless of whether you are using the first or second implementation. Little hint: you probably need to set a new tag (remember how to set a tag from *Chapter 2, Baking Cupcake Towers*?) for the waypoints, and add colliders on them too.

3. **Waypoints that auto-reach themselves**: In more complex waypoint systems, you shouldn't manually create the chain (even though the solution becomes hard to scale when the map becomes bigger). As such, try to design and implement a system where the waypoints auto-connect themselves once placed.

4. **Create a Gizmo path displayer**: Back in `Chapter 2`, *Baking Cupcake Towers*, we saw how it was possible to use some Gizmo functions to draw useful stuff on the scene. Use those functions, and in particular `Gizmos.DrawLine()`, to show the chain of waypoints on the **Scene** view.

And finally, there is a challenge for you:

5. **Easy waypoint**: In the second implementation, we use a different game object for each one of the waypoints. Design and implement a system that is as easy as the one implemented in this chapter for designers (so they can drag around the waypoints in the **Scene** view, and possibly see the chain from the previous exercise), but at the same time is efficient, since it won't use game objects for waypoints (but rather an array stored somewhere).

Summary

In this chapter, we learnt the very basics of artificial intelligence in video games. We went through an overview about navigation and some common techniques used.

Then, we built our navigation system for our game, based on waypoints. In particular, we have implemented two types of waypoint systems for our game, to learn different ways of achieving the same results.

Finally, we had another general overview about AI in games.

In the next chapter we will finish our game! Already excited? Well, what are you waiting for? The next chapter is just a page away.

7

Trading Cupcakes and the Ultimate Battle for the Cake – Gameplay Programming

After going through different parts of the Unity engine, it's time to come back to our game and finish it up. In doing this, we will explore another big topic: **gameplay programming**. In particular, we will see how data can be exchanged between different parts of a game. Since in our tower defense game there are still many parts to connect, and they can be implemented in thousands of different ways, I tried to choose different techniques in order to give you a different perspective on how things can be implemented within Unity.

Specifically, in this chapter we will cover:

- How to implement a trading system to allow the player to buy, sell, and upgrade cupcake towers
- Scripting how the player can place cupcake towers on the map once they are bought
- How game over conditions can be triggered to display a winning or losing screen
- Keeping track of the progress made by the player during the level
- Creating a spawn system for our Pandas, based on dividing the Pandas into waves
- Designing and implementing a main menu
- How to change a scene in Unity

As always, at the end of the chapter you can find the *Homework* section, which is full of exercises for you to bring your skills to a higher level. Some of these exercises will challenge you about the concepts learnt in the chapter, and they will guide you in improving our tower defense game.

But before we go straight into gameplay programming for our game, let's spend some time learning about gameplay programming in general.

Getting ready

To better understand this chapter, you should have followed all of the other chapters, since we are going to implement our scripts here on top of the ones we have previously created throughout the book.

For simplicity, for those readers who only did the first implementation in the previous chapter, I have kept the code of the first implementation. However, for those who did the second implementation, you shouldn't have a problem doing the same modifications to the code. In any case, it's recommended that you have the second implementation of the code in the game, because the next chapter will give us some ways to exploit its potential in the context of a larger game.

What does gameplay programming mean?

There is not a unique definition for gameplay programming. Of course, it deals with building and developing the game, but for instance, does it include programming artificial intelligence? Or UIs? Or database connections? Or animation machines? Therefore, the definition depends on the context. However, it is interesting to note how the definition changes again, when you seek a job position. As a rule of thumb, based only on experience, the bigger and larger the company is, the better the gameplay programmer job position will be. In fact, in small companies, teams can be resource limited and therefore having a gameplay programmer means that he/she will do everything, whereas in larger teams where there are AI, UI, and animation programmers, the gameplay programmer is likely to be more a coordinator of all such roles, and therefore it is a higher position.

I would like to close this section with a quote from a blog of a game developer (Ask a Game Dev at `http://askagamedev.tumblr.com/post/72792621882/roles-in-the-industry-th e-gameplay-programmer`), who describes what it feels like to be a gameplay programmer:

> *"As you can see, being a gameplay programmer is about solving problems even moreso than the designer – you have to really figure out all of the bits of the problem and solve them all. But you also have much more in-depth knowledge of how the entire system works. You get to create those systems. You get to be the first to see something awesome happen."*

Now, it's time to go into the specifics and get our tower defense game done!

Planning what is left to implement for our game

The first thing to do before we complete our game is to reorganize the ideas after having written down what we have done so far.

In Chapter 1, *A Flat World in Unity*, we imported all the Sprites and set them up properly. Then, in Chapter 2, *Baking Cupcake Towers*, we implemented the Projectile and Cupcake tower classes. In Chapter 3, *Communicating with the Player – the User Interface*, we implemented the health and the sugar of the player, whereas in Chapter 4, *No Longer Alone – Sweet-Toothed Pandas Strike*, we focused on animating our sweet-toothed Panda. Finally, in Chapter 5, *The Secret Ingredient Is a Dash of Physics*, we explored physics and how we can use it within our game, and in Chapter 6, *Through a Sea of Sprinkles – Navigation in Artificial Intelligence*, we gave the Pandas the possibility of moving along the path towards the sweet cake.

So, what's left to do is the following:

- Integrate a trading system so the player can buy, sell, and upgrade cupcake towers
- Create a mechanism to place the cupcake towers once they have been bought
- Specify how the player can select a specific cupcake tower
- Set up game over conditions.
- Keeping track of the progress of the player during gameplay
- Implement a spawning system for our Pandas
- Create a main menu for our game

After we have done all of this, we will basically have a functioning game. So, let's get started with the first on the list.

Trading cupcake towers

In this section, we will see how to allow the player to trade towers. In particular, the player can either buy, sell, or upgrade a cupcake tower. Since these three actions have something in common, we will implement them by using **inheritance**. If you remember, we talked a bit about it in Chapter 2, *Baking Cupcake Towers*, but now we have the possibility of seeing it in action. As a result, along the way we will have a better understanding of abstract methods and static variables, since we will use them again.

In any case, each one of these trading actions that the player can perform are implemented separately. This is the structure we will implement:

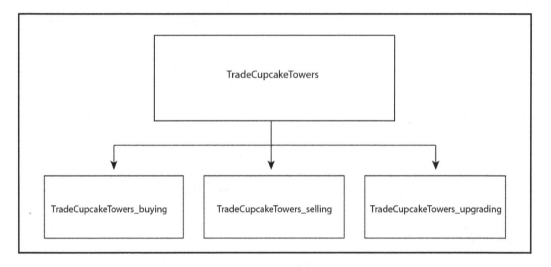

Each of the child scripts can be attached to a UI element, and that will be transformed into a button to perform that specific action. Let's start with the parent class.

The trading parent class

Let's start to create a general class named `TradeCupcakeTower`, and open it with your favorite code editor.

Buying, selling, and upgrading require the user to click on their icon in the user interface (we will create the UI in the scene for the trading actions after we have scripted the whole trading system first), and so we need to provide a way to detect the click (or the tap in case of a mobile application) of the player. As we have talked about it in Chapter 3, *Communicating with the Player – the User Interface*, we can use a handler. Thus, we need to add the following library at the beginning of our script:

```
using UnityEngine.EventSystems;
```

Now, in the definition of the class, we can add the click handler. Moreover, since this will be an abstract class, we need to specify it in the following way:

```
public abstract class TradeCupcakeTowers : MonoBehaviour,
    IPointerClickHandler {
```

When trading, we want to check the player's sugar level (which is the currency of our game). As a result, we need to have a reference to the Sugar Meter, which is also shared among all the trading classes. Thus, we can make the variable protected and static:

```
// Variable to store the Sugar Meter
protected static SugarMeterScript sugarMeter;
```

Similar to what we did in the last chapter when we had to get the reference to the game manager for all the Pandas (since also, in that case the variable was static), we need to get the reference to the Sugar Meter only once. As such, in the Start() function we can write:

```
void Start () {
  //If the reference to the Sugar Meter is missing, the script gets it
  if (sugarMeter == null) {
    sugarMeter = FindObjectOfType<SugarMeterScript>();
  }
}
```

When the player sells or upgrades a tower, the trading system should know which tower the player is referring to (how the player selects a tower is left for later in *Selecting the towers* section). Therefore, again we can use a protected and static variable shared across all the trading operation classes:

```
//Variable to store the current selected tower by the player
protected static CupcakeTowerScript currentActiveTower;
```

Then, we need a function to set the selection (the current active tower), and it needs to be static, so it can be easily set by other scripts (as we will see later). The function just assigns the tower passed as a parameter to the static variable:

```
// Static function that allows other scripts to assign the new/current
  selected tower
public static void setActiveTower(CupcakeTowerScript cupcakeTower) {
  currentActiveTower = cupcakeTower;
}
```

Finally, we need to implement the interface for handling the click. However, the sequence of actions that should be performed depends on if the player is either buying, selling, or upgrading. Therefore, we can leave the implementation to the child classes, and leave this as an abstract function (refer to Chapter 2, *Baking Cupcake Towers*, on how abstract and virtual methods work) as shown here:

```
// Abstract function triggered when one of the trading buttons is
  pressed, however the
// implementation is specific for each trade operation.
public abstract void OnPointerClick(PointerEventData eventData);
```

We can save the script, and as a result our parent class is ready. Now, before we implement its children for specific trading actions that the player can perform, we need to modify the CupcakeTowerScript.

Modifying the CupcakeTowerScript

Back in Chapter 2, *Baking Cupcake Towers*, we implemented many functionalities for our cupcake towers. However, there is more work to do on their script. In particular, we need to add some variables to store their prices and costs.

Let's start by adding the following self-explanatory variables, which we may want to set into the **Inspector** later:

```
// How much this tower costs when it is bought
public int initialCost;

// How much this tower costs when it is upgraded
public int upgradingCost;

// How much this tower is valuable if sold
public int sellingValue;
```

Every time we upgrade the cupcake tower, we want to raise both the `sellingValue`, because an upgraded tower is more valuable, and the `UpgradingCost`, because upgrading to higher levels requires more sugar. So, we can add the following lines of code in the `Upgrade()` function (the values may depend on your very specific balance of the game, but the next chapter will go into more detail on this and how to handle costs of towers in a dynamic way):

```
//Increase the value of the tower;
sellingValue += 5;

//Increase the upgrading cost
upgradingCost += 10;
```

Save the script, and go into your cupcake tower prefabs and change the values of these three, new variables in the **Inspector** (again, feel free to use the values you prefer). Here is an example:

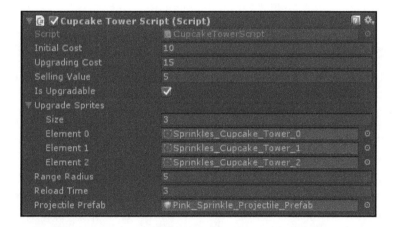

Now, we are ready to implement the trading actions, starting with buying.

Buying cupcake towers

In this section, we will implement the script that handles the buying action. Let's start by creating a new script and name it TradeCupcakeTowers_Buying and open it.

First of all, we still need to import the event systems library from the Unity engine:

```
using UnityEngine.EventSystems;
```

In the class declaration, we need to specify that we are going to extend the `TradeCupcakeTowers` class, instead of `MonoBehaviour`, in the following way:

```
public class TradeCupcakeTowers_Buying : TradeCupcakeTowers {
```

If you look at the design of our user interface back in `Chapter 3`, *Communicating with the Player – the User Interface*, we have three different kinds of towers that the player can buy. Each one of the buttons, once clicked, will instantiate a different tower. Therefore, we need to specify which cupcake tower prefab this instance of the script is referring to. Of course, its values should be set in the **Inspector** (we will see this later). So, let's add the following variable:

```
/* Public variable to identify which tower this script is selling.
 * Ideally, you could have many instances of this script selling
   different
 * Cupcake towers, and the tower is specified in the Inspector */
public GameObject cupcakeTowerPrefab;
```

Then, we need to implement the abstract function inherited from its parent, to handle what happens when the player clicks on its icon. As such, we need to use the `override` property, and declare the method in the following way:

```
public override void OnPointerClick(PointerEventData eventData) {
  //Rest of the code
}
```

Now, the first thing to do when the player clicks is to retrieve the price of the cupcake tower that the player wants to buy:

```
//Retrieve from the prefab which is its initial cost
int price = cupcakeTowerPrefab.GetComponent<CupcakeTowerScript
  ().initialCost;
```

Next, we need to check if the player has enough sugar, by using the shared static variable, `sugarMeter`. If the player has enough sugar, then a new cupcake tower is instantiated (we will see how the player places the tower later in the chapter) and it is assigned as the active tower among the trading classes:

```
// Check if the player can afford to buy the tower
if (price <= sugarMeter.getSugarAmount()) {
  //Payment succeeds, and the cost is removed from the player's sugar
  sugarMeter.ChangeSugar(-price);
  //A new cupcake tower is created
```

```
GameObject newTower = Instantiate(cupcakeTowerPrefab);
//The new cupcake tower is also assigned as the current selection
currentActiveTower = newTower.GetComponent<CupcakeTowerScript>();
}
```

Save the script, and the buy functionality is implemented. Let's see how the player can sell the cupcake towers to get some sugar back.

Selling cupcake towers

In this section, we will implement the script that handles the selling action. Create a new script and name it `TradeCupcakeTowers_Selling`, then open it.

Once again, we still need to import the event systems library from the Unity engine:

```
using UnityEngine.EventSystems;
```

As we did for the `TradeCupcakeTowers_Buying`, we need to inherit from the `TradeCupcakeTowers` class in the following way:

```
public class TradeCupcakeTowers_Selling : TradeCupcakeTowers {
```

Then, we need to implement the abstract function, to handle what happens when the player clicks on the selling icon. Again, we need to use the `override` property, like the following:

```
public override void OnPointerClick(PointerEventData eventData) {
    //Rest of code
}
```

Since selling is an action that the player is always able to perform, we don't need to do any checks (except if there is an active tower), but rather retrieve the value of the cupcake tower and add that amount to the player's savings. Then, remove the cupcake tower from the scene:

```
//Check if there is a tower selected before to proceed
if (currentActiveTower == null)
    return;

//Add to the player's sugar the value of the tower
sugarMeter.ChangeSugar(currentActiveTower.sellingValue);
//Remove the cupcake tower from the scene
Destroy(currentActiveTower);
```

Finally, we can save the script. As a result, the selling functionality is also implemented. Only the upgrading one is left.

Upgrading cupcakes towers

Here we get to create the upgrading button. Create a script and name it `TradeCupcakeTowers_Upgrading`, then open it.

Once again, we still need to import the event systems library from the Unity engine:

```
using UnityEngine.EventSystems;
```

As we did for the other trading classes, we need to inherit from the `TradeCupcakeTowers` class in the following way:

```
public class TradeCupcakeTowers_Upgrading : TradeCupcakeTowers {
```

Then, we need to implement the abstract function, to handle what happens when the player clicks on the upgrading button. Once more, we need to use the `override` property, like the following:

```
public override void OnPointerClick(PointerEventData eventData) {
  //Rest of the code
}
```

Similar to what we did with the buying button, we need to check if the player can afford to upgrade the tower, and if the tower is actually upgradable (we had a Boolean flag for that, set back in *Chapter 2*, *Baking Cupcake Towers*). If so, the cost of the upgrade is subtracted from the player's sugar, and the tower is finally upgraded:

```
//Check if the player can afford to upgrade the tower
if(currentActiveTower.isUpgradable && currentActiveTower.upgradingCost
  <=sugarMeter.getSugarAmount()) {
  //The payment is executed and the sugar removed from the player
  sugarMeter.ChangeSugar(-currentActiveTower.upgradingCost);
  //The tower is upgraded
  currentActiveTower.Upgrade();
}
```

Save this script, and as a result we have completed all the trading functionalities. However, they are not present in the scene, so let's add them to our interface.

Adding the trading options to the user interface

Now that we have the scripts to implement all the different trading buttons, we need to actually place them within our scene/level.

Therefore, let's start to create three UI images, and attach to each one of them, the `TradeCupcakeTowers_Buying` script. As their **Source Image**, you can select the icons we have in our graphical package for the three different kind of towers we have. In case you didn't implement them all, that's alright, just remove the buttons you don't need. If on the contrary, you have implemented more with your own graphics, feel free to add more of these buttons. Then, after you have properly scaled the buttons, place them within our interface as shown in the following screenshot:

Then, in the **Inspector**, we need to assign their respective **Cupcake Tower Prefab**. Here is just one of the three buttons, shown as an example for you:

Very well, now the player can buy towers! What about selling and upgrading them?

Let's create another two UI images, and attach respectively, the `TradeCupcakeTowers_Selling` and `TradeCupcakeTowers_Upgrading` scripts to them. Then, use the icons for selling and upgrading you can find in our graphical package as **Source Image**. Scale the buttons properly, and place them within our interface as shown in the following screenshot:

We don't have any variables to assign in the **Inspector**, so we can consider our trading system ready! Although to make it work properly, we still need to have a way to place our towers and a way to select the towers. These will be explored in the next sections.

Placing the towers

Once the player has bought a cupcake tower, he or she should be able to decide where to place it. This section will explore how to implement this mechanism, which may be simple, but requires you pay attention to many things.

Sketching the idea of how it works

There are many ways in which we can implement this system, but we will use colliders and a second script on the cupcake tower. As a result, you will also be able to learn new ways to handle situations in which information should be exchanged among the different game elements.

In particular, we will define some areas where it is allowed to place a tower, and we will do this through the use of colliders. Then, the game manager registers if the pointer of the player is within allowed areas. A second script, attached to the cupcake towers, uses this information from the game manager to actually allow the player to place cupcake towers. Moreover, once the tower is placed, the script attaches a collider to the cupcake tower. This will prevent a tower from being placed on top of others, and it will also be useful for implementing the selection system.

 In the *Homework* section, you will find some exercises to improve what we are going to implement in this section.

Allowed areas

To begin, we should notice that the player is not free to place his towers wherever he wants to on the map. In fact, he cannot place them along the path where the Pandas are moving or in areas where there is water or other obstacles. Therefore, we need to specify this constraint within our game. Thus, we need to look at our map and find all the spots where the player can place the tower. In our case, the spots that we are looking for are the following:

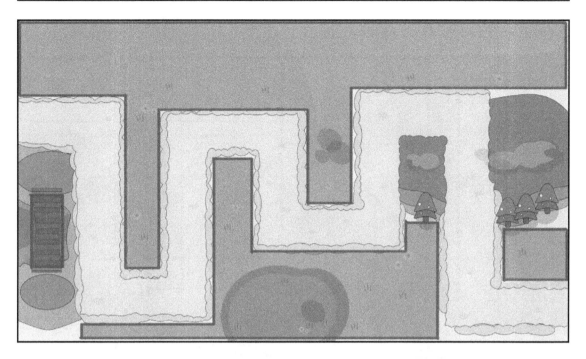

As we can see, they have a custom shape. Even if it is possible to implement custom shapes (which is left as an exercise to readers who want to challenge themselves), it can be much more convenient to think in terms of rectangles and thus to split our shapes into rectangles. Of course, this can be done in more than one way; however, the less rectangles that cover the entire area, the better from a computational point of view. On the other hand, by using more rectangles, you are able to better approximate your areas. So find your tradeoff.

A possible choice could be the following:

In the end, we have found 11 areas.

The idea here is that all these areas are **Box Colliders 2D** attached to the Game Manager object, which will check if the mouse is within one of these areas or not by toggling a flag. This flag will be read by the script we are going to implement in the next section.

Let's start by adding a **Box Collider 2D** on the **Game Manager** by clicking on **Component |
Physics 2D | Box Collider 2D**. Then, we need to resize it to the same dimensions as one of the rectangles we have found, and by using the offset parameter, place it onto the map. At this stage in the book, you should be able to repeat this operation for all the areas of the map, without having their exact values written down here in the book.

Now, the next stage is to modify the GameManagerScript to toggle the flag. Once we have opened the script, we can already add the flag as a Boolean variable:

```
//Private variable to check if the mouse is hovering an area where
//Cupcake tower can be placed
private bool _isPointerOnAllowedArea = true;
```

Since we don't want other scripts to change this variable, it is private, and therefore we need to expose a function to retrieve its value:

```
//Function that returns true if the mouse is hovering an area where a
//Cupcake tower can be placed
public bool isPointerOnAllowedArea() {
  return _isPointerOnAllowedArea;
}
```

Unity offers us a couple of very handy functions to detect when the pointer of the player enters within an area. Their names are self-explanatory: OnMouseEnter() and OnMouseExit(). In the first function, we will set the flag to true, whereas in the second we will set the flag to false:

```
//Function which is called when the mouse enters in one of the
//colliders of the Game Manager
void OnMouseEnter() {
  //Set that the mouse is now hovering an area where placing Cupcake
  //towers is allowed
  _isPointerOnAllowedArea = true;
}

//Function which is called when the mouse exits from one of the
//colliders of the Game Manager
void OnMouseExit() {
  //Set that the mouse is not hovering anymore an area where placing
  //Cupcake towers is allowed
  _isPointerOnAllowedArea = false;
}
```

Save the script, and the setup for the allowed areas is ready.

Scripting the placement script

For placing the cupcake towers after having been bought, we need to create another script for our cupcake towers. You can rename it PlacingCupcakeTowerScript, and add it to the **Cupcake Tower Prefabs**.

Before modifying it, we need to uncheck the CupcakeTowerScript from the prefabs of our cupcake towers. In fact, a tower enters in the scene for the first time because the player has bought it. While in placing mode, the cupcake tower should not shoot. Once placed, the CupcakeTowerScript is enabled, and the tower is operative again.

Now, we can open the newly-created script. We need to retrieve the `Game Manager`, since we will need it to check when the mouse is on an area where cupcake towers can be placed. As such, we can write the following code, which is the same we used in Chapter 6, *Through a Sea of Sprinkles – Navigation in Artificial Intelligence*, to retrieve the `Game Manager` for the first time:

```
// Private variable to store the reference to the Game Manager
private GameManagerScript gameManager;

void Start () {
  //Get the reference to the Game Manager
  gameManager = FindObjectOfType<GameManagerScript>();
}
```

In the `Update()` function we are moving the tower to the mouse location (so at each frame, the tower will move with the mouse of the player), and if the player presses a key, we check if the pointer is actually over an allowed area. If so, the tower is placed, which means that the script that moves the tower is destroyed. Moreover, the `CupcakeTowerScript` is enabled again, and a collider is placed on the cupcake tower. In fact, this additional collider prevents the placing of other towers on top of this (and to select the tower in the next section):

```
void Update () {
  //Get the mouse position
  float x = Input.mousePosition.x;
  float y = Input.mousePosition.y;

  /* Place the cupcake Tower where the mouse is, transformed in game
    coordinates
   * from the Main Camera. Since the Camera is placed at -10 and we
     want the
   * tower to be at -3, we need to use 7 as z-axis coordinate */
  transform.position = Camera.main.ScreenToWorldPoint(new Vector3(x,
    y, 7));

  //If the player clicks, the second condition checks if the current
    position is
  //within an area where cupcake towers can be placed
  if (Input.GetMouseButtonDown(0) &&
    gameManager.isPointerOnAllowedArea()) {
  //Enabling again the main cupcake tower script, so to make it
    operative
  GetComponent<CupcakeTowerScript>().enabled = true;
  //Place a collider on the Cupcake tower
  gameObject.AddComponent<BoxCollider2D>();
  //Remove this script, so to not keeping the Cupcake Tower on the
```

```
      mouse
   Destroy(this);
 }
```

Save the script, and as a result the player is able to place cupcake towers once they are bought.

Selecting the towers

If you remember, all the trading operations have a selected tower to deal with. In fact, when the player presses the sell button, the game should know which cupcake tower the player intends to sell. As such, the player should be able to select (and unselect) a tower, and this tower should notify the trading system.

To achieve this, we need to slightly modify the CupcakeTowerScript. From the previous section, we know that when the tower is active, it has a collider to prevent placing other towers on top of it as well. But, we can also use this collider to detect if the player clicks on this very specific tower. In particular, we can use the self-explanatory function, OnMouseDown() in the following way:

```
//Function called when the player clicks on the cupcake Tower
void OnMouseDown() {
  //Assign this tower as the active tower for trading operations
  TradeCupcakeTowers.setActiveTower(this);
}
```

After saving the script, the player is able to select a specific tower among the ones he or she has in the game, and sell or upgrade it through the trading system.

The Game Manager

In the previous chapter, we introduced the GameMangerScript, but even after the second implementation of waypoints, we have left this script empty with no use. However, we do indeed need a game manager in our game to handle a couple of things. So, in case you have erased it from the last chapter, recreate it, along with a game object in the scene with such a script attached (the same way as if you erased the reference from the PandaScript, because we will need it later on).

We will use the `Game Manager` as a hub for exchanging information between the player's health and the Pandas. In fact, the `Game Manager` will spawn Pandas in the scene divided into waves, and it's the only script to be aware of when the level starts and finishes and/or if the player has lost all the health. This makes the Game Manager the perfect candidate to handle and trigger the game over conditions. Let's start with them.

Game over conditions

When does our game reach an end? Well, there are two cases: when the player loses his/her health, which means the Pandas have eaten all the cake (losing condition), or when the player has shot down all the Pandas (winning condition). In either case, we need to show to the player the outcome and terminate the game.

Game over feedback

In our graphic package, there are two screens ready for when the game is over. Respectively, these are *Game Over*, used for the losing condition, and *You Win*, used for the winning condition.

Create two UI images, as we learnt in Chapter 3, *Communicating with the Player – the User Interface*, and place the two sprites of our package, one for each UI image. You probably want to press the **Set Native Size** button, and then scale and move them, so that they are in the middle of the scene, as shown here:

Now, we can disable them, since they shouldn't be displayed until the game ends. However, we need to add a reference to them in the `Game Manager`.

As such, open the `GameManagerScript` and let's add these variables:

```
//Variable to store the the screen displayed when the player loses
public GameObject losingScreen;

//Variable to store the screen displayed when the player wins
public GameObject winningScreen;
```

Save the script, and from the **Inspector** assign the UI images we created previously, as shown here:

As a result, the `Game Manager` is able to activate one of the two when certain conditions are met. Let's see how to implement a function for that in the next section.

The GameOver function

To keep things ordered within our `GameManagerScript`, let's create a function to trigger what happens when the game ends. It will have a Boolean as a parameter to determine if the player has won or not.

Of course, what exactly should happen when the game ends is up to you. You can save statistics and the score (if you have any), trigger nice and cool animations, display buttons to load next levels, and so on. In this book, we will just display the UI images created in the previous section, because the goal is to show you where and how to insert code for game over. Feel free to add your own implementation to it.

Therefore, let's write down this function that, based on the parameter, will display the right screen to the player. Then, it stops the time of the game to create a kind of pause situation in the game. As a result, the game won't be running when the game over screen appears (if any UI is present, it will still be possible for the player to press on it):

```
//Private function called when some gameover conditions are met, and
    displays
//the winning or losing screen depending from the value of the
    parameter passed.
private void GameOver(bool playerHasWon) {
  //Check if the player has won from the parameter
  if (playerHasWon) {
    //Display the winning screen
    winningScreen.SetActive(true);
  }else {
    //Display the losing screen
    losingScreen.SetActive(true);
  }

  //Freeze the game time, so to stop in some way the level to be
    executed
  Time.timeScale = 0;
}
```

 You can find out more about timeScale here in the official documentation for Unity:
https://docs.unity3d.com/ScriptReference/Time-timeScale.html

Save the GameManagerScript, and let's explore when to trigger this function in the next sections.

Keeping track of the game's progress

Keeping track of the game's progress is one of the fundamental functions of a Game Manager. So, the first thing we want to ask is: what should we keep track of?

Definitely not the sugar possessed by the player, since it is separately handled within the Sugar Meter and the trading scripts. What about the player's health? Well, we do indeed want to keep track of it. In fact, when the player loses his/her health, the game ends as well, and the Game Manager needs to handle this case. What else? The Game Manager needs to keep track of how many Pandas the player shoots down, because in this way, the game manager is able to determine when the player wins.

Thus, the first thing we need to do is to get a reference to the health of the player. We can add the following variable:

```
//Private variable to store the reference to the Player's health
private HealthBarScript playerHealth;
```

We can initialize it in the `Start()` function, by adding this line at the beginning:

```
void Start () {
  //Get the reference to the Player's health
  playerHealth = FindObjectOfType<HealthBarScript>();
}
```

Then, we need a variable to keep track of how many Pandas there are still to defeat, hence we can add the following variable:

```
//Private variable which acts as a counter of how many Pandas are
  remained to defeat
private int numberOfPandasToDefeat;
```

It will be initialized by our spawning system, which we will implement soon.

Finally, we need to implement a couple of functions, which will be called, respectively, when a Panda is shot down, and when the player loses his/her health.

For the first, we don't need any parameters or return values, since the Game Manager just acknowledges that a Panda has been shot down by decreasing the number of Pandas that still need to be defeated:

```
//Function that decreases the number of Pandas still to defeat every
  time a Panda dies
public void OneMorePandaInHeaven() {
  numberOfPandasToDefeat--;
}
```

Regarding the second function, we want to create a hub of communication between the Panda that is eating the cake and the player's health. As such, we need to implement a function that takes the damage of the Panda as a parameter and subtract it from the player's health. Then, it checks if the player is still alive, because if he/she is not, the GameOver function is triggered. In either case, at the end we need to decrease the number of Pandas still to defeat, because we remember that Pandas eat so much cake that they explode:

```
//Function that damages the player when a Panda reaches the player's
  cake.
//Moreover, it monitors the player's health to trigger the GameOver
  function when needed
public void BiteTheCake(int damage) {
```

```
    //Apply damage to the player and retrieve a Boolean to see if the
      cake has been eaten all
    bool IsCakeAllEaten = playerHealth.ApplyDamage(damage);
    //If the cake has been eaten all, the GameOver function is called in
      "losing mode"
    if (IsCakeAllEaten) {
      GameOver(false);
    }
    //The Panda that bit the cake will also explode, and therefore we
      have a Panda less to defeat
    OneMorePandaInHeaven();
  }
```

Save the script, and open the `PandaScript` since now we need to slightly modify it. In particular, we need to call the functions just created in the Game Manager. From Chapter 6, *Through a Sea of Sprinkles – Navigation in Artificial Intelligence*, we already have a reference to the Game Manager, which we can use to trigger these functions.

The first modification is to add the following variable to determine how much cake this specific Panda can eat when it bites (its value needs to be set in the Inspector, don't forget it!):

```
    //The amount of cake that the Panda eats
    public int cakeEatenPerBite;
```

The second modification is in the `FixedUpdate()` function. In fact, we need to detract health from the player by using the `BiteTheCake()` function in the Game Manager. The highlighted part is what we have modified:

```
    void FixedUpdate() {
      //if the Panda has reached the cake, then it will eat it, by
        triggering the right animation,
      //and remove this script, since the State Machine Behaviour will take
        care of removing the Panda
      if (currentWaypointNumber == gameManager.waypoints.Length) {
        animator.SetTrigger(AnimEatTriggerHash);
        gameManager.BiteTheCake(cakeEatenPerBite);
        Destroy(this);
        return;
      }
      // [...] The remaining code of the function
```

The third and last modification is in the Hit() function, in which we also need to trigger the OneMorePandaInHeaven() function of the Game Manager. We can do it in the following way (again the highlighted part is what is changed):

```
private void Hit(float damage) {
  //Subtract the damage to the health of the Panda
  health -= damage;
  //Then it triggers the Die or the Hit animations based if the Panda
    is still alive
  if(health <= 0) {
    animator.SetTrigger(AnimDieTriggerHash);
    gameManager.OneMorePandaInHeaven();
  }
  else {
    animator.SetTrigger(AnimHitTriggerHash);
  }
}
```

Save the script, because we are going to explore how the Pandas are created/spawned in the next section.

Panda invasion – spawning Pandas

In this section, we will implement the spawning system of the game. This can be done in many ways. However, since we have only one kind of Panda (at least for the moment), we will implement it in a simple way. In any case, we will use coroutines to implement the system, and we will see a template structure which we might also use in more complex spawning systems (in the next chapter, some ideas of more complex spawning systems will be provided).

What is a coroutine?

It is a structure that Unity provides to allow functions to be interrupted and continued in other frames of the game. In the case of our spawning system, we don't want to spawn all the Pandas at the same time, but a little bit over time. This over time can be controlled with coroutines. You can definitely learn more and see some examples in the official documentation here: https://docs.unity3d.com/Manual/Coroutines.html

However, the most important things to know about coroutines are listed here:

- They are special functions which have an `IEnumerator` as a return value.
- They can be started with the `StartCoroutine()` function and stopped with the `StopCourotine()` function.
- They cannot run/start within any `Update()` function. The reason is because the `Update()` function's nature is to be called one time per frame (or more), whereas the coroutine's nature is to run at the time they specify.
- They can use a special instruction; yield: It allows them to wait for something, such as a fixed amount of time, the end of the frame, or even another coroutine. In any case, after the yield, they expect a return value. Common functions that are used with yield are:
    - `WaitForEndOfFrame()`: Waits until the next frame (official documentation: `https://docs.unity3d.com/ScriptReference/WaitForEndOfFrame.html`)
    - `WaitForSeconds()`: Waits a specific amount of time specified in seconds as a parameter (official documentation: `https://docs.unity3d.com/ScriptReference/WaitForSeconds.html`)
    - `WaitUntil()`: Waits until a certain condition is met (official documentation: `https://docs.unity3d.com/ScriptReference/WaitUntil.html`)

Moreover, you can even implement custom yield instructions, as shown in the official documentation here: `https://docs.unity3d.com/ScriptReference/CustomYieldInstruction.html`

 For the most curious of you, coroutines are not threads. In fact, coroutines run on the same thread as the rest of the game.

It takes time to get used to them, since they are hard to make work when you have complex environments, and as such they are often considered as an advanced topic. But they unlock many potentialities in what can be done, which is fundamental for good gameplay programming. Unfortunately, in this book we don't have enough space to dedicate them a proper space, but I hope that with the official documentation, this small explanation, and the example of the spawning system in the next section, you will be able to better understand coroutines.

Sketching the idea of how it works

We will divide our game into waves. Each wave has a determined number of Pandas, which will be spawned over time at an increasing intensity. Once all of the Pandas of that wave have been shot down, the game will increase the number of spawned Pandas for the next wave and start it. When all the waves are completed by the player, the level can be considered as a win.

In particular, we will have a cycle in a coroutine which will manage the different waves and wait till the end of a wave before starting another one. A second routine will take care of the single wave, to spawn Pandas for it, and check when all the Pandas have been shot down by the player.

Setting up the spawning system

Designers should be provided with a way to place where the Pandas will be spawned. As such, we can create an empty game object, and call it `SpawningPoint`. Moreover, you can attach to it a gizmo, similar to what we have done with waypoints in the previous chapter. As a result, it will be visible in the **Scene** view. So, at the end you should have something like this:

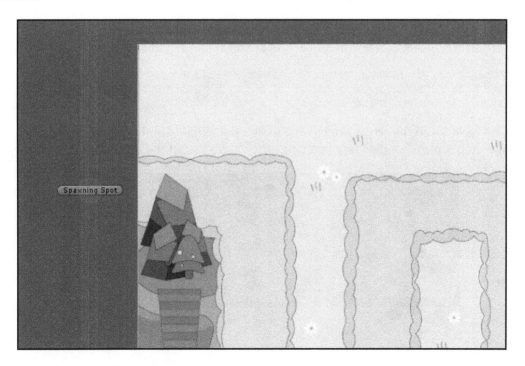

Open the GameManagerScript and let's add a variable to keep track of where this SpawningPoint is. Since we just need the position, we can just take the Transform, instead of the whole game object:

```
//The Spawning Point transform so to get where the Pandas should be
  spawned
private Transform spawner;
```

To set its value, let's change the Start() function like the following:

```
void Start () {
  //Get the reference to the Player's health
  playerHealth = FindObjectOfType<HealthBarScript>();

  //Get the reference to the Spawner
  spawner = GameObject.Find("Spawning Spot").transform;
}
```

Also, we need three more variables. One is for the prefab of the Panda to instantiate the right enemy, another is for the number of waves that the player has to face, and the last one for the number of Pandas per wave (which will increase between waves):

```
//The Panda Prefab that should be spawned as enemy
public GameObject pandaPrefab;

//The number of waves that the player has to face in this level
public int numberOfWaves;

//The number of Pandas that the player as to face per wave.
//It increase when a wave is won.
public int numberOfPandasPerWave;
```

After we have saved the script, we have to assign the variable in the **Inspector**, as shown in the following screenshot (feel free to change the values to suit the balance of your game):

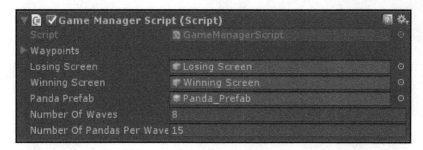

Managing waves

In this section, we are going to implement the first of the two coroutines aforementioned. In fact, this coroutine will cycle over all the waves, and call the second one to handle the single wave. Between waves, the number of spawned enemies is increased. If the player has won all the waves, then the GameOver() function is called in the winning mode.

Thus, open the GameManagerScript and we can start to write the following:

```
//Coroutine that spawns the different waves of Pandas
private IEnumerator WavesSpawner() {
  //For each wave
  for(int i = 0; i < numberOfWaves; i++) {
    //Let the PandaSpawner coroutine to handle the single wave. When it
      finishes
    //also the wave is finished, and so this coroutine can continue.
    yield return PandaSpawner();
    //Increase the number of Pandas that are generated per wave
    numberOfPandasPerWave += 3;
  }
  //If the Player won all the waves, call the GameOver function in
    "winning" mode
  GameOver(true);
}
```

As you can see from the code, we call call the PandaSpawner() coroutine, which we implement in the next section.

The single wave

Now for the tough part. Here we need to write a coroutine that is able to handle a whole wave of Pandas. Therefore, let's look at it step-by-step, starting with creating the coroutine:

```
//Coroutine that spawns the Pandas for a single wave, and waits until
  "all the Pandas are in Heaven"
private IEnumerator PandaSpawner() {
  //Rest of the code
}
```

The first thing to do is to initialize the `numberOfPandasToDefeat` variable, to keep track of how many Pandas the player has defeated so far. Of course, we will initialize this number to be the same as the number of Pandas that will be spawned in the wave:

```
//Initialize the number that needs to be defeated for this wave
numberOfPandasToDefeat = numberOfPandasPerWave;
```

The next step is to cycle through all the Pandas to spawn, to progressively spawn them:

```
//Progressively spawn Pandas
for(int i=0; i < numberOfPandasPerWave; i++) {
  //Rest of the code inside the cycle
}
//Rest of the code outside the cycle
```

Inside the cycle, we need to first spawn the Pandas at their spawned position (with no rotation, which means having the identity as a **quaternion**). Then, we need to wait for a time that depends both on how many Pandas are left and by a random number. In particular, we will calculate the ratio of how many Pandas are left, and use it to interpolate between two times. As a result, the greater the number of Pandas spawned so far, the less time to wait. Then, this is added to a random number, to add a bit of chance in our game. Here is the code:

```
//Spawn/Instantiate a Panda at the Spawner position
Instantiate(pandaPrefab, spawner.position, Quaternion.identity);

//Wait a time that depends both on how many Pandas are left to be
//spawned and by a random number
float ratio = (i * 1f) / (numberOfPandasPerWave - 1);
float timeToWait = Mathf.Lerp(3f, 5f, ratio) + Random.Range(0f, 2f);
yield return new WaitForSeconds(timeToWait);
```

 Of course, this is not the only way to implement this and the numbers in the code are arbitrary. In a real game, everything should be decided in order to balance the game, by the hard work of designing and play testing. You can find a bit more about this in the next chapter.

Outside the cycle, instead, we need to wait until all the Pandas have been shot down by the player (or some game over conditions have been met) before ending the coroutine, and so give back control to the `WavesSpawner()` coroutine for the next wave:

```
//Once all the Pandas are spawned, wait until all of them are defeated
//by the player (or a gameover condition occurred before)
yield return new WaitUntil(() => numberOfPandasToDefeat <= 0);
```

Save the script, and as a result, the player has to face many, terrible waves of sweet-toothed Pandas!

The main menu

As in many games, there is a main menu when the game starts, and so, also, in our game we cannot forget a main menu. This will give us the possibility to explore a bit more of what we have touched upon in Chapter 1, *A Flat World in Unity*, about changing scenes in Unity.

Designing the main menu

As we learnt back in Chapter 3, *Communicating with the Player – the User Interface*, it's good practice to have a design of the user interface, and the main menu is an extension of the user interface. As such, it should be designed with the same principles of UI design in mind.

The menu for our game is very simple: we have a cool background, and three buttons placed just below the center of the screen. They are respectively:

- **NEW GAME**: Creates a new game for the player, by loading the level we have been creating so far
- **SETTINGS**: Triggers a setting screen, where the player can manipulate some options (this is left as an exercise, in the *Homework* section)
- **QUIT**: As the name suggests, it closes the game

So, our design will look something like the following:

Creating the main menu in another scene

To create another scene in Unity, you can select **File** | **New Scene** from the top bar, but it's preferable to navigate in the **Project** panel within the `Scene` folder so that by right-clicking you can select **Create** | **Scene**. In this second way, the scene will be directly created within the right folder; as a result, your project is ordered and tidy.

You can name the scene `Main Menu`, and then double-click to open it. And here from scratch again, there is an empty void to fill up with your creativity and fantasies!

Now, you should have the skills to do the following without a step-by-step explanation:

1. Create a UI image (which will automatically generate a **Canvas** as well as the **Event System**), and name it `Background`. Then, extend it to the whole screen, and place the cool background you have in mind.
2. Tweak the canvas settings if you need to achieve what you have in mind.
3. Create three buttons, change their graphics if you want, and their texts so to match **NEW GAME**, **SETTINGS**, and **QUIT** respectively. Place them, as in the design of the previous section.
4. Create an empty GameObject where we will attach a script to handle all the different interactions.
5. On the three buttons, add an `OnClick()` event and drag the new empty object into the `object` variable

Once the menu is created, we can save the scene.

Since we have two scenes, if we want to include them in the final version of the game, we need to include them in the **Scenes In Build**. To do so, we need to open the building settings from the top bar menu by clicking on **File** | **Building Settings...** . You can drag and drop the scene in the **Scenes In Build** area from your **Project** panel, and they will appear there in a determined order. The numbers you see next to the scenes are the identifiers of the scene. For instance, we can use this identifier to specify which scene to load.

In our case, be sure that the `Main Menu` scene is before our `Level_01`, as shown in the following screenshot:

Now, it's time to create the script with all the functionalities.

Loading scenes through scripts

Create a new script and call it `MainMenuFunctionalities`. Since its functions will be triggered by the `OnClick()` event, we need to make them public.

In particular, we have a function for loading the level of our game. If you remember, its ID is 1. To load a scene in Unity, you use a special class called `SceneManager`. As such, we need to import its library by adding the following line of code at the beginning of our script:

```
using UnityEngine.SceneManagement;
```

The `SceneManager` class along with the `UnityEngine.SceneManagement` library are relatively new in Unity. In fact, these allow you to perform many actions on scenes, such as loading them together, loading them dynamically, and unloading them, all at runtime. This gives you a new universe of possibilities, which I hope you will have chance to explore, since in this book we don't have time to go through everything in detail. In any case, a good starting point is, as usual, the official documentation that you can find here: https://docs.unity3d.com/ScriptReference/SceneManagement.SceneManager.html.

For the more curious of you, before the `SceneManager` class, scenes were handled by the `Application` class. So, in case you have some outdated code, which still uses the `Application` class to load scenes, you know that it was written for previous versions of Unity. If that code belongs to your project, consider (if possible, due to legal issues) to update it using the `SceneManager` class.

The most common function of the `SceneManager` class is `LoadScene()`, which can load another scene. One way to specify the scene is with its identifier (as we will do in our script), but there are also other ways, such as with a string containing the name of the scene.

We can implement the function that will be called by the **NEW GAME** button in the following way, which is really simple and straight forward:

```
//Function that loads the first level
public void NewGame() {
    SceneManager.LoadScene(1);
}
```

The function related to the **SETTINGS** button, instead, is left as an exercise (see *Homework* section):

```
//Function that displays the settings
public void Settings() {
    //Your own code here
}
```

Finally, the function to quit the game uses the `Application` class (more on this class in the official documentation here: https://docs.unity3d.com/ScriptReference/Application.html), where there is a specific function to quit your game:

```
//Function that closes the game
public void Quit() {
```

```
        Application.Quit();
    }
```

Keep in mind that this function doesn't work in some circumstances, such as when the game is running in the editor (in Unity itself), or for instance, for web-based games. As such, closing a game that should be shipped on different platforms might require more work. More about multi-platform games in the next chapter.

Save the script, and come back to the `OnClick()` events on the three buttons.

Assign the correct function to each of them. Here is the example of how the **NEW GAME** button event should look:

And also, the main menu has been implemented. With this, our game is basically completed and functioning. Let's recap what we have done and learnt so far in the next section.

Techniques we learnt in this chapter

If you have reached this point of the chapter and book, it means that your game is completed. Let's recap what we have learnt in terms of techniques, instead of topics:

- **Inheritance**: We have implemented our trading system by using inheritance, and this gave us the possibility to explore it. In particular, we learnt a bit more about:
  - **Abstract classes and methods**: So that their full implementation is left to child classes
  - **Protected variables**: Which can be seen by some scripts but not all of them
  - **UI handlers**: Can be automatically linked to have an interaction with the UI without settings events in the **Inspector**
- **Interaction between mouse and camera**: To implement the placing script, we needed to transform the mouse coordinates into game coordinates.

- **Enabling/disabling scripts**: To implement functionalities, always in the placing script, we learnt how it is possible to disable and enable scripts to trigger functionalities when they are needed.
- **Storing information**: Within the `Game Manager`, we learnt how other scripts can have access to them. Throughout all the chapters we have done this, and in different ways. In particular, we used public functions on the `Game Manager` that have been called by the other scripts. As a result, the **Game Manager** became a hub to exchange data between the different parts of the game.
- **Using static functions**: To assign generic variables again, in the trading system, we have implemented a static function to set the active tower. As a result, any script can have access to that function without the need to get a reference to the specific trading class instance (moreover the parent class is abstract so it doesn't have instances). This could have been done without many problems, because the variable assigned was already static and shared among all the instances of the trading classes.
- **Implementing coroutines**: To handle events that last over time in implementing the spawning system, we have used coroutines. These are special functions which have the possibility to be interrupted and continue in other frames of the game. This is the most powerful tool we have seen in this chapter, although it requires a bit more practice than other tools to master it, but it is definitely worth it.
- **Using UI events**: To implement the functions, in our main menu, we have implemented functions within a script to be triggered by the `OnClick()` event of the buttons. In this way, you avoid using UI handlers. The advantages of this method is that you can place all the functions within a single script and have a specific instance of that script to trigger (in case the script can be instantiated). On the other hand the disadvantage is that a lot of manual work for linking the events in the **Inspector** is required. UI handlers, on the contrary, have advantages and disadvantages flipped. As such, UI handlers are suitable for big scripts with many functions implemented in that which require a bit of interaction with the UI. For small functions, instead, it is better to have them all in a single script that creates a different script for each one of them. In any case, the best solution depends on the situation and which one is your goal.
- **Using colliders to identify zones**: We used the physics engine to detect if the mouse is hovering over certain zones when placing cupcake towers is allowed. Moreover, we used a collider on the cupcake towers to detect a click on it (so as to be selected) and to avoid placing other cupcake towers on top of others. These are just one of the many ways to use the Physics engine for non-physics related calculations.

I hope you have learnt a lot in this chapter, and that you have grasped the basic concepts of each of the different techniques we have used. To improve both the game and your skills, I invite you do the exercises in the following section.

Homework

In this chapter, we have covered many techniques on how to exchange information between different parts of our game, and learnt a bit about gameplay programming. Here there are some exercises to improve your skills and become a better game developer:

1. **Sweet capital**: When the the game begins, Pandas start coming and the player should buy some cupcake tower to defend his/her cake. But, at the very beginning, the player doesn't have any sugar to buy towers, nor he/she can kill some Pandas to get some sugar. Thus, add an initial sugar amount variable in the Game Manager (so that it can be set from the Inspector), and set this quantity in the Sugar Meter within the Start() function. As a result, the player will be immediately ready to fight Pandas.

2. **The calm before the storm**: At this stage, when the game starts, the Pandas immediately come to eat the player's delicious cake. However, the player should have the time to buy and place some cupcake towers at the beginning, with the capital set from the previous exercise. In the wavesSpawner() coroutine, set a timer before each wave to give the player the time to assess. Then, expose the right variables in the **Inspector**, so as to tweak the timer depending on the level. Consider, as a variant, that you can increase or decrease such a timer between waves.

3. **Wave bonus (Part I)**: If you are planning to increase the number of Pandas spawned significantly between waves, then you should consider rewarding the player with some sugar once the wave is completed. Modify the wavesSpawner() coroutine to include a sweet bonus for the player. Then, expose the right variables in the Inspector to tweak the bonus for each level.

4. **Wave bonus (Part II)**: After have done the previous exercise, make an array of bonuses, where its dimension changes according to the number of waves. Then, at the end of each wave, assign the right bonus to the player, so as to have the possibility to tweak the bonus not only for each level, but also for each wave.

5. **Singleton pattern (Part I)**: In our game, there are some scripts that should have a single instance at the time, such as the `Game manager`, the `Health Bar`, or the `Sugar Meter`. As such, it's best practice to make them unique, since some of our scripts rely on the implicit (but not granted) fact that there is only one instance of such classes. Therefore, you should implement a pattern called **singleton**. You can definitely search on the Internet how to implement it, but try to come up with your own personal solution. Many online implementations rely on a static variable to retrieve the single instance of the class. Since our script will find these classes with the `FindObjectOfType()` function, you can try to explore other ways. So, try to give your solution to the problem and implement it for the `GameMangerScript`, the `HealthBarScript`, and the `SugarMeterScript`.

6. **Singleton pattern (Part II)**: After Part I, you should have implemented the singleton pattern in your way. Now, look at the following two links: `http://wiki.unity3d.com/index.php/Singleton` and `https://unity3d.com/learn/tutorials/projects/2d-roguelike-tutorial/writing-game-manager`, since both implement the singleton pattern. Compare those to the ones you came up with, and highlight for each approach, the advantages and the disadvantages. Which approach do you think would work better in our game? Does the approach differ for the `Game Manager`, the `Health Bar`, or the `Sugar Meter`? Implement the singleton pattern you consider worthwhile for our tower defense game.

7. **Improving the allowed areas (Part I)**: We have seen how it is possible to use colliders to check if the mouse is hovering over allowed areas, so that the placing script knows if it is a suitable place or not when it needs to release the cupcake towers. But what happens in the `Game Manager`? Even if there is no tower to place, it stills checks for allowed areas and updates its internal state. Think about a solution in which the `Game Manager` checks if the mouse is hovering over allowed areas only when the placing scripts asks for it. As a result, your new solution should improve the performance of the `Game Manager`.

8. **Improving the allowed areas (Part II)**: This exercise is independent from part I. In the allowed areas system, we have considered only the mouse. What about if you want to export the game on a mobile platform, such as on an Android device? In this situation, should the allowed area system be completely redesign or changed? As such, design and implement a system which is suitable for as many platforms as possible.

9. **Improving the allowed areas (Part III)**: This exercise is independent from Parts I and II. The system of allowed areas we came up with is not really easy to use for a multi-level game (something that, most likely, you have), since you cannot place colliders in the `Game Manager Prefab` as they depend on the particular level. Can you think of an easier solution for level designers to tell the `Game Manager` which areas are allowed, level by level? Once you have designed such a system, implement it in our tower defense game.

10. **Improving the allowed areas (Part IV)**: Consider all the solutions you have found for the different problems faced in Parts I, II, and III. Try to merge them together into an ultimate solution for the allowed areas. The goal is to create a system which is efficient (from a computational point of view), easy-to-use (for game and level designers), and multi-platform (so as to deploy the game on more than one platform) at the same time.

11. **Feedback to the player (Part I)**: This is a series of exercises all independent of each other, and they aim to improve the feedback that the game provides to the player, which is of vital importance for a game to be appealing. When the player trades, he/she sells, buys, or upgrades towers, but there is no feedback that the operation was a success. Therefore, you need to implement some visual feedback. Consider the following as smaller exercises:

    - When sugar is detracted or added to the `Sugar Meter`, add an animation so that a big number appears on the `Sugar Meter` showing the quantity that changed. Moreover, consider changing the color of this number based on the amount, and whether it is added or subtracted.
    - When the sugar is detracted or added to the `Sugar Meter`, add an animation to show the numbers of the `Sugar Meter` changing, instead of suddenly changing the number displayed.
    - When a tower is upgraded, consider placing an animation that plays on the tower. Same for when the tower is sold or placed (after have bought it).

12. **Feedback to the player (Part II)**: This is a series of exercises all independent of each other, and they aim to improve the feedback that the game provides to the player, which is of vital importance for a game to be appealing. When the player trades, he/she sells, buys, or upgrades towers, but there is no feedback about what the operations are going to do/change, such as: which one is the price of buying a tower? Therefore, you need to implement some visual feedback. Consider the following as smaller exercises:

    - When the player hovers over one of the trading buttons, make the price (or the value in case of the selling button) appear somewhere (which needs to be decided carefully, since it impacts the design we did in

Chapter 3, *Communicating with the Player – the User Interface*), so the player can read it before, to perform the action.

- When no tower is selected, both the selling and the upgrading buttons shouldn't be displayed as active. Change this, to display a disable button when the `currentActiveTower` variable is null.

13. **Implementing a setting menu (Part I)**: In this chapter, we left this as an exercise, so let's see what we need to do. The first thing to decide is what settings the player can change and how (a toggle? A slider? A drop-down menu?). In particular, you should have at least an audio toggle, and a quality settings drop-down menu, plus any options you would like to include. Then, make a complete design of the UI. Finally, in Unity create a new scene (or screen, whichever you prefer) and implement the settings screen by using UI elements.

14. **Implementing a setting menu (Part II)**: In Part I, we did the design and implemented it within Unity. Now, we need to implement the functionalities (except the audio for now, which is left for the next chapter). So, create a script, and similar to what we did with the main menu, implement all the functionalities there, and link them to the UI elements through the use of events in the **Inspector**. To modify the quality settings and the audio settings, search the official documentation on how to do it (this is part of the exercise). Moreover, keep in mind that the next chapter might give you some other ideas of the kind of settings to implement.

15. **Magic numbers (Part I)**: We already have encountered magic numbers in the previous chapters. They are numbers that appear within a script and without an explanation, and good practice says that it is better to avoid them as much as possible. Also in this chapter, we have left many of them; let's try to remove them. The first magic number is the number 7 from the placing script when we create a new vector for the position of our tower. This number depends on the position of the camera and where the tower should be placed along the z-axis. As such, add some lines of code to calculate this number in a dynamic way (so if we decide to change the camera position or the z-depth of the towers, we can do it without changing the script, as a bonus, you will have the possibility of also having different kinds of towers on different z-depth layers, which can be useful to you in the same way). In particular, you need to subtract the z-axis of the tower from the z-axis of the camera.

16. **Magic numbers (Part II)** : We have also left some magic numbers in the `Upgrade()` function of the `CupcakeTowerScript`. Create variables that can be set in the **Inspector**, to remove any magic numbers that are left (such as increasing the selling value or the upgrade cost).

Summary

In this chapter, we have explored many techniques to exchange information and data between different scripts. In doing so, we have finished the implementation of our tower defense game.

The Pandas walk towards the player's cake to eat it, the cupcake towers shoot at them, and so Pandas die and they are periodically spawned as well. The player can buy, sell, and upgrade cupcake towers. A main menu is present and the player can either win or lose. So, our game is complete. Or is it not? Can we go even further? Let's find it out in the next chapter.

8

What Is beyond the Cake?

"From colorful cupcakes to delectable desserts, discover how to tantalize the taste buds of consumers!"

In the first part of the chapter, we will present a series of ideas on how to improve your game. Some of these sections have already been anticipated in previous chapters. In order to have these sections explained in detail, and by also showing the code, we would have required much more time and space, which we unfortunately don't have. Therefore, you need to consider these sections as exercises. In fact, this is the only chapter in which the *Homework* section is not present (although there are some explicit exercises). Please, feel free to expand and implement what captures your interest most. After all, nothing can teach you better than experience, and trial and error!

Later in the chapter, we will discover what's beyond the cake. In fact, game development is not limited to the game itself; there are many things built around that you should consider. These things may include, teamwork, playtesting, marketing, and localization! Of course, this is not a book about video game marketing, but it provides some ground to start to go beyond the mere game!

Finally, I have to say that you should congratulate yourself since you have reached this far! In fact, not only have you finished a *Tower Defense* game and learnt a lot about Unity, but also you are still here, standing for the last chapter! So, to keep yourself motivated, go and grab a slice of cake before continuing to read this last chapter.

Enhancing and improving your game

The aim of this section is to give you an idea of the potentiality of your game and a direction to work toward. After all, if you have reached this far, you will also be able to walk by yourself, and so I won't explain everything in detail.

Improving cupcake towers

Here we will focus on how we can improve our cupcake towers by exploring some ideas and new directions, such as shooting policies or a special kind of sprinkles.

Shooting policies

Back in `Chapter 2`, *Baking Cupcake Towers*, we implemented the first cupcake tower that shot the Panda closest to the tower. However, this is not the only policy that you can pick. Actually, you can also allow the player to pick one that suits better for his/her strategy.

These policies may include:

- Shoot the weaker/stronger Panda
- Shoot the Panda with less/more health
- Shoot the furthest Panda within the range
- Shoot the first/last Panda that enters in the range

Feel free to add more and implement your own.

How to implement these:

In `CupcakeTowerScript`, we loop over all the Pandas (actually colliders, but we filter them by tag). We have found and calculated the distance from each one of them. Some concepts can be applied with the preceding list. In the case of the furthest Panda, this is immediate, because instead of having the `min` variable, you can have a `max` variable. The same holds true for weaker/stronger and with less/more health Pandas, in which you still need to have a `min` or `max` variable, but instead of the distance, you take some properties from the `PandaScript`. The case in which we are searching the first or last Panda that has entered the range is a bit trickier. In fact, you need to have a data structure for the Pandas that enters and exits from the range, and then retrieve the Panda to shoot from this structure.

Special sprinkles

In our game, all of the sprinkles just have a damage and a speed, which can be set by the Cupcake towers that shoots them. However, you can have more types of sprinkles, and some of them can have special effects.

Some examples of these effects might be the following:

- **Freeze**: A probability to slow down the enemy for a limited period of time.
- **Poison**: A probability to poison the Panda; that will decrease its health over time (usually within a short period of time).
- **Explosive**: They don't damage only the Panda that they hit, but also surrounding Pandas.
- **Critical hit**: A probability that the sprinkle could kill the Panda regardless of its remaining life. But for instance, it is not applicable for bosses, which in a critical hit just receive double the damage.

Feel free to add your own.

How to implement these:
You can create special sprinkle classes that derive from the ProjectileScript class by using inheritance. This derivative class can contain additional data about their effects. In PandaScript, you can retrieve in the OnTriggerEnter2D() function which kind of sprinkle hit the Panda, so as to retrieve its information and apply an effect to the Panda.
In the case of the explosive effect, the Panda that was hit should use the Physics2D.OverlapCircleAll() function (as in CupcakeTowerScript) to find nearby Pandas.

Moreover, you can animate them so that they have nice and smooth animation. Even just a rotation animation could be awesome to see.

Aging and pricing model

Who said that a tower cannot get old? Given that a Cupcake tower is shooting at Pandas continually from its creation, it might be subjected to usury. As such, its performance may decrease over time and also its value if the player tries to sell it.

What Is beyond the Cake?

You can add another trading option to repair a cupcake tower and get it back to work as it should.

How to implement this:

You can implement a coroutine within `CupcakeTowerScript` that after a fixed amount of time, it ages the tower, by lowering its stats, eventually until it stops to work. If you also want to implement a repair functionality, you need to store the original values of the tower somewhere in order to restore them after the repairing option.

Besides aging, what about the various prices and costs that change over time dynamically? Ideally, you would like to create a real pricing model for that (which takes a lot of design efforts), but it would be greatly appreciated once it works. In fact, it's something to take into consideration when you balance your game.

How to implement this:

Again, you can create a coroutine within `CupcakeTowerScript` that, based on the current state of the tower (and potentially of the game), changes its costs. As a result, when the trading system fetches these values, they are updated based on your model price.

Improving the user interface

Also, the user interface of our game can be improved, for instance, a notification indicating to the player how many waves he/she has still to defeat. Adding this kind of information can be extremely useful. The next step is then to determine, where?. This is another design choice that should be taken into account, because it might affect the balance we reached when we designed the current UI back in Chapter 3, *Communicating with the Player – the User Interface*.

So a good exercise would be to iterate the design of the whole interface of the game by taking into account as many things as possible (including showing the prices and costs in the trading system; there was an exercise on this in the previous chapter).

A really good book on how to design user interfaces is *Designing with the Mind in Mind* by Jeff Johnson, but this is just one of many, so be sure to check out other more specific books about UI in video games.

Improving levels

Here we will focus on things we can do to improve our levels. As for the cupcake towers in the previous section, we will explore new ideas and directions, such as including more levels, enemies, and paths to follow.

Multilevel

Of course, your game must contain more than one level! We have implemented only one level, but you should definitely expand your game to more than one.

At this stage, you are able to create your own map and level. But here are a few hints and considerations that you might find useful:

- Remember that static variables are persistent. Therefore, they need to be reassigned with the correct values when you change the scene.
- You can make some objects persistent between scenes by using the `DontDestroyOnLoad()` function (useful when you need to implement music; we will see this in *Audio* section).
- You have to take designing choices, such as: is the sugar collected by the player preserved among levels? And his/her health?

Large maps

We can implement very large maps in the game, so large that they cannot be displayed all at once on the screen. In this way, we need to implement a way that the user can move the camera so as to move the level (or you can also implement that the camera is fixed, and all the rest moves).

How to implement this:
Attached to the camera, you can create a script, which detects when the player drags the mouse, so as to move the camera in the opposite direction (left drag, camera moves right).

Many paths

Nothing prevents us from creating a map where the path for the Pandas at a certain point splits or merges with other paths. We can even have more spawning points, or more than one way of access to the cake.

All of this can be taken care of by our waypoint system. In fact, the Pandas call the GetNextWaypoint() function, which can return any waypoint in the map.

As such, you can create many different waypoints that inherit from the parent class of waypoint. In the case of a split, you can randomly choose where to send the Panda. Here is a fragment of code to give you an example when the path splits in two:

```
[SerializeField]
private Waypoint waypoint1, waypoint2;

public override Waypoint GetNextWaypoint() {
  if(Random.Range(0,2) == 0) {
    return waypoint1;
  }else {
    return waypoint2;
  }
}
```

But you can really implement whatever you have in mind as far as you reason in terms of waypoints! You can also make GetNextWaypoint() accept some parameter, such as the Panda itself, and based on the Panda also decide on which waypoint to send the Panda! Basically the possibilities are many, and the structure to have waypoints as single entities allows us to do this kind of stuff.

Many Pandas

We cannot limit ourselves to just one type of Panda! We can make green, red, and purple Pandas too! Each one of them can have different stats. For instance, some are really slow, have a lot of health, and do eat a lot of cake. Others are really fast, have low health, and eat just a moderate bite of the player's cake when they reach it.

You might even think about giving them different abilities, and again you can use the concept of inheritance to implement other Panda classes that derive from the PandaScript. However, remember to keep in mind that you also need to change the spawning system!

Multiphase bosses

Among the different kinds of Pandas, you can add at the end of the level a boss to defeat a giant Panda with a crown on its head:

The different phases of the boss can be structured with a finite state machine, and the different transitions triggered by the amount of its health or how close it is to the player's cake. It might also have the possibility to get really angry and go off the track to eat a cupcake tower!

A better spawning system

Since we added so many different kinds of Pandas, we need to restructure our spawning system. Ideally you want to find a solution easier for designers to show in the **Inspector** an array with the different waves, and for each wave how many enemies of one kind and how many enemies of another kind, like this image:

```
SPAWNING SYSTEM

  WAVE #1
    RED PANDAS      [ 12                        ]
    BLUE PANDAS     [ 7                         ]
    GREEN PANDAS    [ 3                         ]

  WAVE #2
    RED PANDAS      [ 16                        ]
    BLUE PANDAS     [ 10                        ]
    GREEN PANDAS    [ 5                         ]

  WAVE #3
    RED PANDAS      [ 20                        ]
    BLUE PANDAS     [ 16                        ]
    GREEN PANDAS    [ 9                         ]
```

You may be wondering whether this can really be done in the Unity Inspector. The answer is yes; in fact, the Unity Editor can be extended (we will see later in this chapter).

Switching difficulty at runtime

Another great way to adapt the game to a large audience might be to switch the difficulty of the game at runtime, based on the player's performance. In fact, you may want to keep players who seek challenges engaged by increasing the level of difficulty if they are progressing relatively easily through the game, or help players that are struggling.

There are different ways to do it. The simplest one includes if-chains, based on the player's score to increase or decrease the difficulty; whereas the most complex ones include adaptive learning algorithms.

How to implement this:

Whichever your way is, the first thing to do is to link your entire game to a difficulty parameter, maybe within the `Game Manager`. Whenever, this parameter is changed, all the parts of the game dependent on it change (refer the *More about communication between scripts* section). Then on a separate script, you can implement your adaptive algorithm, which, fed with the different states of the game, can determine whether to increase or decrease the difficulty.

Training and extending your Unity skills to become a better game developer

In this section, we will give some ideas on how to improve your Unity skills and overall improve any game, including this *Tower Defense* game.

Making things easier for other team members

When you program your scripts in Unity, you need to keep in mind that your code will be used by different team members (we will see more about teamwork later in the chapter). So keep in mind the following:

- Increase the readability of your code through documentation (we will see later in *Teamwork* section) for your programmer's colleagues.
- Make a nice interface in the Inspector (also by using custom inspectors; see later) so that it is easy to use by designers (an example is exposing events, which we are going to explore in the next section).

Exposing events

If you are programming a very cool script that needs to interact with other elements in the game, you can actually expose your own event in your scripts.

In fact, you can add this library to your code:

```
using UnityEngine.Events;
```

As a result, you will be able declare and trigger events in the following way:

```
//Float variable just for test. Can be set in the Inspector.
public float myFloat;

//Declaration of the event class. It has a float as parameter to pass.
[System.Serializable]
public class OnEveryFrame : UnityEvent<float> { }

//Declare the variable event which will be shown in the Inspector
public OnEveryFrame OnEveryFrameEvent;

//Function that is called every frame
void Update() {
  //fire the event at every frame
  OnEveryFrameEvent.Invoke(myFloat);
}
```

This is how it appears in the **Inspector**:

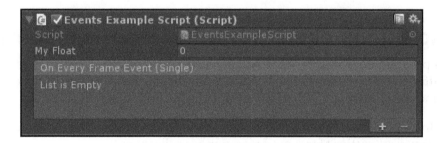

Cool, isn't' it?

Sprinkles pooling

Instantiating a game object in Unity is a slow operation; as such, every time the cupcake tower shoots, a new sprinkle is instantiated and then removed from the game.

A much better solution would be to do object pooling, which is an optimization technique (we anticipated something about this in Chapter 2, *Baking Cupcake Towers*). The concept is to instantiate a fixed number of sprinkles at the beginning and keep them off-screen. When a cupcake tower shoots a sprinkle, it just takes a sprinkle from this pool and shoots that. When the sprinkle is supposed to be destroyed, instead, it is moved back into the pool off-screen so that it can be picked again by another tower.

In a scenario where there are many towers shooting, this can dramatically improve the performance of your game, especially if you are targeting a mobile platform.

Saving your data

We haven't discussed saving the data for the game (unfortunately we couldn't cover everything in this book). However, Unity offers a class called `PlayerPrefs` (official documentation: `https://docs.unity3d.com/ScriptReference/PlayerPrefs.html`), which is great to save some values between sessions of your game, such as the score.

If you need to save many things, you should implement your own solution by saving your own file. What format to use for the file is up to you. Unity offers built-in support for XML since many versions, and just recently Unity has also included built-in support for JSON files.

Lastly, you should also consider saving data to the cloud, such as on an online database.

Debugging

Bugs are nasty to fix, but you have a very powerful ally: the console. Don't underestimate the value of this tool. This is because it will save you from many situations, and although at the beginning it could seem that what it is logging doesn't make sense, with time you will learn how to interpret those messages and correct bugs fast.

Another great way to use the console is by inserting debug logs. In Unity, they can be printed with the `Debug` class. Here is an example:

```
Debug.Log("This is a string that will be printed on the console");
```

Placing this line of code in strategic places can help you identify the bug and eventually correct it.

Remote Logs

Unity offers the possibility to use your powerful ally (the console) remotely if you are targeting another platform. For instance, for Android devices, you can read this (which actually allows you to have not only the console by using an ADB connection but also a debugger):

```
https://docs.unity3d.com/Manual/AttachingMonoDevelopDebuggerToAnAndroidDevice.html
```

Otherwise, you can implement your own solution to show console logs or check out code written by other people. For instance, you may want to give this free asset a look:

```
https://www.assetstore.unity3d.com/en/#!/content/12294
```

Cleaning the release version

However, you should remember to remove these lines of code from the final version; otherwise, they consume computational power that you could've used in another way.

A great way to deal with debug statements is to create another class that prints a debug message. If you include the `Diagnostics` library, you can define a conditional attribute such as the following class:

```
using UnityEngine;
using System.Diagnostics; //Needed for the Conditional attribute

public class myDebug : MonoBehaviour {

  [Conditional("DEBUG_MODE")] // Conditional attribute
  public static void Log(string message) {
    //Print the message in the console
    UnityEngine.Debug.Log(message);
  }
}
```

As a result, you can use the following line of code, instead of the preceding one:

```
myDebug.Log("Hello World");
```

This line will be compiled only if the DEBUG_MODE attribute is defined within your game. You can check which attributes are present in your game by navigating through **Edit** | **Project Settings** | **Player**. In the following screenshot, you will find where to define such attributes/symbols highlighted, and as you can see, I've also added the DEBUG_MODE attribute (which you should remove before shipping your game):

For a very nice implementation of this system, you can take a look at the code in this link: https://gist.github.com/kimsama/4123043.

More about communication between scripts

In the last chapter, we saw many ways in which scripts can communicate with each other. However, Unity offers many other ways. One of these is messages to trigger functions. In fact, you can send a message to a game object asking to trigger a certain function if that function exists in any of the scripts attached to that game object.

However, this is an expensive (from a computational point of view) method to communicate between scripts, and it should be used only when necessary.

Moreover, Unity offers more than one messaging system, each one of them with their advantages and disadvantages.

In any case, these systems can be used to create your custom message system, which is a great way to broadcast messages to many scripts when certain events happen, for instance, when you need to switch difficulty at runtime and many scripts should be aware of the change (refer the *Switching difficulty at runtime* section, for more information). You can find many implementations online, such as http://wiki.unity3d.com/index.php/Advanced_CSharp_Messenger, but I strongly advise you to create your own, since you will definitely learn more in this way. For instance, you can follow this tutorial: https://unity3d.com/learn/tutorials/topics/scripting/events-creating-simple-messaging-system.

Documenting the code

When you work in a team, you need to properly comment all of the code you write. There are tools to help you automatically generate documentation, but you need to take the efforts to comment everything!

It may be worthwhile to also use the summary tag, which I didn't use in creating the tower defense project in order to increase the readability of the code for this book: https://msdn.microsoft.com/library/2d6dt3kf.aspx.

In any case, when you write your code, you should always maintain a balance between performance and readability, which often are in contrast. If the documentation is rich and full enough, even the most complicated performance optimization that makes code unreadable can be understood. Keep in mind: maintaining a level of elegance in your code should be your guiding principle when you writing it.

Protecting your game

Once you have your game, you may want to protect it from piracy and/or game hacks. About this, there is an extensive literature, as well as different opinions about it. In fact, one of the major critique to these systems is that they make hackers' lives more difficult, as well as legitimate players' ones; the game will be eventually cracked, and you will end up with upset players. On the other hand, the opposite school of thought says that the major amount of revenue that is generated from a game happens in the first month from the release date (we are talking about non-online games) and therefore a protection system that lasts on month has done its job.

One of the most popular (among both players and hackers) anti-piracy system used for games is Denuvo (`www.denuvo.com`). Although Devuno has received many critiques, it has kept many games from by being immediately cracked and is still giving a hard time for cracking others. You can find a list of games protected with this system (whether they have been cracked yet or not) here on Wikipedia:
`https://en.wikipedia.org/wiki/Denuvo.`
For the most curios of you, Denuvo is an anti-tamper and not a **Digital Rights Management** (**DRM**) system (which binds a legitimate copy of the game to an user). An anti-tamper makes harder to reverse engineering a DRM system in order to by-pass it.

However, in case you decide to include some kind of protection for your game, but you don't have time to develop your own systems, you can buy inexpensive and useful security tools from the Asset Store, such as these ones: *Anti-Cheat Toolkit* (`www.assetstore.unity3d.com/en/#!/content/10395`) or *PlayerPrefs Elite* (`www.assetstore.unity3d.com/en/#!/content/18920`).

For more advanced protection systems (such as the aforementioned Denuvo), of course the price increases, making it hard for Indie game developers to afford one of them. In conclusion, before you spend part of your budget on a protection system, think carefully if it is necessary for your game.

Here is a short, fun, and easy historical overview of DRM systems:
`https://www.youtube.com/watch?v=HjEbpMgiL7U`.

Building for more than one platform

When you consider shipping your game on different platforms, you should keep in mind the different platforms you are going to target. Do they have touch input? Do they support controllers? Based on this, you need to modify the code in your application so that it can work in more than one platform.

Unity offers the possibility to insert some assembly directives to compile the code in a certain way. For instance, you may want to compile a small bit of the code in a certain way when the game is built for Android rather than for Windows. Here is the link to the documentation:
`https://docs.unity3d.com/Manual/PlatformDependentCompilation.html`.

For fast prototyping on devices, you should consider some emulators (we will see later in the chapter). However, Unity provides for Android devices an application called Unity Remote (you can find it here on the Play Store:
`https://play.google.com/store/apps/details?id=com.unity3d.generi cremote`), which allows you to test your game directly with your device from the Unity Editor through an USB connection.

Input/output devices

What will the player use to play your game and how will it be used during gameplay? From consoles to peripherals, there is a large spectrum of different hardware devices that can be utilized by your game. To get you started, here is a basic list of input/output devices that you should keep in mind when you are developing your idea and choice of platform:

- Xbox (360, One):
    - Kinect
    - Controller (wired, wireless)
    - Various peripherals (microphone, DJ control station, guitar, and so on)
- Playstation (1, 2, 3, 4):
    - Move controllers

- EyeToy
- Controllers (wired, wireless)
- Various peripherals (microphone, DJ control station, guitar, and so on)

- Wii:
  - Controller/Nunchuck
  - Motion sensor
  - Balance board
  - Various peripherals and add on (microphone, DJ control station, guitar, steering wheel, sporting equipment, and so on)
- Mac/PC:
  - Operating system (OS X, Windows, Linux)
  - Graphics card
  - Video card
  - Motherboard
  - Sound card
  - Network card
  - Processor
  - Storage space
  - Mouse
  - Keyboard
  - Screen
  - Joystick
  - Controller
  - Various other peripherals (steering wheel)
- Portable devices (Phone, Tablet):
  - Android
  - Apple
  - Windows
- Audio devices:
  - Speakers
  - Headsets
- Required network connection:
  - High-speed Internet
  - LAN connectivity

- Mobile network
- Wi-Fi
- Bluetooth

- Virtual reality (VR) headsets (such as Oculus Rift or HTC Vive):
  - Head tracking
  - Touch controllers
  - Oculus remote (only for Oculus Rift)
  - Camera (only for HTC Vive)
- Leap motion:
  - Hand and gesture tracking
- Brain-scanning headsets (such as Emotiv headset):
  - Electroencephalography (EEG)

Virtual reality in Unity

Recent versions of Unity support virtual reality devices (such as Oculus Rift, HTC Vive, or Samsung Gear).

To start developing for virtual reality in Unity, you should first download the appropriate SDK and install it. Then, from the top menu bar select **Edit** | **Project Settings** | **Player**. Under **Other Settings**, there is the **Virtual Reality Supported** option. Once this is checked, you can check which SDKs are ready to be used in the menu below the option, as shown in in the following screenshot (in this example, there is the Oculus SDK):

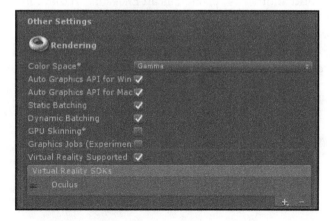

Balancing the game

Don't forget to balance the game. This is very important and can determine the success or not of your game. In order to proper balance your game, you need to do a lot of playtesting (we will see more about this later).

Imagine that we are playing a co-op game and I have a magical wand, special powers, and an invincibility. You, on the other hand have a flashlight. This clearly isn't balanced unless the flashlight was a compact version of all the stuff I had, which unluckily for you it's not. Now, this isn't just an issue when it comes to two player or even multiplayer games but also single player games where the AI are highly powered and drain all of your resources just to defeat them, if you can at all. The same goes for having limited opportunities to get power ups while other players are clearly not having any issues.

Balancing games is important for many reasons because it provides an even playing field and gives everyone the opportunity to win, lose, and progress. With every iteration of your game, and every subsequent update (especially if you change something significant), make sure that your game is balanced. For single and co-op games, this will be something that you can iron out with playtesting. For large-scale MMOs, you are able to playtest but there are likely to be unbalanced things that will come to light the longer people play, explore the world, develop and upgrade their character, and progress through the world.

One of the many ways that you can approach the balance of games is via a cost analysis approach. In this approach, you can begin by adding, removing, and substituting different features in your game. For example, instead of adding a new character, make an existing one more powerful, or replace it with a more powerful version of itself. So, instead of a *Special Wizard*, substitute it with an *Epic Wizard*. Alternatively, you could remove the *Special Wizard* altogether, or add another type, such as an *Elemental Wizard*. In each case, their abilities will change (or be removed) and as a result it will affect the overall dynamics of play, including how other characters will be able to battle against it. Some real-life examples of this are in games such as *Clash of Clans* and *Clash Royale*, where adjustments are made on a regular basis in order to balance gameplay.

For further reading, check out this link:
https://gamedesignconcepts.wordpress.com/2009/08/20/level-16-game-balance.

Extending the Unity editor

The Unity Editor can actually be extended. In fact, some scripts can use the Unity Editor library to get access to all the editor related functions. It can be imported by adding the following line of code at the beginning of such scripts:

```
using UnityEditor;
```

This is a very powerful tool since you can implement custom functionalities, or provide easy interfaces to your scripts.

Here is the link to the official documentation:
`https://docs.unity3d.com/Manual/ExtendingTheEditor.html`.

However, since this is such an extensive topic, I advise you to read a tutorial from some blog post or buy a specific book, such as, *Extending Unity with Editor Scripting*, by Angelo Tadres, Packt Publishing, which you can find here:

`https://www.packtpub.com/game-development/extending-unity-editor-scripting`.

Multiplayer and networking

Wouldn't it be fun if you and your friend could build Cupcake towers together and face hordes of waves of sweet-toothed Pandas in cooperation? Wouldn't it be even awesome if one of you two could control the pandas and the other one the cupcake towers? What if you could connect many players together across the world? All these scenarios are possible by transforming your game into a multiplayer game, which could be potentially played by many different players over a network.

Unity offers many built-in functions to for multiplayer games, but they are not as easy as you would expect. But if you have money, there are many third-party plugins to make managing multiplayer games easier. The asset store of Unity is full of them!

In either case, programming a multiplayer game is not easy, because there are many different parts (such as the server, the client, security protocols, and so on) should work perfectly together, and that is not simple at all. As such, multiplayer and networking is one of the most difficult topics to face in game development (although possible, otherwise you wouldn't see so many online games around).

The best way to start to understand the principle of multiplayer programming is to read a book about it and (if you're using the built-in functions of Unity) read the official documentation about it, which can be found here: `https://docs.unity3d.com/Manual/UNet.html`.

Practice makes perfect

Nobody is born with knowledge of game programming or of Unity. You need to gain it with hard work, and regardless of your level of experience, there is always something new to learn (as we mentioned back in Chapter 1, *A Flat World in Unity*).

In order to become an expert game developer, you need to keep practicing (as everything in life), because there is something to learn around any corner. Challenge yourself, work in projects, and give yourself homework. In fact, in this book, I have provided you with some homework, but often you need to be your own teacher, and force yourself to do homework to improve your skills.

In doing this, don't forget to learn from those who have preceded us, and have found some methods and techniques, which work great in most cases. In fact, you should learn and develop your own best practices. In the case of Unity, you can start by visiting this link: https://docs.unity3d.com/Manual/BestPracticeGuides.html.

Improving the atmosphere of the game

Have you ever played a game or watched a movie and felt like you were there, you felt entranced, immersed, and completely a part of the world... the moment? This is all relates to the atmosphere. Creating the right mood requires a number of different things, it's not just about how it looks but what it sounds like; it also has a way of communicating something to the player. Unfortunately, we cannot yet tap into touch (although there is a lot of research going on haptic interfaces), taste, or smell (with the exception of the Nosulus, a prototype device created by Ubisoft; it can be found at http://nosulusrift.ubisoft.com). Therefore, how they look and sound is imperative to the atmosphere!

Visuals

Games don't necessarily have to look amazing to be immersive, but they need to provide a visual environment that makes sense. Visuals can range from skyboxes, aesthetic style of objects and environment.

Color schemes

Color represents mood, and anyone who has ever taken an art class learns early on that colors help to express emotions to the viewer. Although there is not a unique interpretation of colors, you could stick with a convention throughout all of your game.

A great tool for developing color schemes (as we covered back in Chapter 3, *Communicating with the Player – the User Interface*) is with Adobe Color CC, which you can find at https://color.adobe.com:

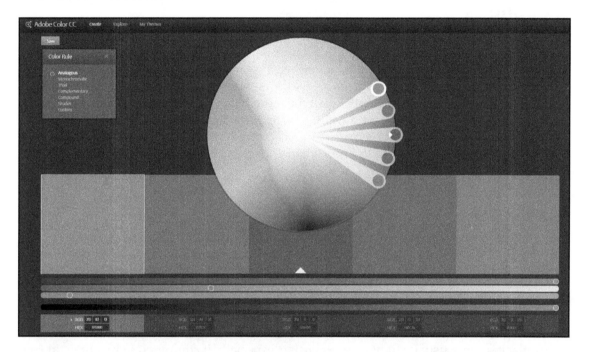

 Did you know that the concept of colors relating to our emotions originated from a man named Robert Plutchik, who created the first color wheel of emotions in 1980?

Homework

Look at some games. Do they have a particular color dominant over others? If so, what would happen if you change the color to something that is opposite? For example, if it's mostly blues, what would happen if you changed it to reds or yellows? Make a list of what objects are affected by the dominant color. And why or why not? If they are/aren't, how would it affect the atmosphere if you changed them?

Lighting

When you walk into a room full of light, you might feel fresh, energized, and positive. Imagine, on the other hand, walking into a dark room without any light to gauge what is inside, or how big it is; it may feel a bit daunting. This may be the same room, but two different lighting conditions provide two very different atmospheres. Pairing it with other sensory cues such as sounds can make it all the more terrifying or uplifting. Of course, these are your stereotypic environments; a well-lit room doesn't always mean that nothing nasty will jump out just like a dark room means that it's full of enemies. These are some things to consider, especially for 3D environments when it comes to understanding how to communicate a sense of danger or peace.

Lights in Unity

Unity implements different kinds of lights, which can be placed within our scenes. We didn't cover them, because they are strongly related to 3D games, although you may use them also for UIs (and therefore also in 2D games).

As mentioned in the preceding section, you need to consider lights in your scene as an art expression so as to create an atmosphere. Surprisingly, good-looking scenes don't have realistic lights at all. As many things in game development, there is a trade off with performances, since usually lights are expensive, especially if computed in real time. In fact, one of the most used techniques is to "*bake*" the lights, which means to pre-calculate them. Of course, this method has many limitations, and that's why there are intermediate solutions as well. A good level designer should be able to place the right kind and number of lights in the scene to enhance the look without overloading the CPU and GPU, leading to a drop of the frame rate.

Image by Divine Unity Shrine, Shadowood Productions, Example of use of lights in Unity

We won't go any further in the details, but you can read more about them at the following links:

- https://unity3d.com/learn/tutorials/topics/graphics/lighting-overview
- https://docs.unity3d.com/Manual/LightingOverview.html
- https://unity3d.com/learn/tutorials/topics/graphics/introduction-lighting-and-rendering

Homework

Think of a particular part of a game that you might like. It can be inside or outside, but it has to be a single location. Now, try and find similar locations within other games. For example, let's choose a laboratory facility; compare one found in a game such as *Portal* to one from *Half-Life*. Keep going until you found at least five other examples and then pay attention to the lighting in each scene. Are they similar or dissimilar? Do they convey the same meaning or something different? For games that you haven't played before, watch online play through to get a sense of the environment.

Environment

Is your game set miles below earth in a secluded dungeon, a faraway castle, enchanted forest, or perhaps inside a foreign utopian world with mountains and glorious landscapes? How you convey your environment can add to your atmosphere. For example, creating a desert may not necessarily be a large plane of sand. There is vegetation (even if very few), animals, and in some cases wreckage. However, a desert on Mars is going to be very different from a desert in Egypt, or one in Australia. The same goes for mountains, waterfalls, hills, frozen lands, forests, and beneath the Earth's surface

Image by Open-World demo collection of Unreal Engine: An example of a detailed forest

Image by Alto's Adventure (`www.altosadventure.com`): A minimalist environment, but it provides a great feel of the atmosphere that surrounds the scene

Homework

Similar to what we did with lighting, we can do with the environment. For example, look at many different types of forests. Are they dense or sparse? Do they have tracks to guide the player or not? Are they occupied by wildlife or are they empty? Pay attention to how they are structured and consider why they are like this. It will give you some ideas how to go about designing your own environments, what works or doesn't work, and it maybe even some inspiration to try alternative approaches to the same environment.

Special effects

A spell isn't much of anything without some magical effects behind it, just like a magician would look a little crazy if nothing happened when he or she moved their hands or wand. Special effects add that something special to action. It also provides the player with a bit of feedback when they do something. For example, when they fire a deadly spell, you will expect at least something pretty grand will happen. Even subtle effects, such as when you heal yourself, can go a long way in creating a more immersive experience.

Particle systems

Unity offers a great built-in particle system that can be used to create atmospheres in the scene. Here is a list of different types of particle effects that you could implement into you game:

- Fireworks
- Rain
- Snow
- Fireflies
- Embers
- Dust
- Bubbles
- Smoke
- Leaves
- Fireworks

Of course, these are just a few suggestions, and in reality, anything can become a particle effect. Who knows, maybe Pandas could be made like that, given the right context.

Keep in mind that particle systems aren't usually computationally cheap additions to your game, but they are for sure a way to enhance the visual aspect of your game.

Image by the Fireworks Showcase Video for Unity 5.5: Fireworks made in Unity by using particle systems

It's worthwhile to mention that from Unity 5.5 a new light module has been implemented. As a result, the particles of a particle system can now cast light, with the opportunity to create amazing effects. As such, I suggest you to watch these three videos taken from the showcase of the beta version of Unity 5.5 illustrating the new features of particle systems:

Fireworks: `https://www.youtube.com/watch?v=xAzmNo2fxWA`
Embers: `https://www.youtube.com/watch?v=copE2b_XfTc`
Trails: `https://www.youtube.com/watch?v=rQpgaP-r_lc`

Here you can find the official documentation about particle systems:
`https://docs.unity3d.com/Manual/ParticleSystems.html`.

Whereas, here is an introductory tutorial that can help you to get started (although it is for a previous version of Unity, many of the concepts apply to the new version of Unity as well):
`https://unity3d.com/learn/tutorials/topics/graphics/particle-system`.

Post processing

Post processing effects can greatly enhance the visual look of your game at a relatively cheap cost (from a computational point of view). Here is an example taken from the official documentation of Unity; it shows the difference between a scene without post processing and the same with it:

Images by the official documentation of Unity

You can even program your own post processing effect. You could start with this link:

```
https://docs.unity3d.com/Manual/WritingImageEffects.html
```

Therefore, you should definitely consider adding some post processing effect to your game, because they can really help you in giving the look you have in mind. In any case, the full documentation for post processing in Unity can be found here:

```
https://docs.unity3d.com/Manual/comp-ImageEffects.html
```

Other visual effects

Unity offers other rendering effects that can be placed in the 3D world. These include Line and Trail renders to draw lines or trails. Imaging a shooting star in the most romantic scene of your game. It needs to have a trail or else it's just a point moving in the sky. Another example could be in an RTS with characters leaving a small trail, which increases the visual looking of your game although it is not realistic.

It's worthwhile to point out that these visual effects have been largely improved in Unity 5.5, so if you are working with previous versions, you might find them really different.

Image by the official documentation of Unity: An example of the Trail Render component of Unity in action

 Some of these effects are really expensive from a computational point of view. By knowing how to program in a **Graphic Library** (**GL**), it's possible to re-implement simpler versions (so without all of the features they have) of these effects within Unity in such a way they are highly optimized to reduce the performance overhead.

Other effects include Halos, Lens flares, and Projectors. Halos can be used to highlight objects in your scene, or just to simulate some really fine dust. Lens flares can simulate the effect of the sun on a camera. Projectors can be used to create relatively low-cost shadows:

Image by Battlefield 3 (DICE, 2011): An example of flare lenses used in video games

Audio

Audio can move us, bring us to tears, motivate, excite, and sometimes terrify us. In some cases, it can help to place us *in* an environment. The power of music is something that can really add a nice special touch if done right. At the same time as it being incredibly amazing, it can be incredibly annoying. The pace, intensity, and even instrument can all create a different mood.

Music

Music can serve a specific purpose such as being used as background music. It can provide a level of ambience and drama to an experience that visuals alone cannot provide. Depending on the part of the game, the music is likely to change. We can think of such an example in real life, the music we would use to meditate is likely to be quite different from the music when we are lifting weights in a gym.

In saying that, background music tends to remain consistent and continues to play throughout an entire level. Whereas, gameplay tends to be dynamic and music can also reflect this. For example, a beautifully created piece of background music with strings playing softly; as soon as a dragon appears, the mood is likely to change and so is the music. Some more examples may include the following:

- Opening/closing credits, sequences, and cut-scenes.
- A character encountering combat.
- Being chased.
- When a character enters a dangerous area. An example of this is in *Assassin's Creed* when a player enters a restricted area.
- When using vehicles.
- During dialogue sequences.
- Ambient sounds:
  - Traffic
  - Talking
  - Machinery
  - Gunfire/Artillery
  - Water (waterfalls, river, creek, and so on)
  - Wind
  - Room noises (air conditioner, computer's humming, typing, closing/opening doors, cabinets, drawers, telephone ringing, and so on)
  - Animals/Insects (crickets, frogs, owls, birds, and so on)

Sound effects

Sound taps into one of our five senses and it can be an important component of a gaming experience. The use of sound can range from setting the atmosphere, indicating feedback, acknowledging an action, providing sound effects to various items (such as weapons), to indicating an event has occurred.

Using sounds are not just limited to background music. When we do things, anything, we make a noise, and gameplay is no exception. When a character knocks something over, it should make a noise, when they walk, open a door, draw a weapon, they should all make some sort of sound. Some sound effects that you may use in your game include:

- Spells being cast
- Ricochet
- Bullets whizzing by
- Splashing in water
- Cable/robes breaking when cut
- Doors creaking
- Glass shattering
- Footsteps
- Flying down a zip line

Eliciting emotions

In some instances, you'd want to elicit a certain emotion from a player such as when a character dies or when the player is triumphant. Just like movies, when we want to increase the emotion with a particular aspect of the game, albeit during a cut-scene or gameplay, music can do this. Think of some moments during gameplay when you have been moved in both a negative and positive way. Here is a list of some moments when you may want to elicit the player's emotion:

- Introduction of a new character(s)
- Death/Birth of a character
- Sadness/Happiness
- Anger/Happiness
- Victory/Defeat
- Dramatic
- Creepy
- Romantic/Envy
- Tension

These are just some of the many emotions that your game can evoke.

Homework

A great exercise to do before you start to decide what sounds to add into your own game is to play a range of different games and make note of what sounds they use. Do this for background music and sound effects. You might be surprised about the amount of different sounds that each game has. Also take note of how the music in levels transition, do the sounds effects also change?

Keep in mind that you don't just have to play games; watching movies and even TV series can also be useful to see the types of noises that are made, when, and if they add any kind of element (scare, represents happiness) within the scene/movie.

Audio in Unity

Audio is another extensive topic in Unity, which from Unity 5.x has greatly improved. Unfortunately, we didn't have enough time to have dedicated a whole chapter on how to handle audio in Unity. However, the foundational concept is that there is a component that works as listeners. There should be only one (active) listener per each scene, otherwise Unity gives you a warning about, and it is good practice to keep in that way. Then, there is another component that works as an audio source, which can produce a sound or play some music. Moreover, audio sources can be set to act in 3D, which means that they can be placed in the environment so as to have a spatial sound (the closer the player from the audio source, the higher the volume of the audio source will be).

In the official website, there is a series of video tutorials on how to use audio in Unity, which can be found here:
`https://unity3d.com/learn/tutorials/topics/audio`

External audio systems

In case you are aiming high and the built-in audio system of Unity is not enough for your game, there are pieces of third-party software you can integrate into Unity.

One of the most used is called FMOD (`www.fmod.org`), which is a complete solution to integrate spatial sounds in your game.

Another similar tool, which is less used due to its high price but offers many features, is Wwise (`https://www.audiokinetic.com/products/wwise`). You probably have seen its logo in some games you play.

Both FMOD and Wwise are really powerful tools, but in order to appreciate their features, you should see them in action. There are many videos available online, and I encourage you to check them out.

Teamwork

They say it takes a village to raise a child, well, it can take a team to build a game, and a team that works well together can achieve incredible things. However, choosing the right people, dealing with conflict and working on a daily basis together isn't always straightforward. Next, we will look at a few ideas about the roles in a game development team, considerations that need to be made, and a few other things that will get you all on your way.

It is not just about you, it is about working in a team

A good team is like any good relationship; you need to have communication, consideration, and understanding, and most importantly you must acknowledge the other person. There is no *I* in a team, but too often people get caught up in the *me*. In such cases, neglecting others within the team can be for many reasons, from ego, skillset (or lack of), impatience, financial gain and so on. Of course, this is not to say that such traits are negative, but in the wrong amount (just like anything), they are a sure way to end up in a disaster.

Another issue when it comes to teams is the amount of time that you have known the others. This is not bad thing, nor can it always be a good one. The idea, especially if you're going into business with each other is to keep it professional. You have a product that you need to deliver, deadlines that need to be met, and potentially stakeholders who are involved in your project. You must be able to separate business and friendship. The dynamics will change, and you need to avoid making it personal.

A game development team will consist of different roles, and how big your team is determines how those roles are carried out. In a perfect world, you will have a team member for each role, but in most cases you will have to double up on responsibilities. In saying this, a typical team is likely to consist of the following members:

- **The project manager**: Who sets milestones for the team and makes sure that they are achieved. But it is not just time management; the project manager should also encourage and motivate the team and members who fall behind deadlines. They help to boost team morale and keep the project running smoothly and, more importantly, on time.

- **The producer**: Who will be the person who deals with the business side of the things. They are responsible for maintaining budgets, schedules, and marketing strategies. They differ from the project manager in the sense that they are more about logistics and the technical details than managing the group's functioning.

- **The social media strategist**: Who is someone who is dedicated to all social media and marketing aspects of your game. Typically, the producer is also responsible for this, but in some cases, depending on the extent of social media that you will want, having someone dedicated to promoting you game can help free up time for budgets and the financial aspect of your group's producer.

- **The designer**: Who will be the one who ties all the elements together to create the overall experience. They ensure that what is created complements the story; they decide how it is revealed to the player and ultimately how the player interacts with its flow.

- **The artist**: Who is responsible for creating the look of the game, from concept art of characters, assets, and levels all the way to their models and textures. It is ideal to have more than one artist if you are able to, especially if your game is large. Art takes time, especially if you want your game to be aesthetically magical.

- **The programmer**: Who is like the arm to the hand of the project; without them, you are likely to struggle to make your wonderful ideas come to life. In saying all of this, if you are unlucky to not have a Programmer in your team (or not enough for all the functionalities that you may want to develop), many game engines offer visual scripting that allows you to link commands together to create actions. A great example of this is Blueprints in Unreal Engine (`www.unrealengine.com`), as shown here:

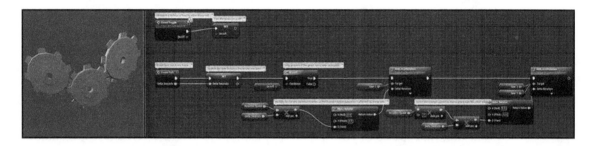

Image by Unreal Engine, Blueprints visual scripting (`https://docs.unrealengine.com/latest/INT/Engine/Blueprints`)

- **The sound designer/composer**: Who makes your game sound great. The sound designer ensures that every action has some sort of audio feedback. Audio in a game includes sound effects and background music. Sound designers contribute to the atmosphere by making it sound alive. Even the subtlest effects, such as when a player nears some dark and dangerous room, can arouse all kinds of emotions.

- **The quality assurance (QA) tester**: Who is the person (or people) dedicated to making sure that the game works. This can range from friends, family and professional gamers and QA testers. Ideally, you will want people who are not involved in the creation of your project to be QA testers, because even though you will be testing it yourself, it is easy to look past aspects of your game that may impact the overall gameplay experience.

- **The writer**: Who is usually responsible developing the story of the game. Elements of the story can include the overall plot, the characters, setting, and other narrative elements such as dialogue and narrative pathways such as alternate endings. In essence, the writer is responsible for ensuring that the story not only entices and captivates leaving them wanting for more but also to set the atmosphere and enhance the overall game experiences. In addition, the writer must also ensure that the story makes sense, follows a logical progression and is explanative. Lastly, one thing to keep in mind is that writing for games requires a different approach than movies or reading text because it is interactive.

Sharing a common vision

When you're working in a team, it is important to have a common goal and shared interest. While it goes without saying, morale is key when it comes to working on team projects. There will be difficult moments in the project, late nights, and points where stress levels will rise, but having the support of others can improve the way that everyone is able to cope through it all. There will be moments when you are busy, not able to, or just overloaded with work that inhibits your ability to get it done. Of course, if you've been lazy, that is an entirely different situation, but you should always communicate any difficulty with the other team members, and as soon as possible. To really illustrate this point, consider the poetic notion of the Butterfly Effect: *Does the flap of a butterfly's wings in Brazil set off a tornado in Texas?* Small (unresolved) problems in the beginning become bigger problems later.

Managing expectations

Having a common vision is not always the same as having the same expectations. For example, you and your team might want to make a high selling and popular application, but the amount of time and effort that will be given from each team member can vary. Therefore, it is important to establish expectations too, early on, for a number of reasons.

In addition to expectations, be sure to take the time to plan the development of your game properly. You don't want to over-plan what you intend to do, if you have little time or your game contains necessary components. Along the same lines, the same can be said for under-planning, where you decide on the design of the game but not allow yourself enough time to complete it in. You will get to a point where your team will begin to cut back on sections, in order to meet the goals. In the end, you might end up with something equivalent to a demo version of your game without the exciting full version to keep players interested in your work, or worse, you won't have a completed game at all.

Lastly, never assume anything. Assumptions are likely to result in disasters later on. For example, you look at the wonderfully planned Gantt chart of things to do, and at this stage your artists should be modeling assets, but in reality they aren't; or at least one of them isn't because they thought that the other artist was. Having a regular meetings and a good project manager and producer will likely avoid this situation from occurring, but always keep up to date with what others are up to.

Collaboration and communication are key

The worst thing that can happen within a group is to stop talking. Maybe things have hit a lull and people become busy, maybe something happened in a member's personal life, in any case, things happen that may draw our attention elsewhere; it's life after all. However, this is no reason for teams to stop talking. If communication breaks down, find out why and do something about it early on. Perhaps the issue is something small and can be dealt with easily. In other cases, it can be damaging to a project's success, such as work not being completed because a team member is too embarrassed to admit that they are unable to complete a task or is simply too busy, but fails to notify anyone until the last minute. One way to avoid such problems is to make it easy to communicate within the group and to communicate often.

Ways to communicate

While it is obvious, there are a few relatively simple ways to keep in touch by using the following:

- **E-mail:** The electronic snail mail is great for keeping a thread for conversations, but it can become quite difficult to manage. In these situations, it would ideal to schedule a regular (for example, weekly or monthly) progress update. Give it a deadline and a template. For example, a list of things that they need to cover such as currently working on, problems, and future work. In this way, you're able to keep up-to-date with how everyone is going, and so is everyone else. To make the whole process a bit easier to manage, there are functions such as tagging and filtering in most (if not all) e-mail software. In these instances, e-mails relating to specified criteria, such as e-mail address or subject are then directed to a specific folder and/or given a tag to make it easier to retrieve later on.
- **WhatsApp**: You are likely to have the phone numbers of your other team members, albeit personal or business numbers. Therefore, phone messaging services like WhatsApp are great ways to keep in touch and make calls regardless of where they are in the world.
- **Social media groups and chats such as Facebook**. With Facebook, you can keep communication lines open in a number of ways. You can create a message group or a private group. The difference between the two is minimal, in that they function in much the same way, you can upload documents and discuss. However, a group functions much the same way as a Facebook page. So if you upload an image, it creates a separate post, as opposed to within a chat, where it would just be added as the next part of dialogue in the conversation.
  The advantages of creating a Facebook group is that it is easier to manage in terms of finding certain items, and keeping conversations more specific to a post

(or topic).

- **Skype/Google Hangouts, and so on:** Save time in typing something, and give someone a call. Never underestimate the power of a voice/video call. While sometimes, especially if you're working over distance, it is important to maintain contact that is beyond text communication. It adds a more personal level to your work relationship, and you get a better sense of the other person, than trying to read between the lines.

Version control

An effective solution for artists to share files, such as textures and meshes, between them, is by using a cloud storage service (such as Google Drive or Dropbox, which we will discuss later). However, when it comes to programmers and developers, sharing files is a different situation. During the development of a game, programmers tend to work collaboratively with their code and script files. As a result, there are some important needs that should be taken into consideration:

1. Programmers work together on the same source code. This may involve (but is not limited to) collaborating on different areas within a project, as well as the same file(s). As a result, without having some sort of file control, it can become quite messy with no way to keep track of what has been modified.
2. The general nature of programming in a project will involve utilizing a range of different techniques and trying varying solutions to a range of problems that will be the best for the project. Therefore, if large changes are made or changes that are not necessarily the right solution, programmers need to have a way to go back to a previous version.
3. Reusing all or part of code from other sources, like libraries and source-files, where it's relevant can help to save a lot of time later on. By doing this, it is possible to save time for parts of the project that have similar elements to existing projects leaving more time for more complicated parts.

By having some kind of version control in place, coders are able to utilize a file-system that not only identifies and tracks file changes, but allows programmers to reverse them. In addition, version control can also help to facilitate programmers to reuse and integrate code form external sources and/or projects. These features, and more, are supported by a piece of version control software.

Git is a free and open source program for version control. You can download it by visiting the Git home page here: www.git-scm.com. Once installed and properly configured, it can be used to apply version control to your files, thus being an incredible asset to your workflow.

> There are some visual tools to manage Git in an easier way. One of the most complete is SourceTree (www.sourcetreeapp.com) by Atlassian. However, if you are a newcomer, probably you'll find it easier to use GitKraken (www.gitkraken.com) by Axosoft.
> Moreover, if you want to learn Git, here there is a quick and nice interactive tutorial:
> https://try.github.io.

Make a GDD and stick to it

When starting out, everyone will have an idea, concept, or something to add to the overall development of the game. At this stage, this is fantastic because it will give you lots to mull over when it comes to refining your game and provide you with an array of different choices to make.

A **game design document** (GDD) is a neat way to have a current version of what your game is and will be. Think of the GDD as a manual that defines your aesthetic, audio, naming conventions, story, characters, and other bits and pieces of your game. It is a point of a reference, a game bible if you will. The structure of a GDD varies, and there is no right or wrong way to do it, as it will all depend on what your game is. However, there are some sections that define the substance of your game. For example:

1. **Introduction**:
    - What is your game about? Think of this like an elevator pitch. Keep it short, sharp, and to the point. You don't want to go into too many specifics but enough to give the overall gist of your game. For example, Sugar mountain, Panda invasion is a 2D real-time tower defense game where the player must defeat Pandas with various edible projectiles.
    - Who is your game aimed towards? Children, adults, perhaps both? Ideally, this is where you consider the demographics that you want to engage your game with.
    - Where will your game be featured / what devices? Android, iOS, Windows, Mac, Linux, all come with different challenges and require different considerations, so keep this in mind and defined early on to minimize headaches later on down the track.

2. **Art**:
- Mood boards that define the aesthetic style that you're wanting to achieve. These can be general or specific for a character or level. That help to guide the art direction when it comes to creating concept art.
- Concept art includes anything that defines the current state of the game. Of course, previous art can be kept in the GDD, but it is ideal to move it to an appendix, or separate section to maintain the relevancy of the document.
- UI/GUI/HUD all relates to how the interactive elements will look, and basically how anything else that isn't in the game will appear. For example, if you have a HUD (heads-up display), how will it appear in-game. How much for the screen will it take up, and how will it work with the current aesthetic style?
- Characters will need to be illustrated in order to provide an idea about their appearance, which will then be modeled (or drawn in the case of 2D) and animated. Drawing characters in various poses, environments and situations will help to illustrate more about the character's personality and overall appearance.
- Assets that will populate your game environment that will then be created (drawn or modeled) later on.

3. **Audio**:
- The background music that will set the atmosphere for the game. It can be as simple as music that provides an ambient soundtrack to exploring environments or act as audio cues when the player is approaching some significant part of the level.
- Sound effects that not only provide a source of feedback for actions such as when an object makes contact with a surface but also when an event occurs such as the player winning or losing.

4. **Story**:
- Character biographies will include information that relates to each character from their general information (age and appearance), background story, personality and their relationships with other characters within the game. Depending on your type of game it will be general or extremely detailed (as with role-playing games).
- The general plot of your game will provide everyone with what the game is about. Like character biographies, the level of detail will depend on the type of game. For instance, you might not even have a story if it's a game like *Sudoku* (unless of course your solutions unlock doors to free a princess).

- Narrative flow will explain how the narrative is revealed as the game progresses. Think of it like a map that indicates when and how parts of the narrative is revealed to the player and how each part of the game relates to the narrative. For example, having a player cross through an underground cave is not going to save the princess who is stuck in the castle on the other side of the map, unless of course the cave has a secret passage to get you there. Just like gameplay, your narrative needs to relate to what you are doing in the game, and vice versa.

5. **Technical**:
   - Pipeline overview will briefly explain the software that is going to be used to build the game (game engines, third-party plugins, and so on) and how to connect them together. Moreover, it establishes a connection between the art and the software, and how these can communicate (such as, how the graphics should be packed to be used in the software/game).
   - Technical design will explain how the different parts of your game are connected and establish conventions. Moreover, it contains how interfaces should be implemented so in order to maintain consistency within the project, and how to encapsulate the work in tasks (which can be done by different people) and how to integrate them together. Often the technical design is in a technical design document, separate from the game design, since it only used by programmers.
   - System limitations will explain which are the limitations of the technology used, to other members of the team who are not programmers (in fact, more detailed limitations are in the technical design document). Like the pipeline overview, this document provides a bridge between programmers, designers and artists.

6. **Game flow**: It explains, in brief, how the game will play out. From one level/cut-scene/and so on, to the next. Similar to the narrative flow, game flow discusses what the player will be doing within the game as they progress through the narrative. For example, they will go to part A of the map, kill 20 dragons and then discover the magical elixir, cue cut-scene revealing the truth about his father, then the player is transported to a magical island to explore the family archives. By doing this, you begin to see the holes in your gameplay and/or story and are able to make sure that it not only makes sense but it progresses at pace that the player will enjoy; that is the game is neither too fast nor boring and confusing.

7. **Timeline**: It refers to the time that it takes your game from start to finish and all the progress milestones and deadlines to ensure that your game will reach the release date:

- Milestones are like the stepping stones to progress your project further. These are generally when the game reaches a significant point, such as art assets completed, cool function implemented, first working prototype, and so on. Milestones can be as frequent or infrequent as you want, but they are one way to keep on top of what everyone is up to, to ensure that work is delivered within a timeframe to reach a ranger of different project targets.
- Deadlines can be as daunting as they sound, because if it's an important one, it can ruin a project and end up costing (albeit money and time).
- Important dates are well important. They are the days where everyone will either need to be present, on site (if you have a physical location), online (if you have a virtual location), or present in any other shape or form. These dates can be for a range of different reasons from stakeholder, client, and even potential employer meetings. Members of a team should take these meetings seriously, arrive on time, and be prepared. Meeting notes should also be taken, in order to keep a log of what happens.

Keeping it tidy with project management tools

No one likes a cluttered workspace; even an organized chaos has its limits when you need that one document. The same goes for when you are developing games that are likely to have a lot of files. Therefore, we must find ways to not only manage the files, but also the team members so that we all know where the files are but a way to communicate with others about them. There are many programs out there for team and file management, some of the most popular and useful ones are discussed next.

Slack

Slack (www.slack.com) is one of the most effective team management tools. It keeps all your conversations, topics, to-do lists, notes, and many other bits and pieces from your project all in the one place.

Some of these features are explained here:

- Channels keep topics separated and the discussion focused. Think of them like rooms that have a specific topic of discussion. For example, you may have an art channel that focuses directly on the art of your project. It also provides a place for other team members to request or check on the progress of certain items. Channels can be as broad or as narrow as you want them to be.

- The app makes Slack a much easier app to manage on the go. It allows you to receive real-time updates when members of your group upload and/or post anything. In addition, it allows you to also interact with Slack whenever and wherever. For example, you get a great idea or you might see something that is useful to a concept that you're developing, with the Slack application, all you have to do is post or snap your idea and submit it to the channel. You can think of channels like groups.

- Slack's App Directory allow you to integrate other applications (some of which we will explore later) into Slack to make it the ultimate project management software. You can find the App Directory at `https://slack.com/apps`.

Image by Slack tutorial video (`https://slack.com/is`)

HacknPlan

Similar to Slack, HacknPlan (`www.hacknplan.com`) is another team management software. However, it is more directed towards game development. For example, you are able to provide timelines to work towards, assign points or value to each task, which can then be used to determine the payment of a particular part of the game and/or contribution from the creator. It allows you to have, at a glance, a relatively detailed overview of project in its most current state. If you have a look at the following screenshot, you can see that there are a number of different boards, each indicating a different part of the production pipeline, from things that have yet to commence in **Planned** to things that have been finishing in **Completed**. I recommend that you try it out because it is one of my favorite tools!

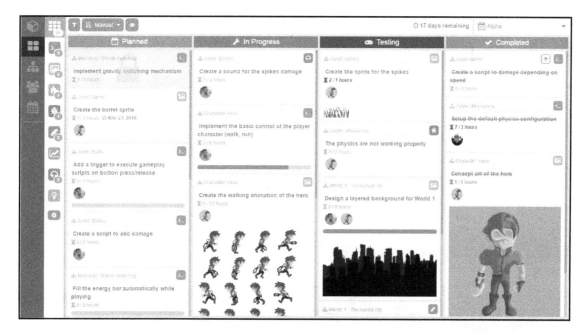

Image by Press Kit (`http://hacknplan.com/press/#!`)

Drive

Google Drive (`https://drive.google.com`), along with all of its program suite, is quite versatile and useful as a communal resource. Not only does it offer programs that are like those from other well-known commercial products, but also it has sharing capabilities that make the whole process much easier. You can easily create and share documents, files and folders with as many or as few people as you want either via a private link or through permission. There are many ways you can control access to files (from editing to read-only); it will all come down to the purpose of sharing them in the first place.

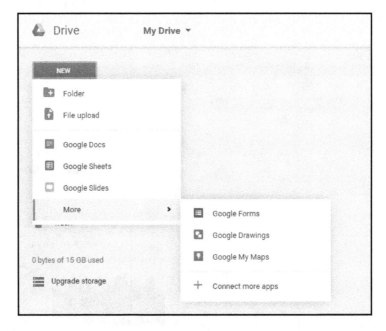

Image by Google Drive

 Some alternatives to Drive in terms of files and document creation are Apache OpenOffice (`www.openoffice.org`) and ONLYOFFICE (`www.onlyoffice.com`).

Dropbox

Like Google Drive, except with the addition of other software, Dropbox (www.dropbox.com) provides a versatile tool for managing project files. It allows you to upload files, create folders, and share them and the files within them. As a result, it is a nice alternative to Drive in terms of sharing files. In addition, for documents such as Word files, it allows you to edit them in real time along with other team members, while showing you what edits are being or were made.

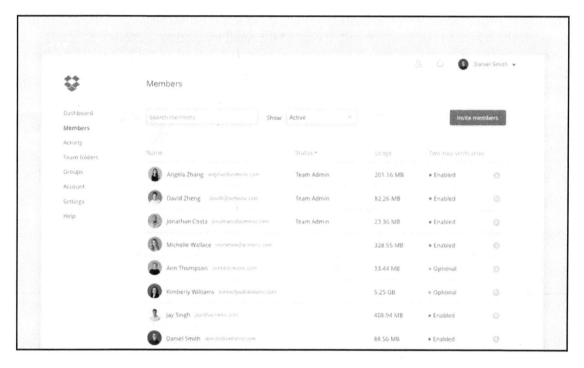

Image by Dropbox Press Kit (http://tinyurl.com/DropboxPressKitScreenshot)

Trello

Trello (www.trello.com) is somewhat like a virtual pin board for task management. It allows you to create a board, where all your tasks are kept. Each board features different panels that feature tasks. Of course, these are ordered as you prefer, depending on what kind of process you are intending to use Trello for. For example, developing a pipeline style Trello board may feature different areas such as art, design, programming, and audio; all of these are then assigned tasks specific to their area. For example, the art section may feature tasks such as concepts for main menu or concept art of the princess tower, and so on. Each task can then also be assigned to specific people, or be left open for anyone in the group to engage with. Once a task is completed, it could be moved to another section, which of course, is appropriately named finished or simply left and moved to the bottom of the list. How you use Trello is ultimately up to you, but it definitely helps to keep the process streamlined.

Image by Trello Tour (https://trello.com/tour)

Redbooth

Another option, which is somewhat a mixture of Trello and Dropbox is Redbooth (`https://redbooth.com`), which is also known as Teambox. Redbooth allows users to share files, assign tasks to team members, and send direct messages. Like a number of other applications that we have looked at here, it also alerts you whenever the status of a project is updated.

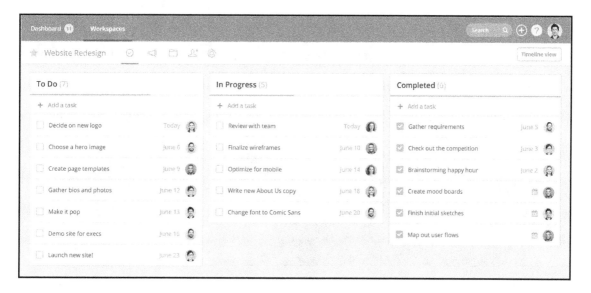

Image by Redbooth (`https://redbooth.com/?ref=teambox#!/dash`)

GitHub

Earlier, we talked about Version Control. However, you still need a place to keep your repositories. GitHub (`www.github.com`) offers hosting for Git repositories. It is free for public repositories, which means that everybody can see what you upload (this choice was made to encourage open source software). Otherwise, it offers paid hosting plans for your repositories.

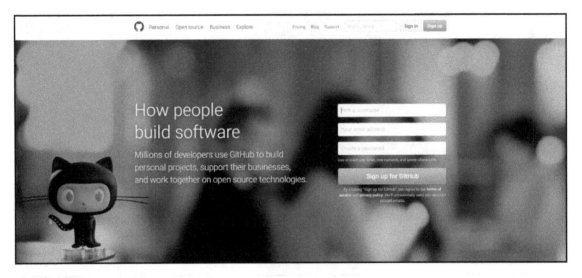

Image by GitHub

BitBucket

Bitbucket (`https://bitbucket.org`) is a service very similar to GitHub to host your Git repositories. Here you can have private repositories for free, but the limitation is on the number of users. Up to five users is free (which is perfect for small teams); otherwise, you need to switch to a paid plan.

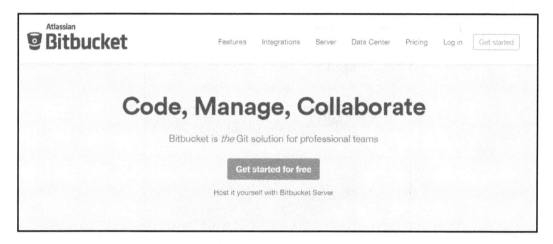

Image by Bitbucket

Calendar

Another intuitive piece of software (or even hardware) to have is a calendar, but more importantly a calendar that is shared among your group. It is important to set deadlines, but to ensure that everyone sticks to them, use a communal calendar; it will send notifications to everyone when upcoming events, meetings, and milestones are approaching.

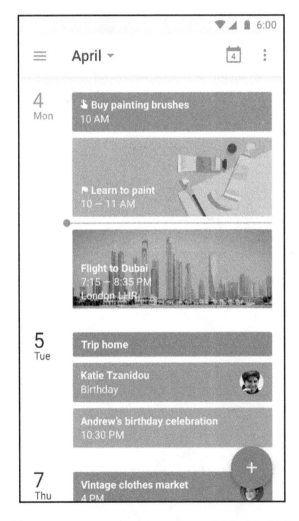

Image by Google Calendar (https://play.google.com/store/apps/details?id=com.google.android.calendar&hl=en)

Pinterest

A great way to communicate the aesthetic part of your idea(s) is mood boards. Pinterest (www.pinterest.com) is an absolutely fantastic tool for this. Not only can you create different boards to pin images to, but also they can be shared among team members and be made private.

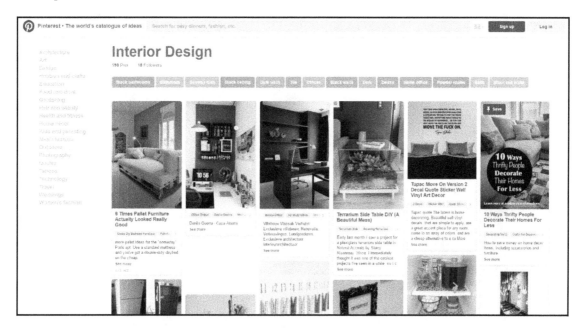

Image by Pinterest

Hootsuite

One simple way to manage a number of social media channels in the one place would have to be Hootsuite (www.hootsuite.com). It allows you to schedule posts on various platforms (Facebook, Instagram, and Twitter to name a few, we will see later) so that you can worry about other important things with your application.

In addition, it also allows you to view, at a glance, how each post has been interacted with, such as Likes, Tweets, and Favorites.

Image by Hootsuite (http://signupnow.hootsuite.com)

Polishing your game

Well, we've filed and buffed our game to shape it into a masterpiece, it's now time to add some shine. To make our gem shine, we need to polish it up with a few things to make it work better, as well as ensure that it will work as we want it to. By now, you should have already tested it (more than once), so you will have a few ideas about what needs to be improved, such as lag. In the following sections, we will explore ways to optimize various parts of the game so that by the time you publish it, you will have something that runs smoothly and effectively.

Processing the power

One thing that you will want to make sure to do before you really get stuck into the development of your game is to determine whether or not it is optimized for the device(s) that you are targeting it towards. Often optimization is seen as the last step in game development, but it is not true. The sooner you consider optimization in your development workflow, the less the effort required later on to optimize your game.

 Unity provides great resources for optimizing for mobile platforms such as specific optimizations such as script and graphics. You can find them here:
https://docs.unity3d.com/Manual/MobileOptimizationPracticalGuide.html.

Different devices come with their own issues that you need to overcome. Just like our own brains, mobile devices (and computers in general) can process so much at any one time. As a result, this will ultimately impact the overall performance of your game. For example, certain parts such as graphics (both 2D and 3D), or just inefficient code can be extremely draining. Ultimately, this will impact the running of your game, causing it to lag. In addition to the device, depending on what dimension that you designed in (2D or 3D) will require different considerations, of which we are going to explore in the following sections.

Checking the build size

One of the many things you you need to take into account, is the dimension of your game, especially since it will impact how it will be distributed and/or released. Thus, checking how the size of your build is key in understanding the dimensions of your game. You can just build the game (how to do it, it's explained later in the chapter), and check its size. However, this doesn't give us much information on what we could reduce.

After you have built the game, you can right-click on the **Console** window and then select **Open Editor Log**, as shown in the following screenshot:

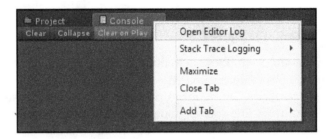

Your operating system will open the Editor.txt file with your default text editor; near the end, you can find some statistics about your last build, and in particular the size divided by the different elements of your game. You should have something similar to this:

```
Textures        81.1 mb    94.7%
Meshes          0.0 kb     0.0%
Animations      9.1 kb     0.0%
Sounds          0.0 kb     0.0%
Shaders         9.0 kb     0.0%
Other Assets    28.4 kb    0.0%
Levels          14.3 kb    0.0%
Scripts         542.9 kb   0.6%
Included DLLs   3.9 mb     4.6%
File headers    9.2 kb     0.0%
Complete size   85.6 mb    100.0%
```

There are details related to individual files (only a fragment is shown) as follows:

```
Used Assets and files from the Resources folder, sorted by uncompressed size:
 16.8 mb        19.6% Assets/Graphics/towers/cupcake_tower_sheet-01.png
 14.3 mb        16.7% Assets/Graphics/enemies/animation_panda_sprite_sheet.png
 12.0 mb        14.0% Assets/Graphics/maps/candy_mountain_asset_overaly-01.png
 12.0 mb        14.0% Assets/Graphics/maps/candy_mountain_without_bar-01.png
 12.0 mb        14.0% Assets/Graphics/maps/candy_mountain-01.png
  7.0 mb  8.1% Assets/Graphics/projetiles/projectiles_sheet_01.png
  2.0 mb  2.3% Assets/Graphics/UI/map_complete.png
  1.9 mb  2.2% Assets/Graphics/UI/ui_health_bar_frame.png
  1.7 mb  2.0% Assets/Graphics/UI/ui_blue_top_with_text.png
  1.2 mb  1.3% Assets/Graphics/UI/ui_health_bar_filling.png
346.9 kb        0.4% Assets/Graphics/UI/ui_sugar_meter.png
  9.2 kb  0.0% Resources/unity_builtin_extra
  4.1 kb  0.0% Assets/Animations/PandaAnimatorController.controller
  4.1 kb  0.0% C:/Program Files/Unity
5.5.0f3/Editor/Data/UnityExtensions/Unity/GUISystem/UnityEngine.UI.dll
  4.1 kb  0.0% C:/Program Files/Unity
5.5.0f3/Editor/Data/UnityExtensions/Unity/GUISystem/Standalone/UnityEngine.UI.dll
  2.5 kb  0.0% Assets/Animations/Panda_Eat_Animation.anim
  2.3 kb  0.0% Assets/Animations/Panda_Walk_Animation.anim
  2.3 kb  0.0% Assets/Animations/Panda_Die_Animation.anim
  2.1 kb  0.0% Assets/Animations/Panda_Hit_Animation.anim
```

As you can see, most of our game size is taken by **Textures**, which is common in 2D games. Let's explore how we can reduce the size of the textures in the following section.

Texture optimitation

Some image formats can be problematic, such as file size. Thankfully, in Unity you can reduce the file size in a number of ways:

1. Change the image resolution.
2. Change how Unity will handle that specific image.

In Unity, you can change these in the importing settings. To do this, just select an `Asset` from your `Project` folder, and the following screen will appear:

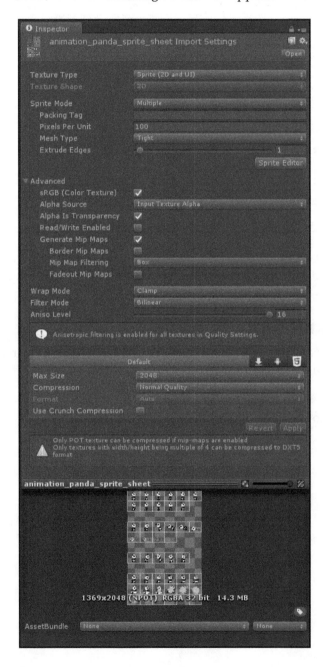

In the past chapters, we explained some of these settings, mainly the ones related to the game. But as you can see from the preceding screenshot, there are many other options to set the texture in perfect conditions for your game.

As you can see from the previous screenshot, there is a warning about POT textures. What are those? **Power Of Two** (**POT**) textures are squared images in which the length of the side is a power of 2 (such as 2, 4, 8, 16, 32, 64, 128, 256, 512, 1024, 2048, 4092, and so on). Since the hardware we have, runs with a binary system, the power of 2 is really important, because some techniques allow it to be processed in a certain way. As a result, performance can improve. In the specific case of the warning, to be compressed into DXT5 format. Therefore, although it's hard to have all the textures of your game as POT textures, you should consider having as many as you can.

As you can read from the previous screenshot, our Panda sprite sheet is an **NPOT** (**Non-Power-Of-Two**) texture, because this sprite sheet was designed for clarity to learn animations back in `Chapter 4`, *No Longer Alone – Sweet-Toothed Pandas Strike*, and not to be optimized.

To improve the performance of your game, the most important parameters are: **Generate Mip Maps**, **Filter Mode**, **Max Size**, **Compression**, and **Format**. To make it easier to understand, they have been highlighted in the previous screenshot:

- **Generate Mip Maps**: It is an option that, if checked, creates smaller versions of the texture/sprite. Therefore, when the sprite is far or small with respect to the camera, the smaller version is rendered. As a result, there is a gain performance at runtime, but it could increase the size of your build.

- **Filter Mode**: It allows you to apply a filter to the image, in particular to make the borders a little blurry. It might be useful, when working with pixel art, to have some filters can be handy. This is because filter makes your asset less pixelated. **Filter Mode** selects how the texture is filtered when it gets stretched by transformations:

  - **Point**: The texture becomes blocky up close
  - **Bilinear**: The texture becomes blurry up close
  - **Trilinear**: This is like **Bilinear**, but the texture also blurs between the different mip levels

- **Max Size**: As the name suggests, places a limit on the maximum size that the image can have within that specific platform. In fact, while it may be ideal to have hi-res pictures or graphics to enhance the experience, it is not not the best for an application in terms of performance. This option allows you to drastically reduce your build size, in case you have problems with it, at the cost of quality.

- **Compression** and **Format**: Specify whether or not the image will be compressed when the game will be compiled/built. It is important to remember, that if your target device is a particular platform, or really old, it is possible that it might not be able to support some compression formats. Again, there is a trade-off between quality and performance.

Exercise:
Since we don't have the time to go through all the single options in detail, as an exercise, find out how all the other settings work in the official documentation. Then, play with them a bit until you are comfortable and really understand how they effect the development workflow.

Stats and profiling

When creating your games, optimization will become a difficult process, especially if you have waited until the last minute to worry about it. One of the main issues (at least in 3D games) is polycounts, which are the number of faces that your 3D assets have. For instance, if you think of a cube, each face is a polygon, and therefore a cube would have a total of six polygons (some graphic cards don't support quads, and so the six faces of the cube should be split into two triangles each, resulting in a total of 12 polygons). In saying this, it is the cumulative total that needs to be kept into consideration. Get it too low and you are going to have a game that looks relatively blocky; too much and it's likely (especially for mobile devices) to lag. To check the polycount inside your Unity scene, head to the top-right hand corner of the **Game** view, and check the **Stats** option, as highlighted in this image:

To get a better idea of how you should model, in the User Manual for Unity, there is a page that explains how to model assets and characters in order for them to be optimized. You can read it here: `http://polycount.com/discussion/130371/polygon-count-for-smartphon e-applications`.

Once you have done this, a popup as shown in the next screenshot should appear. The statistics in this popup shows you information related to the performance of different things, such as draw calls. In addition, it also indicates how many polygons are present in your current view of the scene. In fact, one of the great advantages of this **Stats** screen is that you can use it in real time when you press play so that you can observe which parts of your games are more resource heavy than others (we mentioned this back in `Chapter 2`, *Baking Cupcake Towers*):

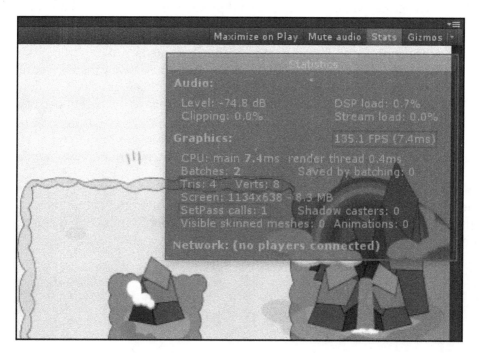

The most important parameters to check (highlighted in the screenshot) are:

- **FPS** (Frames-Per-Seconds): As the name suggests, this shows how many frames your game can produce per second. Of course, this value could change drastically between different devices and/or computers depending on their hardware. You should ensure that your game is able to run at least at 50/60 FPS on each one of your target platforms.

> In some cases, you'd want to limit the maximum amount of FPS, for two reasons:
> Some monitors have a limited refresh rate
> The human eye has a limited refresh rate too
> Therefore, you may want to avoid producing more frames than you actually need, resulting in a waste of computational resources.

- **Tris** (Triangles) and **Verts** (Vertices): They indicate how many triangles and vertices are rendered in the current frame from the active cameras (more than one camera might be active). Especially in 3D games, this is crucial. The more the **Tris** and **Verts**, the more details you can include, but it's at the cost of performance.
- **SetPass calls**: This indicates how many iterations Unity needs to go through to render that specific frame. You should do everything you can to try to reduce this number. The smaller the number of iterations, the faster Unity will render that specific frame, and hence increasing your FPS.

If you need more sophisticated statistics about the use of resources in your game, you can access the **Profiler** by navigating through **Window** | **Profiler** from the top menu bar. You should have a screen like the following:

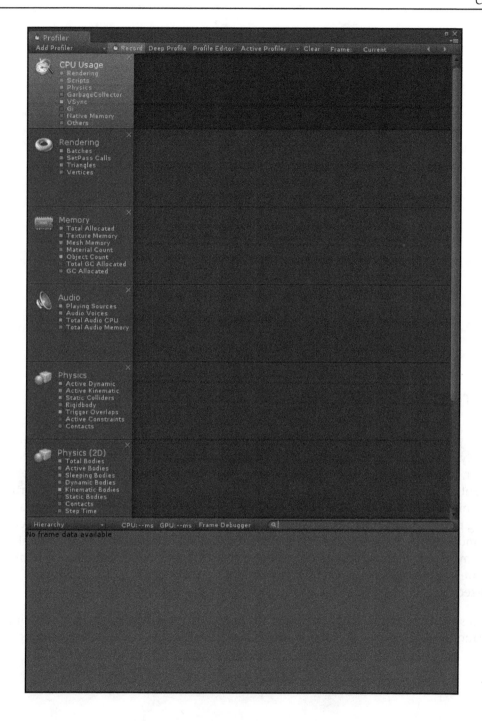

The window has been stretched vertically in order to show you as many categories as possible. However, since the empty spaces will be filled up with graphs and the different parts of your game, the profiling window should be enlarged as much as possible. If you have a dual monitor setup, consider placing the profiling window in your second monitor.

This powerful tool allows you to monitor in detail how the different components of your game use resources. The Profiler helps you to optimize your game by analyzing the performance of the GPU, CPU, memory, rendering, and audio. Therefore, you can have an idea of how much computational power is spent in the different areas of your game. For example, you might want to know the percentage of time spent rendering, animating, or even in your game logic.

 You can find more about the Profiler in the official documentation (`https://docs.unity3d.com/Manual/Profiler.html`) or in a video tutorial from the official website at `https://unity3d.com/learn/tutorials/topics/interface-essentials/introduction-profiler`. In addition, you can do remote profiling as well; on `https://docs.unity3d.com/Manual/ProfilerWindow.html`, towards the end, you will find a section named *Remote profiling*. It explains how to do it based on the platform you want to remote profile.

Other optimization tips

Another option to optimize your game is to limit the amount of materials (which is the way that Unity can apply a shader on a game object) on 3D assets. For example, sometimes you can apply many different materials (and maps) to an object to give it a range of cool effects; however, less is more. For games that are played on computer or console, this is not a big issue, but one that needs to be considered. For games on mobile devices, it is important to keep in mind that they are capable of handling some cool effects, but everything has a limit. Keeping this in mind in the early stages of your game's development will help to reduce the stress and amount of work in the later stages if you need to adjust some components of your game. Some materials could be really expensive from a computational point of view. There are shaders which replicate (with a good approximation) cool effects but are optimized for mobile (such as the bloom effect we discussed earlier).

The ideas explored in this small paragraph is just scratching the surface in optimizing your application from a graphical point of you. However, you can continue your reading here: `https://docs.unity3d.com/Manual/OptimizingGraphicsPerformance.html`.

Another way in which you can optimize your game is to pay attention to your code.

In previous versions of Unity (before version 5), there was the need to cache the Transform component. As you can read at the end of this article at `https://blogs.unity3d.com/2014/06/23/unity5-api-changes-automatic-script-updating`, there is no more need for this. However, there are still developers that use it; now it should be avoided since it reduces the code readability a lot, and therefore the development process as well. In any case, you should still cache other components into variables, as we did for the UI back in `Chapter 3`, *Communicating with the Player – the User Interface*.

> In case you are using an old version of Unity, or you just want to understand what was the caching of the Transform component, look at this line of code:
>
> `transform.position = Vector3.zero;`
>
> When it was compiled (in past versions of Unity), it was equivalent to:
>
> `GetComponent<Transform>().position = Vector3.zero;`
>
> And, as we already mentioned in various chapters, the `GetComponent()` function is slow and it should be avoided when possible. So, you should have considered to cache the Transform component into a variable (as we did back in `Chapter 3`, *Communicating with the Player – the User Interface*, where we stored the reference to the UI component into a variable). Thus, in the case of the Transform, you could have done it within a `Start()` or `Awake()` function with the following line of code (of course, after have declared the `thisTransform` variable of type Transform):
>
> `thisTransform = GetComponent<Transform>();`

Other tips deal with strings, which are extensively used everywhere in Unity. However, unless you are doing particular intense string manipulation, you should avoid doing the optimizations presented here for strings, since the performance gain may not be worth the time spent and the reduction of readability of the code. Here are these tips:

- Remember that if you are concatenating different strings together in a single call (which means, for example, doing in a while loop, which is not placed within a Coroutine so that it will be computed all in one frame), the memory could fill up quickly with unused string objects without giving the time to the garbage collector to clean it up. Therefore, you can use the `StringBuilder` class, which is also slightly faster.

- There are many different ways to compare different strings. However, the fastest one is the following:

  `firstString.Equals(secondString, StringComparison.Ordinal);`

- The reason is that the algorithm just needs to walk (go through character by character) the two strings (which the single characters are seen as numbers, thus this method is case sensitive) to see whether any difference is found.

Playtesting

Test, test, test! Not only test with your target device and audience, but test, test, and test again with them! This may seem like an obvious part of the game development process, but at this stage, even when you do it by yourself and with other members of your team, it is absolutely crucial. Make sure that the game works on high-end AND low-end devices that are within the range of your specifications. A great video to watch that will give you an overview on the process is extra credits video on playtesting, which can be found here: `http://tinyurl.com/PlaytestingExtraCredits`.

Don't assume that if it works on your or your friends' devices that it will work on everyones'. There have been cases where games don't run on specific model of phone. Given this, test on as many as possible. However, thankfully, if you can't get a hold of a range of different devices, you are able to use an emulator to simulate it running on a particular device (or devices). Genymotion (`www.genymotion.com`) is a product that offers a great way to emulate different devices.

Why are you even playtesting?

The is the most fundamental question of the whole playtesting: why are you playtesting your application? Sure, the answer is obvious: to get feedback. But why? For example, do you want to see if the additional feature is necessary? Perhaps you want to find out whether the sound effects are too frequent and irritating; or perhaps they're not enough.

Exercise

Call a team meeting, sit down and go through the features that your application has, what have been difficult to get working, which ones are novel/experimental, or even which ones should be removed. Has there been any informal testing that has offered an another perspective about the game? Do you need to redefine the project, and does everyone have the same concept of the game in their head? It is likely that you have already done this, even a few times, but if you haven't it is good practice to have constant reviews of your game and its development.

Whom do you need to playtest?

Whom do you want and need to playtest your game? Is it a multiplayer, single player or cooperative game? Ideally, when you are conducting a playtest, you want people who are from your target group. While they are playtesting, you'd want to encourage them to take notes, before the playtest (what are their expectations?), during the playtest (what are they thinking/feeling?), and after the playtest (what could be improved, what is good/bad about the game, what is missing, and so on).

The solo test run

It is better to test your game before you ask anyone outside of your group to test it. While this might seem like an obvious thing, but even if you think that your game is infallible, it is more than likely something doesn't work the way that it should. This is why it is important to playtest with yourself and/or your team because if you get bugs and glitches out of the way, then players spend less time trying to play your game and more time playing it to give you valuable feedback. In saying this, it is even worthwhile to playtest with a small group of others before conducting an actual playtesting session. Ideally, this could be easily done within your team itself. While you are doing this, it is useful to not only get a better idea how you want to test the application with others, but it will also help you to shape your questions about their experience for the real thing.

Making it a social occasion

The more the merrier, and it's the same with playtesting; but at the same time, make sure it is manageable with the resources that you have available to you. When you are organizing a group test, it is important to have a mix of people from both your target demographic and outside of it. This is because you can get feedback different perspective, which could offer insight into how the game works or doesn't work.

Putting it within boundaries

This is the same as asking whether your playtest will be public or private. At this stage, you need to ask yourself whether the game contains sensitive components that could effect the release. As a result, you may require players to sign a **non-disclosure agreement** (**NDA**), which prevents them from discussing the game publically, sharing screenshots, and legal consequences for doing so. In contrast, it may be fine for them to freely and openly talk about the game to anyone after they have played.

It is very important that this is made clear to playtesters in the beginning, even before they sign up. You don't want to be logging onto Facebook or Twitter with people publishing screenshots about your app when it's still being developed. Other considerations can be asking playtesters not to take any video or pictures during the actual testing, including selfies, check-ins, and social media posts. In some cases, the print screen option is disabled for this very purpose. Of course, people are smart and they find many workarounds to this. But if you have certain measures and consequences in place, ensuring that participants adhere to a set of rules prior to playtesting and acknowledge them (for example, signing an agreement), you can avoid any unwanted publicity later.

Reaching out to family and friends

Now, playtesting can always start with your friends, family, and other close associates. This limits the amount of time that is required to get superficial issues out of the way, such as navigation functionality, certain aspects not working properly, and so on. Make sure that they don't tell you want you want to hear either. Family and friends know you on a more personal level and will know what you are looking for, so make sure that they are honest with their feedback and constructive with their critiques.

Those who are strangers

In saying all of that, it's great to get comments from those that we know because there really isn't anything unknown and you're comfortable to communicate with them. But like we mentioned before, you need an objective opinion from someone you don't know and who doesn't know anything about your game other than the synopsis that you gave them prior to testing.

Those who you want to play your game

Given all this talk about people, it is important to keep in mind who you are intending your game for. For this group of users, you really need to define your target audience (age, location, and experience level). By developing a user profile early on, then you are able to define the kind of attributes that they may have and that you need to cater for. Not only will this will help you to improve the design of your game but also to define how you will need to conduct your playtest. By doing this, you are able to focus the questions that are related to the application, and to them, and find out (if it's not), what could make it more relevant.

Some simple steps that can get you refining this group of people are the following:

- Look at who is already using your products (if you have more than one). If you don't already have a user-base, then create a list of what would be your most ideal one. Start broad and then work your way to refining it to becoming a bit more specific. This will help to improve how you also market your game later. Look at things like age group, gender, location to help develop a better picture.
- See what others, who are similar to you, are doing. This will help you to also refine (or redefine) your target audience. Make a list of games that are similar to yours and see how their audiences are being targeted.
- Analyze the products and/or services that you already have available. Have they done well, if so why, if not why not?
- Choose specific characteristics of your audience to focus on. For example, while all of them may be gamers, maybe some are more casual than others. Perhaps your game is more targeted towards adults than children, and so on. While we aim to please everyone, we can't, so it's better to a more directed focus.
- Take a step back and evaluate your target audience. Are there things that could be added to help improve or specify them?

These are only some of the things that you will need to consider when defining your target audience, so I encourage you to also check out other, and more relevant text (on the web, books) that are more relevant to your game.

When

The time that you decide to run your play-set is also an important consideration. Especially if you require people to be physically present. When deciding on a time think about what your group would most likely to be doing at that time. For example, if your target group students, it is more than likely that during the day they will be at school, therefore, weekend testing sessions are probably going to be more suited for them. On the other hand, if your group are people who run, early mornings or after work are probably more ideal times to have sessions. Of course, these are dependent on the type of game that you have as well. If your game requires more time commitment, then having a longer period of time for them to play your game is going to be better suited both for you and their lifestyle. Remember, they are helping you, so flexibility is key.

 A good way to ensure that people will turn up on time to your test group is to either add them to your calendar or to call or send them reminder a few days before the proposed play date.

Where

If playtesting is all done virtually, either by downloading and executable or by logging in to a website, then feel free to skip this section. However, if you require participants to come to a physical location, you want to make it as accessible as possible. Ideally you want it to be somewhere that is close public transport and in an area that is likely to be a central point for people to come to. For example, a city center is generally close to public transport, and it is likely to be close to people's places of work, or even school.

What

What are you expecting from the playtest and what are your playtesters expecting to do are two questions that you need to consider. For example, are you wanting them to play the tutorial and then provide feedback to you, either written or verbal? Perhaps they are thinking that they will need to play the entire game. The what of your playtest is essential to define and to make clear to the playtesters, that way you're not wasting their time and they aren't wasting you by giving feedback to irrelevant parts of the application.

A little goes a long way

What will you provide your playtesters during playtest, and/or for their time? If you are unable to compensate them, make sure to provide food and beverages. This is not to say you need to get a caterer to provide you with cakes and sandwiches, but having tea and coffee with some snacks (cut up some fruit, chips, candy, biscuits, even make your own sandwiches) will help to keep them sharp, especially if they are there for a long time. Scheduling breaks during long playtest sessions is also important, because you don't want them to be sitting there for hours. Having breaks every 45 minutes is a great way to also check-in with them and see how things are going.

How

How are the playtesters going to, well play and how will you manage this? How are you going to get their feedback? What kind of equipment (recording devices or computers) and software (questionnaire) will you need? Prior to the test, make sure that they work, batteries are charged and you have all the necessary equipment (cables and adapters) available. In addition, make sure you have a backup plan if for some reason sometime goes wrong on the day (which it does happen).

Methods of playtesting

There are different ways to approach a playtest. You can let the players figure it all out on their own (after you've provided a bit of context), or guide them through the rules. With each approach, the way that you gain feedback during the playtest will differ. The following are some ways that you can playtest your game.

Observe

Observe how your testers are playing. For example, do they do things in a particular way or that is not expected? Perhaps this is because of a glitch or from other experiences that they have with games, and as a result they use certain features (or try to) in the same way. The same concept can happen in reverse, for example if players are supposed to obtain or do something but they don't, or the game won't allow them to then this needs to be fixed. At these points, future players are likely to find the game difficult to use because of a technical issue and head towards the **Uninstall** button.

Question and explain

There is no better way to check your understanding of something than to explain it to someone else. Therefore, one way to get feedback from your playtesters is to ask them to explain the game to you. Do they explain something different, that has you asking if you gave them the right game? Or do they explain the game in the same way that you intended it to be like? While they are explaining the game to you, make sure that you keep the conversation on what the game is, and not what it could be. Of course, any improvements are great suggestions, but for the purpose of the explanation, you will want them to tell you what they just experienced.

Reflect and follow up

By now, you're left with an empty testing space and a whole bunch of notes, ideas, and different thoughts whizzing around your mind. Now is the time to get them out and documented. Have a group meeting. Write it up on a whiteboard, paper, document, or somewhere that is easily accessible later. This is an important process because what happens here can greatly impact your game upon release.

Now that the playtest is over, you will want to follow up with them. It's just like being in a meeting, you think of something useful afterwards, the same goes for testing. In a week from the playtest, it might be a nice way to drop them an e-mail, thank them again for their participation and if they have thought of anything else since the playtest. The important thing here is not to spam them with e-mails and questions, but to provide them with an opportunity to suggest it. You can provide them with an online (and anonymous) questionnaire.

Creating your online presence

These days, if it's not on the Internet, it doesn't exist. Well, if you're not social, it will be hard for people to know what you are up to, let alone knowing that you are making a game! You don't spend months or years developing something only to have no one come to the party. But this can be fixed, and it does require a bit of planning and time, so be prepared, but I promise you it will be worth it in the end.

Do your research

If you're going for a job interview, you wouldn't go in there without having done a bit of research about your potential employer, the same goes for making a name for yourself. While it's good to get everyone's attention, ideally, you want to get noticed by the right people. One way to do this is to pay close attention to companies, products, and even individuals who are also in the same market as you; and observe who they interact with, what kind of social media tagging are they utilizing. For example, are they using a particular hashtag such as *#Android*, *#game*, *#AppStore*? Perhaps, there are particular groups that they are targeting, from local, international, big, and small companies, even particular key individuals within the area. The idea is not to mimic their interactions, but to observe them. As you begin to observe you will learn more about the market that you are targeting, the major players, and perhaps come across and opportunity to engage with them. Such opportunities can range from conferences, expos, perhaps a meet and greet for a particular launch. Just remember, time and place is everything.

Conducting an audit

From logos to banners, links and even mission statements, a social media audit will ensure that everything is up-to-date. Do this when you first set up your social media accounts and right before you make any big announcement (such as a game launch). Of course, it is important to maintain these regularly, but if you're going to do it, these are the times to check everything is in order, because you are likely to get a higher influx of traffic to your channels.

Engaging with your audience

If you're documenting the process, ask those who are engaging with your content for their opinions. Create polls, post questions and ask for their responses. Keep them engaged and make sure that you interact with your audience on a regular basis. Even if you're just posting an update about a day in the office or something interesting that happened during the development of your game, it keeps users interested. While posting something is good, make sure that it still somehow ties back to the game or your development studio.

Rewarding engagement

Sites like Kickstarter, Indiegogo, and other crowdfunding platforms provide rewards for certain levels of commitment from their projects backers. Even if you choose not to engage with one of these platforms, you can adopt similar approaches to the development and eventual release of your game:

- **Competitions**: Running competitions is a great way to get people involved. If you don't have the funds to create products, offer discounts, early access or (free) full versions of your game. Another option is to create some exclusive artwork/wallpapers and if possible, get them printed and signed by your team.
- **The power of the crowd**: Competitions are a great way to get people interacting with your company and products. Therefore, when you want to get people involved, instead of asking them to write a comment in response to your question or competition, get them to like, share, and even tag friends to enter into the competition. Perhaps for each friend that they tag, it's an additional entry. In any case, it is a win-win situation because they (and even their friends) have the potential to win something, and you get some publicity.

- **Feedback**: Getting insight from those using your product, albeit during playtesting or after the game has launched is ensuring that your game is as good as it can be. Remember to keep in mind that when take the time to give you detailed feedback, it is time out of their day, committed to helping you and your product out. While not everything is roses, and in cases you will get negative feedback, when it's constructive it can give you ideas about future updates. Therefore, while feedback tends to be altruistic, reward those who make an effort. Rewards can be simple as a discount or large like a (or chance to win) free copy of your game.

Marketing on social media

Don't just be a lurker, get involved! It's easy to stay on the sidelines, but it's better to get in and amongst it. While some of you may be new to social networking, the industry is quite integrated into it, and it does play a major part in it all. However, before you get started, there are a few things you should consider before shouting from the rooftop about your work.

Blog about it

Now that you know about your target audience in a bit more detail, it's time to start setting up your own online presence. To begin, let's start with a blog. A blog offers many different avenues for communicating detailed information about what you do, albeit as a company or during the development of a product. It's one way to gather followers and provide a more personal snapshot into your lives. In this way, you begin to develop a more meaningful connection between you and your audience.

There are a range of different blog platforms to choose from. Some of the most popular ones include Tumblr (`www.tumblr.com`), WordPress (`www.wordpress.com`), and Blogger (`www.blogger.com`). These three, while not being the only ones out there, all offer great platforms for creating your own blog.

Twitter

Have you ever read a really captivating headline that made you want to read more? Well micro blogging platforms are great ways to hook your audience in much the same way. Twitter (`www.twitter.com`) is a perfect example of this because it contains you to a limit of 140 characters or less. So you have to get straight to the point or you will get cut off, and nobody likes th…

Tweeting, there are a number of things to keep in mind when you are tweeting updates about your application, some of which, like time zone. However, Twitter uses a few key methods of interaction:

- **Reply**: As the name suggests it allows users to reply to what you have posted. This allows you to interact with those who have showed interest in what you have said.
- **Retweet**: It is Twitter's version of sharing. So if someone tweets something that you liked, you can retweet it so that your followers can also see it.
- **Favorite**: It is similar to a *Like* on Facebook or a thumbs up on YouTube.
- **Hashtags**: These are probably one of the most fundamental things to keep in mind when sharing content. They are like a filtering system, in terms of categorizing information. Using unique hashtags helps you to not only keep track of content distribution that is related to your game, but it also makes it easier to be heard among other tweets.

> A great way to make sure that you have a unique hashtag is to search it before using it.

Some useful links to get you going with advertising on Twitter:

- `https://business.twitter.com/en/advertising.html`
- `https://marketing.twitter.com/na/en.html`
- `https://business.twitter.com/en/help/troubleshooting/how-twitter-ads-work.html`
- `https://business.twitter.com/en/advertising/campaign-types.html`

Exercise

If you're having trouble condensing something into a short version, try putting a limit on yourself. For example, begin with stating you whole idea, then say it in 15, 10, and 5 seconds. You will begin to notice that each time you try to say your idea, the core concepts will become more obvious, and the shorter the time becomes, the more efficient and simplified your explanation will become. We often feel the need to include everything, that one piece of information is equally as important as the next, but in reality that become padding to the concept.

Instagram

While Twitter is the micro blogging platform, Instagram (`www.instagram.com`) tells a thousand words with a simple picture (and caption). It works in a similar way to Twitter in that you can add hashtags, and connect with a larger audience and perhaps follow some of the key players (optional).

Facebook

Facebook (`www.facebook.com`) offers a range of different options when it comes to creating a place to advertise your game as well as connecting with your audience:

- **Pages**: Create a page and populate it a bit before making it public so that you have a somewhat established online presence. By having content on your page, it gives visitors a reason to stay. While they are there, you need to be able to keep them there for a bit, and there are different ways to get visitors engaged, such as having an interesting blog post about a recent update or feature to an intriguing photo.
- **Posts**: These are a versatile feature to use. For example, if you're asking about a particular component for the game, such as the next feature to include, you could ask them to *Like* for option one, *Comment* for option two, and *Share* for option three. Like we have discussed in this chapter in terms of competitions, you can use option two to encourage people to tag their friends as part of the process. As a result, while you are getting them interacting with your posts, you're also getting a bit of publicity from it all while reaching their friends networks.
- **Polls**: They can be used as a way to quickly gauge users' opinions and see what the common consensus is. It is a bit more linear than post a comment (although this feature is available for the poll in general), but it is quicker. Of course, you can use polls to encourage competitive behavior such as vote now, whichever feature gets the highest amount of votes will be included in the next update. In this way, players will also feel as though their input counts and that they are also part of the development process.
- **Live**: The live feature allows you to stream an event in real-time and have people watch it, well, live. This provides you with a great opportunity to stream things such as live game development or a Q&A. The best part is that if people miss it, then they can view it later and interact with it (for example, via comments, likes, sharing, and so on).

MailChimp

While you're not ready, you still want a place for potential customers to keep in touch and there is no better way to do that then with a mainlining list. MailChimp (`www.mailchimp.com`), as well as many others out there, helps you to not only collate mailing lists but also inform them, all at once, about upcoming events, product releases, and many other special events.

Getting ready to publish

There are a number of things, not just to do with your game or application that need to be taken care of before you finally release your precious gem into the world. In the following sections, we will go through a number of considerations, both with your team and final product, to ensure that the final part of this process is as smooth as possible.

Crowdfunding campaigns

There are a number of different platforms for crowdfunding campaigns and each has its own features. However, the fundamental thing about them all is that they are there to provide a place for you to gather a following and importantly the much-needed funds or you to bring your creation to light. Different crowdfunding platforms operate for different reasons. For example, some are about causes (nature, human rights, or poverty), certain types of products (clothing, music), creative (products or virtual goods), and personal (medical treatments). Your game may meet criteria on more than one, specifically for creative projects, so it is recommended that you spend some time to see where your game is likely to reach those who will be the most interested in it.

Crowdfunding platforms work by the developer (or creator of any product or idea) presenting their idea, what they need the funding for, how it will be allocated, and what's in it for the backers who will be the ones that ultimately will give you money. In general, backers for your product (in this case, game) will be offered by you, with varying levels of backing opportunities to choose from. For example, if a backer contributes $1 then they are able to have their name listed in the credits on the game's website, or even in-game. If they give you $50, then they are able to get a signed copy of your game, $800 will get them two copies and a handwritten thank-you note, and so on. Be careful when you're setting the amounts for each level. Too much and you won't get backers; too little and you will ruin your budget. One last thing to consider is that in some cases, the crowdfunding platform will not only take a certain percentage from the total amount of funds that you raise, but will also add a fee to your backer's contributions.

Therefore, before you decide on a crowdfunding platform make sure that it will be the right one for you and for the funds that you are wanting to raise.

One of the most important things is to keep the risks of your project (both if it is funded and isn't) in mind. There are many risks that can occur, especially when you do get funded that the funds are managed properly and for what they were intended for. You want to have a budget that has been planned well and takes into account likely events that may occur (delays, unexpected costs for hardware, and additional help).

We have barely scratched the surface of what it means to develop and run a crowdfunding platform, but it is not a task for the faint-hearted. A great deal of thought is required when you're determining the levels of rewards for your backers and you must their cost into consideration and whether or not that will impact your budget. For example, digital downloads of your games will definitely be more cost-effective than burning them to a disc, and housing them in a beautifully decorated case, and then shipping them where they need to go. You can either include the cost of postage in the amount that backers are required to pay or ask it to be paid separately. In any event, crowdfunding campaigns require a lot of time and effort to be run successfully. In addition, they are not always a sure way to get funding, so keep this in mind when you're planning your game and its future.

Here is a list of crowdfunding sites to check out:

- Fig: www.fig.co
- Kickstarter: www.kickstarter.com
- Indiegogo: www.indiegogo.com
- RocketHub: www.rockethub.com
- GoFundMe: www.gofundme.com
- Razoo: www.razoo.com
- CrowdRise: www.crowdrise.com

Building in Unity

The first thing to do is to actually compile the game. Otherwise, you won't be able to put it anywhere!

To build a game in Unity, you need to navigate in the top bar menu and select **File** | **Build Settings...**. There, you have the following screen, where you can choose the platform you want to target (and the scenes you want to include):

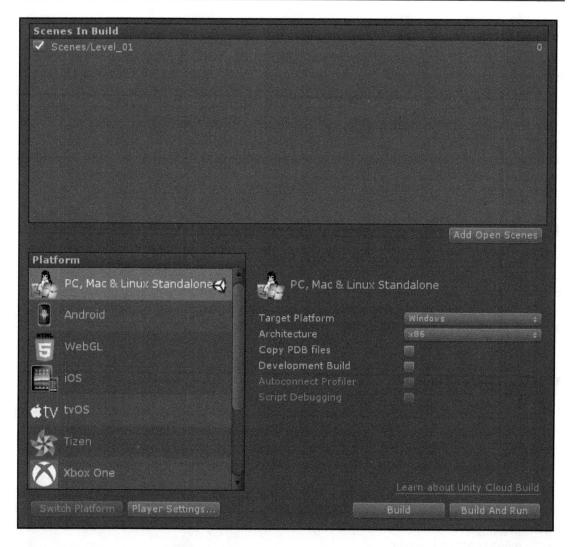

If you click on the **Player Settings…** button, you will go into specific options for your build. Here you can find more information about it:

`https://docs.unity3d.com/Manual/class-PlayerSettings.html`.

Once you click on the **Build**, Unity will actually build the game and you can take a breath (and a break). But here, it's just the beginning of the second stage, in which you actually need to publish and market the game!

Clearing the air

You're getting excited, you're almost at the finished line, but it is imperative at this point to ensure that everyone, and I mean everyone who is involved, is aware of what will happen next. More importantly, make sure that everyone has been accounted for. For example, how the profits/royalties will be divided, their responsibilities post game launch, and so forth. Of course, this would have been outlined in a contract early on in the project, which they would have signed, but we are all guilty of agreeing to terms and conditions without having actually read them. It might even be worthwhile at this stage to remind everyone to revisit their contract.

Accepting terms and conditions

Now that your team are all good to go, you need to make sure that what you're about to put out there for the world to enjoy also abides by the terms and conditions of the platform that you will be targeting. For example, if you are planning to release for Android devices, ensure that you have met their terms and conditions; the same goes for Apple's App Store and any others that you are intending to publish on.

Localization

When you are shipping worldwide, you need to localize your game. Many developers think that publishing only in English should be enough because it is understood by most gamers. However, if you give a look to the marketing and downloading graphs, it's clear that English is just 20% of the market. Therefore, you should definitely take into consideration localizing your game to other audiences.

But localization is much more than just translating your game and/or adding subtitles in other languages. There are so many things you should keep in consideration. Some of the many reasons are as follows:

- In some languages, like German, some words are really long and they might be cut off or overflow from your user interface.
- Some languages, such as Arabic are written in a different direction, for instance, right to left or up to down. Thus, you may have to adjust the design of your UI to support the visual impact that your interface will have.

- In case you have dialogue systems, or just the user interface that uses string concatenation in a certain way within the code, be aware than in other languages, they need to be rewritten if they are not flexible enough! An example would be when you want to place an adjective before the word. In some other languages, it might happen in the opposite direction. For instance, the English sentence the *red hat* becomes *il cappello rosso* in Italian, where *rosso* means red. Thus, the adjective is after the word and not before it, unlike in English. Another (practical) example is the following: you reserve an extra character at the end of your item to add an *s* to make it plural (*potion* can become *potions*). In Italian, you don't need an extra character but change the last one (*pozione* becomes *pozioni* in the plural form). Moreover, in Italian the last character that changes depends on whether the object is female or male (a concept that doesn't exist in English, since objects don't have any sex). Therefore, your solution to reserve a character is not structured enough to support Italian. Imagine applying this to all the other languages, and you quickly realize that it's not so easy to localize you game by just adding a couple of variables.
- In some cultures, the role of the , and of the . is inverted within numbers (For example the number 3,218 can be interpreted as three thousand two hundred eighteen or also as three point two one eight, such as in Italy).
- In some cultures, specific concepts might be not well tolerated, and therefore they should be censured or removed. This is typically with violent games or games that contain certain types of adult content.

All of these problems should be taken into consideration when you translate because it's not as straightforward as getting the translation of your text. Here is a list of examples, by no means exhaustive:

- Translators need to have the context of the game, because in other languages, many shades are lost with direct translation, and in some way, they should be kept when possible
- Biographies of characters are useful in case your collaborators do voice casting for other languages
- Some metaphors or sayings may have no meaning in other languages

As such, you should consider localization from the very beginning of your development flow. However, this is often not possible due time and economic constraints. In any case, keep in mind that the sooner you pay attention to localization, the easier it will be in the long run.

Ethical considerations

Video games are a technology, and like all technologies, they can be dangerous and harm people. They can be used as weapons to hurt people. Unfortunately, this ethical aspect of games is often forgotten. As such, I want to quote Jesse Schell, who wrote in his book (*The Art of Game Design: a book of lenses*):

> *"If you are designing a game that involves strangers talking each other, you must take responsibility for what that might lead to. This is one of the rare cases where your choices in game design could cause lives to be saved or lost. You might think there is a one in a million chance of something dangerous happening in your game, but if that is true, and your game is so successful that five million people play it, that dangerous thing will happen five times."*

You, as a game developer, have certain responsibilities in doing everything you could to make this never happen. If you are not willing to take such responsibilities, probably it's better not to make any game.

In my personal opinion, which is also shared by Jesse Schell as you can read from his book, you have the potential to do something good, and use video games as a tool to enhance human life. You should be inspired by questions like, Is the game I'm developing doing something good? and Can my game in some way improve the life of its players? Of course, these are not questions that game companies care about, but you as game developer should, and answer them inside you. Then, try to make your game a better game for people.

 The same argument, but explained in more detail, can be found in a dedicated chapter of Jesse Schell's book.

Please, in your own way, make this world a better place!

Summary

In this chapter, we faced many topics, and explored many areas, so let's reorganize our ideas.

At the beginning, we discussed about potential improvements for our tower defense game and some hints on their implementation. From there, we extended the improvements to Unity in general, by providing more areas of game development that we didn't have time to cover in detail, but that need your attention if you wish to improve your own skills.

During game development, you are often not alone, but you are within a team, and it is important that each part of the team works as if they all were one (like the human body) so to achieve the finest results. As such, some collaboration tools have been highlighted, so that you are free to try them and choose the one that suits your team best.

Then, we came back to our game, by focusing on optimization and playtesting, which are both wrongly considered as last steps of the game development pipeline, but as we found out, this is not true. The sooner you start iterating on them, the better your game will be. Optimization is needed to run your game efficiently, whereas playtesting is needed to make player's experience smooth.

We didn't stop there, and we went through what's after the game is completed, and we discussed topics ranging from marketing your game, creating an online presence to publish your game, and hopefully get a revenue out of it. As such, we explored many hints on how to use the most common social media platforms as tools to promote your image and your game by engaging and expand your target audience.

At the very end, we scratched the surface of localization, just to have a better idea of what's behind that, since we didn't have the time to face it properly, but it was worthy of mention.

Final notes and goodbye

Unfortunately, this travel in the world of game development has come to an end (although this last chapter should have made you realize that this is just the beginning of your journey). Time flew, and I just realized that I filled up a whole book!

I really want to thank you all, the readers whom I didn't have a chance to meet in person. But when I was writing the words of this book until very late at night, I felt connected to all of you in some way. For me, this has been an amazing travel too (although at sometimes tiring and stressful).

In case you have illegally downloaded this book but you really liked it, please consider buying it. I work hard to deliver high-quality content and this takes time. If you are unable to afford this book, you can always offer me a coffee (`www.francescosapio.com/BuyMeACoffee`) or support this book by sharing the link to buy it (not to torrent and download it) on social media.

Other titles I wrote that might help you in your journey are *Unity UI Cookbook*, Packt Publishing (`www.packtpub.com/game-development/unity-ui-cookbook`) and *Unity 5.x 2D Game Development Blueprints*, Packt Publishing (`www.packtpub.com/game-development/unity-5x-2d-game-development-blueprints`). Furthermore, here is also my mini guide already quoted in `Chapter 1`, *A Flat World in Unity*: *What you need to know about Unity 5*, Packt Publishing (`www.packtpub.com/packt/free-ebook/what-you-need-know-about-unity-5`).

Finally, networking, meeting other people, and sharing ideas are great ways to extend your knowledge and skills. So please feel free to contact me:

I'm very curious and I look forward to hearing about your creations and about what you have learnt from this book. Also, if you have any feedback, be sure to get in touch.

I wish you all the best with your work and maybe our paths will cross again.

FRANCESCO SAPIO

CONTACT
contact@francescosapio.com

WEBSITE
www.francescosapio.com

Index

www.ingramcontent.com/pod-product-compliance
Lightning Source LLC
Chambersburg PA
CBHW081456050326
40690CB00015B/2816